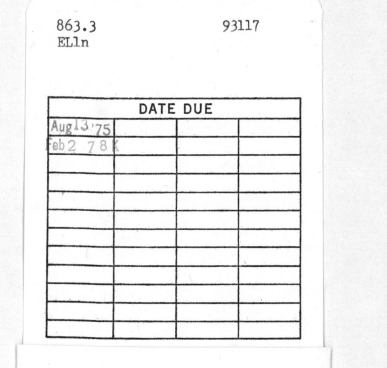

Novel to Romance

Novel to Romance:

A Study of Cervantes's *Novelas ejemplares*

Ruth S. El Saffar

THE JOHNS HOPKINS UNIVERSITY PRESS
BALTIMORE AND LONDON

The Johns Hopkins University Press, Baltimore, Maryland   21218
The Johns Hopkins University Press Ltd., London

Library of Congress Catalog Card Number: 73–19332
ISBN 0-8018-1545-2

Library of Congress Cataloging in Publication data
will be found on the last printed page of this book.

To Zuhair, Ali, and Dena,
who give meaning to everything else.

CONTENTS

PREFACE

his study of Cervantes's *Novelas ejemplares* was made possible by a grant from the National Endowment for the Humanities in the 1970–71 academic year, freeing me from my normal teaching duties. I am grateful for that indispensible material support as well as for the constant, but less easily identifiable, support from students, babysitters, friends, and family, whose encouragement and help in resolving the day-to-day difficulties of the "working mother" greatly facilitated the completion of this book. Equally invaluable was the encouragement I received from colleagues who were willing to spend time discussing problems which arose in my studies and to read parts of my manuscript. I would like especially to thank Elias Rivers for his early interest in this undertaking; R. O. Jones, who took the time and trouble to read an earlier and much longer form of my manuscript and to make helpful and encouraging comments; and J. B. Avalle-Arce, whose suggestions proved very useful in making final revisions. Thanks go finally to my good friends Andrew McKenna and Lucille Braun, who were constantly available for help in reading and criticizing sections of the manuscript.

INTRODUCTION

wentieth-century readers who probe Cervantes's prose fiction beyond *Don Quixote* into the realms of *La Galatea*, the *Novelas ejemplares*, and the *Persiles*, are often disappointed when they discover that very little in those works succeeds in capturing the magic of Cervantes's masterpiece. The problem, ultimately, reduces itself to a vision of Cervantes as a creator either unconscious of his powers, or hopelessly divided within himself between impulses which tend toward works of modern complexity and impulses which draw him back into classical forms.[1] Since *La Galatea* was Cervantes's first published work, its weaknesses are easily explainable as the product of inexperience. The *Persiles* and the *Novelas ejemplares*, however, being published in the last years of Cervantes's life, present more difficult problems. Most efforts to prove that the *Persiles* and many of the *Novelas ejemplares* were written in Cervantes's youth are based on our reluctance, as twentieth-century readers, to envision any development that would not culminate in a work of art that would reflect in technique and content modern man's alienation. For most modern theorists see the novel as a form uniquely adapted to capture man in the anguish of his temporality and his disorientation. J. Hillis Miller's words provide a good statement of our expectations from the novel:

The temporal structure of a novel, whether it is looked at from the point of view of the reader seeking to achieve a total grasp of the novel, or from the point of view of the narrator telling his story, or from the point of view of the characters seeking to fill the hollow in their hearts and come to coincide fully with themselves, is also an expression of the way man is alienated from the ground of his being, that proximity of the distance which haunts him like a tune he cannot quite remember, or like something half-glimpsed out of the corner of his eye. Temporality, as Georg Lukacs in the *Theory of the Novel* long ago saw, is therefore constitutive for fiction in a way it can never be for the epic or for literature of the ages of belief in an independently existing eternal realm.[2]

---

[1] Cesare De Lollis, in *Cervantes reazionario* (1924) offers the best known and most thoroughly argued presentation of this position. However, variations of the same attitude are legion, as much among Spanish as among foreign critics. A fuller discussion of the types of approaches which prevail regarding the question of Cervantes's literary development and the complementary question of the chronology of his works will be taken up in the Appendix (pp. 169–78).

[2] *The Form of Victorian Fiction* (1968), p. 46.

Several recent studies on the *Persiles* demonstrate convincingly that at least the last two books were written at the end of Cervantes's life and that they represent, from Cervantes's point of view, and from that of his contemporaries, the height of modernity. At least as many editions of the *Persiles* were printed in the first hundred years after its publication as of *Don Quixote*. Though Joaquín Casalduero, G. Hainsworth, and other fine critics of Cervantes have reminded us that literary tastes change and that serious consideration must be given to the fact that not only the *Persiles*, but *El amante liberal* enjoyed great acclaim in the seventeenth and eighteenth centuries, twentieth century distaste for such works continues to impede a thorough study of Cervantes's development through his works.

This study will be limited to the *Novelas ejemplares* because there are in that work, in microcosm, problems central to the totality of Cervantes's work. In this study of the *Novelas ejemplares* admitted personal preference for the "realistic" stories will be set aside in an effort to trace the logic of Cervantes's own literary development.[3] The development is one which moves away from perspectivism, away from temporally structured works, and away from representations of "the way man is alienated from the ground of his being." The questions of what is truth, what is reality, what is fiction, what is history—the questions which line the pages of *Don Quixote* I, *El casamiento engañoso*, and *El coloquio de los perros*; and the problematics of characters who can find their way neither within the confines of society nor outside of it—characters like Anselmo, in *El curioso impertinente*; Carrizales, in *El celoso extremeño*; Tomás Rodaja, in *El licenciado Vidriera*; Rincón and Cortado, in *Rinconete y Cortadillo*; characters like Don Quixote himself—dissolve within questions of broader

---

[3] Critics have categorized the twelve stories in the *Novelas ejemplares* in many different ways, subdividing them into as many as four or five different types. The subdivision which I am accepting for the purpose of referring easily to the differences which I consider fundamental in the novelas is the least specialized but most commonly recognized one which labels as "realistic" *Rinconete y Cortadillo*, *El licenciado Vidriera*, *El celoso extremeño*, *El casamiento engañoso*, and *El coloquio de los perros*; and as "idealistic" *Las dos doncellas*, *La fuerza de la sangre*, *La señora Cornelia*, *El amante liberal*, and *La española inglesa*. *La gitanilla* and *La ilustre fregona*, in this scheme, generally fall between the two categories. While there are obvious differences between, for example, *Rinconete* and *El amante liberal*, the labels "realistic" and "idealistic", adopted from nineteenth- and twentieth-century criticism, are clearly unsatisfactory. However, since I have accepted the general division of the novelas into two basic groups, for reasons which I hope this book will make clear, I have also accepted the traditional shorthand labels assigned to them. Henceforth, "realistic" and "idealistic" will appear without quotation marks to avoid a clumsy reading. It should be understood, however, that "A" and "B" would serve as well, for my use of these words is not meant in any way to introduce questions of realism or idealism into the work.

scope in later works. The development traced in this study is one which reflects Cervantes's emergence beyond despair and alienation in his own life to acceptance of an integrating totality the ultimate truth and perfection of which, though impossible to grasp in human terms, serves to obliterate the distinctions in this life which make such questions as individual vs. society, and truth vs. fiction appear relevant. The larger dialectic in which the later works engage involves man's struggle not with other men or with perceived reality, but with his own salvation. The establishment of an external referent—of an eternal truth—is reflected in fundamental alterations in style, characterization, and plot in the later works.

Implicit in J. Hillis Miller's statement is the conclusion toward which my study points. It is faith in an "independently existing eternal realm" that interrupts the continued creation of great novels for Cervantes. The *Persiles*, as Alban Forcione and others have rightly pointed out, is not a novel but a romance. The same division that separates the *Persiles* from *Don Quixote* can also be found within the *Novelas ejemplares*. Some stories, like the ones mentioned above, recall the thematics of Part I of *Don Quixote*, and most are easily shown to have been written, like *Don Quixote* I, between 1600 and 1605. Other stories, like *El amante liberal, La española inglesa, Las dos doncellas,* and *La señora Cornelia,* show characteristics of the romance found in the *Persiles*.[4]

Evidence for the trajectory proposed here can be gathered both by close analysis of the works themselves and by considering the literary theory current in Cervantes's time. While such students of sixteenth- and seventeenth-century literary theory as E. C. Riley, Alban Forcione, and Jean-François Canavaggio reject the notion of significant change in Cervantes's orientation after *La Galatea*, both Riley and Forcione betray suggestions of development which may be significant in considering the chronology of the *Novelas ejemplares*. Forcione and Riley, who agree, with J. B. Avalle-Arce, that the *Persiles*, or at least a large part of it, was Cervantes's last-written work, both suggest that the work reflects a considered development of Cervantes's concept of art. Combined with an increased interest in the marvellous, they detect a continued concern with truth and the role of fiction in capturing it. Forcione's comments suggest

---

[4] Although the *Persiles* is not strictly a romance, in Northrop Frye's sense of the term (*Anatomy of Criticism. Four Essays* [1971], pp. 33–37), I am using that term to indicate the direction toward which the *Persiles* and some of Cervantes's novelas tend when compared with the better known works. Frye's suggestion of a progression in western literature away from myth and romance toward the low mimetic and ironic modes serves as an example of the type of assumption in modern criticism that makes acceptance of a reverse movement in Cervantes's development difficult to accept.

further a theological world view in which fantasy is given greater reign.[5] It is this double-edged development which will be pursued in this study of Cervantes's fiction, especially in the *Novelas ejemplares*.

The model which the Spanish neo-Aristotelian literary theorist El Pinciano offered for the epic was the work of Heliodorus. Although Fernando de Mena's translation of the *Ethiopic History* was available as early as 1587, and another version in Spanish, based on Amyot's French translation, was published even earlier, it was in the seventeenth century that Heliodorus truly came into vogue. The second edition of Mena's translation appeared in 1614, another in 1615, and another in 1616. In 1617, a Spanish version of Achilles Tatius's *Clitophon and Leucippe* came out. The popularity of Heliodorus among intellectuals in the second decade of the seventeenth century corresponds to a period when Cervantes had contact with literary currents, time to develop his literary skills, and the need to keep abreast of literary developments. Cervantes's specific mention, in the prologue to the *Novelas ejemplares*, of his ambition to compete with Heliodorus in the forthcoming *Persiles* makes Cervantes's awareness of Heliodorus by at least 1612 undeniable. What is less frequently recognized is the influence Heliodorus's work may have had on the short works of Cervantes, specifically, the *Novelas ejemplares*.[6]

Las dos doncellas, El amante liberal, La fuerza de la sangre, La señora Cornelia, and *La española inglesa*—all the stories assigned here to the post-1606 period, have frequently been referred to collectively as "Italianate" because of their supposed similarities to the Italian *novella*. Since this form was highly developed by the time Cervantes was in Italy in his youth, and

---

[5] E. C. Riley says: ". . . it remains likely that a wider reading of epic theory and of books of travel and exotic information, increased confidence in his powers as a novelist, and a growing sophistication among the novel-reading public contributed to Cervantes's experiments in controlled fantasy toward the end of his career." (*Cervantes's Theory of the Novel,* [1962], p. 181). Earlier he had said: "His concern with the nature of truth in literary fiction, which impinges on every major aspect of his theory, evidently increases" (p. 11). When Forcione refers to Cervantes's "movement toward Aristotle" (*Cervantes, Aristotle, and the "Persiles,"* [1970], p. 339) and speaks of the reduction of life to a "conceptual scheme provided by law and religion" as something Cervantes was not capable of in *Don Quixote* but which, by the *Persiles,* he was "prepared for" (p. 343); and when he comments on Cervantes's "ultimately anticlassical stance" (p. 343), he is implying a development in Cervantes's works.

[6] Albinio Martín Gabriel ("Heliodoro y la novela española: Apuntes para una tesis" [1950]) makes passing reference to the "bizantinismo" in *El amante liberal* and to the presence, in the *Novelas ejemplares,* of ideas characteristic of the Cervantes of the *Persiles.* But the most complete statement that I know of of the debt to Heliodorus apparent in the *Novelas ejemplares* is made by G. Hainsworth, in *Les "Novelas ejemplares" de Cervantes en France au XVIIe siècle* (1933), pp. 17–26.

since it was popularly imitated in Spain in the sixteenth century by such writers as Juan de Timoneda, the term "Italianate" when applied to Cervantes's tales connotes works written before 1600, when his style was not yet mature. Several critics have taken issue with this denomination,[7] but it is Hainsworth who has most carefully distinguished between the style of the Italian novella and the style of the above-mentioned stories of Cervantes. Hainsworth finds, in fact, very little that resembles the *novella* in Cervantes's short stories. Rather, he relates them in style and content to the *Ethiopic History* or *Clitophon and Leucippe*. Hainsworth emphasizes, against modern prejudices, the originality in Cervantes's idealistic tales that made such seventeenth-century commentators as Scudéry and Florian praise so highly *El amante liberal* and *La fuerza de la sangre*. If the works were indeed "Italianate" they would be no better than those of the sixteenth century which Cervantes criticizes in his prologue to the *Novelas ejemplares*. When we consider the *in medias res* beginnings, the presence of chance, the long voyages and chaste lovers, and the discovery of hidden origins that characterize the idealistic tales, we must agree that they are strongly divergent from the clear-cut, almost anecdotal novellas of the Italian tradition.

When the characteristics Hainsworth isolates as typical of the idealistic tales are related to characteristics of *Don Quixote* Part II and the *Persiles*, a case can be begun to be made for the later dating of the idealistic tales. This conclusion is reinforced by the similarities between the realistic tales and *Don Quixote* I and the fact that all evidence suggests that *Rinconete y Cortadillo*, *El celoso extremeño*, *El licenciado Vidriera*, and *El coloquio de los perros* were written before 1606.

In seeking support for this chronology outside of Cervantes's works, brief reference has been made to the literary theory which appears to have inspired Cervantes's work, with special stress on the importance of Heliodorus's influence in both the *Persiles*, and in the idealistic short novels. But the attraction to the possibilities of fiction exemplified by Heliodorus— possibilities outlined as early as 1604, in chapter 47 of *Don Quixote* I— cannot be seen as independent of Cervantes's attitude toward the more basic questions of truth and man's role in life. Forcione's and Avalle-Arce's references to the theological certainty of the *Persiles* suggests the develop-

---

[7] E.g., Franco Meregalli, "Le *Novelas ejemplares* nello svolgimento della personalità di Cervantes" (1960): 344–51; Alessandro Martinengo, "Cervantes contro il Rinascimento" (1956): 177–222; Paolo Savj-López, *Cervantes*, (1917), pp. 133–66; and Carlos Romero, *Introduzione al "Persiles" di Miguel de Cervantes* (1968), p. cxvii

ment of this other aspect of Cervantes's thinking.[8] Since the idealistic tales combine increased exploration of the possibilities of verisimilitude with religious denouements, it seems likely that the later religious orientation is connected to the interest in fantasy in literature.

When considering this proposed development in Cervantes's thought and works, it is well to remember that not only in an age of faith is such a trajectory possible. The works of Shakespeare, Galdós, Flaubert, Mann, Conrad, and Proust suggest a similar trajectory. The theoretical basis for a retreat from struggle and despair by a novelist and the movement toward transcendence of these problems can be found in the work of René Girard. In Cervantes's case the trajectory suggests acceptance of an absolute truth which changes his view of the particular and concrete. This altered perception of reality radically affects the structure and plot of Cervantes's later works, as will be shown in the detailed study of the *Novelas ejemplares* to follow.

Because the question of chronology is as difficult to settle as it is intriguing for anyone aware of the totality of Cervantes's work, I have included an appendix in which I discuss and present my objections to other suggested orderings of Cervantes's work. I hope that my presentation there and throughout the book will provide enough reasonable evidence for the trajectory I propose to avoid serious problems for the reader in this highly controversial aspect of my work.

---

[8] Forcione, *Cervantes, Aristotle, Persiles,* pp. 342–43, and also his *Cervantes' Christian Romance* (1971), pp. 31–63. Avalle-Arce, "Introducción," *Los trabajos de Persiles y Sigismunda* (1969), pp. 20–27. See also Arturo Farinelli, "El último sueño romántico de Cervantes" (1936), pp. 149–62; and Martín Gabriel, "Heliodoro y la novela," p. 228.

Novel to Romance

I. TYPOLOGICAL AND CHRONOLOGICAL CONSIDERATIONS OF CERVANTES'S WORK

The two Don Quixotes and the Persiles: distinctions and similarities

Because the dates during which *Don Quixote* was written can be determined with reasonable accuracy,[1] an investigation of Cervantes's literary development must begin with a comparison of Part I and Part II. The two parts of *Don Quixote* fall into two periods in Cervantes's life the distinction of which will be the focus of this study. By isolating certain traits in Part II of *Don Quixote* which reveal its kinship to the *Persiles* and its marked deviation from novelistic patterns established in Part I, it will be possible to establish a framework which can be used when turning to the chronological ordering of the *Novelas ejemplares*.[2]

[1] For our purposes, it is enough to acknowledge that Part I of *Don Quixote* was published in 1605. Part II, however, is a little more difficult to date, as it was written in years which are critical to this study. Cervantes mentions as forthcoming the Second Part to *Don Quixote* in his prologue to the *Novelas ejemplares*, written in 1613. Sancho dates a letter to Teresa (II, 36) as July 20, 1614. Avellaneda's apocrpyhal *Don Quixote* was approved for publication on April 18 and July 4, 1614, and was published in September of that year. Cervantes's *Don Quixote* reflects the appearance of Avellaneda's apocryphal version in chapter 59 of Part II and makes numerous references to it from then until the end. This would suggest that Cervantes wrote chapters 36 through 74 between July 1614 and the spring of 1615, when *Don Quixote* must have been completed in order to have been published in the fall of that same year. Although it is not possible to extrapolate from these hints the timing involved in writing the first thirty-six chapters of Part II, it is obvious that they could easily have been written as late as 1613. The point, however, is not important. It is enough to say that *Don Quixote* II is a product of Cervantes's later years and that its ending was written only a year before Cervantes's own death. Further discussion of this problem can be found in Stephen Gilman's *Cervantes y Avellaneda* (1951), pp. 167–76. Although Gilman's arguments seek to establish a longer involvement with Part II by Cervantes, nothing he says makes impossible the supposition that the work was written between, say, 1610 and 1615.

[2] Although there is some dispute about the dating of the *Persiles*, the majority of recent commentaries on the subject appear to agree that at least Books III and IV, and possibly Book II, were written late. See Juan Bautista Avalle-Arce's introduction to his edition of *Los Trabajos de Persiles y Sigismunda* (1969), pp. 12–27. See also Rafael Osuna, "El olvido del *Persiles*" (1968): 55–75; Antonio Vilanova, "El peregrino andante en el *Persiles de Cervantes*" (1949): 97–159; Alban Forcione, *Cer-*

In Part I of *Don Quixote* a dialectic is established between narrator and character. Both appear uncertain of one another and uncertain of their roles with respect to the work in which each is engaged. Don Quixote, though fiercely assertive of his freedom and autonomy, is at the same time the character in Part I most willing to attribute reverses in his fortune to a wise enchanter who has control over his every action. Though he creates his own name, plans his own career, and even projects the book which will be written about him, he takes from Sancho's mouth the name "caballero de la triste figura" and attributes its invention to a power beyond his own (I, 19). The autonomy toward which Don Quixote pretends is strangely linked with a sense of his contingency.[3]

This ambiguity is repeated on the narrator's side by his representation within the novel as both historian and enchanter. The historian is subservient to the actions of his character, while the enchanter controls them completely. The "second author," by emphasizing Cide Hamete's Moorish background, derides the fictional author's repeated claims to truthfulness. Cide Hamete embodies the conflict Cervantes must feel as author between the desire to entertain—which is associated with the creation of fanciful invention—and the desire truthfully to represent reality. The dualism is variously expressed throughout Part I, as each character generates and exaggerates his opposite. Cide Hamete's internal conflict is exteriorized immediately by the presence of the "second author"—the one who has found the lost manuscript in a Toledan market place and who has undertaken to write down the oral translation rendered by an Arabic-speaking boy he has hired. The doubt cast on Cide Hamete's truthfulness suggests not only the specific problem of how a Moor can be relied upon honestly to relate the deeds of a Christian, but the more general problem of how the point of view of the teller affects the substance of the tale.

---

vantes, *Aristotle, and the Persiles* (1970), note 17, p. 264; and Carlos Romero, *Introduzione al "Persiles" di Miguel de Cervantes* (1968), pp. cxiv–cxx. A more recent article by Osuna ("Las fechas del *Persiles*" [1970]: 383–433) modifies somewhat the basic point that Books III and IV were written late by suggesting a 1606–09 dating for Book III, and a 1615–16 for Book IV.

[3] See also chapters 2 and 18 in Part I for explicit references by Don Quixote to the author in charge of his existence. There is, in chapter 17, some fascinating word play by both Don Quixote and Sancho suggesting the relationship between the Moorish muleteer, enchanters, and the author of whom they are supposedly ignorant. Sancho says, "Could this be the enchanted Moor coming back to give us some more punishment, if there is any left in the inkwell?" (I, 17) ("Señor. ¿si será éste, a dicha, el moro encantado, que nos vuelve a castigar, si se dejó algo en el tintero?" Cervantes Saavedra, *Obras Completas*, edited by Angel Valbuena Prat, 15th ed., 1967, p. 1088. Hereafter referred to in footnotes as VP, with pertinent page number). All translations of *Don Quixote* come from Samuel Putnam's translation, *The Ingenious Gentleman Don Quixote de la Mancha*, 2 vols. (1949).

The fictional author's role is further complicated by his tardy appearance within the novel. The work which the reader originally understands to be Cervantes's becomes, after chapter 9, the translation of a manuscript by the Moorish historian Cide Hamete Benengeli. But as early as chapter 1 the narrator had admitted that information for the work had been collected from the archives of La Mancha, and that many inconsistencies had been detected in his researches. Even such fundamental things as the main character's prefictional name and the order of his adventures could not be established with any certainty.[4] It is clear that the author, be he Cervantes or his fictional surrogate, Cide Hamete, is unable to transmit reliably the facts of the history of Don Quixote.

The double presentation of Don Quixote—in his prehistory as bored country squire and in his fictional role as knight-errant—reveals a parallel ambiguity in the character's self-conception. The character—Alonso Quijano-Don Quixote—shares with the author—Cervantes-Cide Hamete— an unstable vision of himself which explains the alternating postures of independence and dependence which both show. This instability also explains their will to create a new story out of nothingness. For both the narrator and the character are shown creating themselves out of a rejection of a past which is to be totally effaced. Don Quixote will create himself in opposition to the sedentary life typical of the country squire Alonso Quijano, and Cide Hamete will create a "true" history in opposition to the fictitious chivalric and pastoral novels.

The narrator, in order to create his "true" history, must write a story that contrasts Don Quixote's actual experience with the "ideal" history of which his character dreams. Cide Hamete places Don Quixote squarely within the context of the reality which he would transform, allowing the novel's truth to emerge out of the ensuing struggle between concrete reality and an abstract ideal. The position the narrator takes with respect to this scene is totally noncommittal.

As a result of the narrator's unwillingness to side either with Don Quixote or with his surrounding cast of characters, Part I is threatened by lack of unity. The presence of the *Curioso impertinente* and the Captive's tale are the most often-cited examples of Cervantes's grappling with the problem of unity and variety in Part I. But the lack of unity is also revealed in the large group of sympathetic characters presented. The

---

[4] Forcione sees this an example of Cervantes's deliberate rejection of the factuality demanded by classical theoreticians: "When, in the following pages [after page 1] he [Cervantes] adds that there is considerable disagreement concerning the real name of Don Quixote and the location of his first adventure, he is saying both that truth is elusive and that those who demand an illusion of truth in a literary work are ignorant of the fundamental nature of art" (*Cervantes, Aristotle, Persiles*, p. 346).

characters in Part I have a genuine existence apart from their association with Don Quixote. Dorotea is the Princess Micomicona for Don Quixote's benefit, but she also has real problems of her own which are as important to the narrator as her skill in fooling Don Quixote. Her equivalent in Part II, the Countess Trifaldí, is never shown apart from the role as Don Quixote's deceiver. Many characters in Part I share with Don Quixote a mixed role as historical, living characters and as characters engaged in deception. As such, they all compete for the attention of the author and challenge, in a way more successful than in Part II, Don Quixote's claims to dominance.

The narrator's uncertainty about theoretical matters can also be seen in the persistent theme of literary discussion in Part I. The characters are often shown discussing literary precepts, outlining the ideal novel, condemning current practices in the theater, and analyzing their own literary responses. Like Don Quixote's consultation with himself about the best way to express his madness so that Dulcinea could know of his love for her (I, 25), this recourse to overt discussion betrays an underlying doubt about the propriety of the actual undertaking.[5]

Still another reflection of the narrator's uncertainty is the narrative disposition of the tale. The story appears to be often on the verge of complete breakdown (e.g., the subdivision into parts, and the protestation at the end of chapter 8 that the author had run out of information). The author's awareness of the absurdity of the conventions to which he nonetheless adheres is made patent.[6]

Part II introduces a different Don Quixote living in different surroundings and controlled by a different type of narrator. Instead of alternating between his desire for self-creation and his sense of helplessness in the face of enchanters who control his existence, Don Quixote appears effectively to be immobilized in Part II, no longer engaged in creating his own image. The enchanters who foiled his plans for glory in Part I move, in Part II, within view of the reader who discovers, in exacting detail, how a succession of characters create situations by which they can deceive and control Don Quixote.

---

[5] See Jean-François Canavaggio, "Alonso López Pinciano y la estética literaria de Cervantes en el *Quijote*" (1958): 79–104, for a discussion of the relationship between theorizing and artistic creation, especially in Part I.

[6] Raymond Willis (*The Phantom Chapters of the "Quijote"* [1953], p. 94) makes this clear: "The disproportion [in Part II] is reduced between the fact of division of the text into chapters and the treatment of the text at the points of division. Thus there is no grotesquely absurd division into *partes* at wholly ridiculous points in the narrative, and, on the other hand, the constructions of overflow and retrospective references are commonly less obvious at the syntactical level."

As Casalduero has pointed out, the mysteries of Part I, many of which befuddled not only Don Quixote and Sancho but the reader as well, dissolve in Part II into a series of mechanistic distortions of reality carried out by their various perpetrators and carefully explained by Cide Hamete.[7] The reader, rather than witnessing with Don Quixote the fearful workings of an autonomous universe, instead observes Don Quixote's manipulation by other characters who intentionally alter the natural order. Universal human confusion, generated by multiple interpretations of natural phenomena, is replaced in Part II by props created and arranged for the specific deception of Don Quixote by other characters who pretend full knowledge and control over the situations they are inventing. The reader must rely on Cide Hamete to explain the various ruses to which Don Quixote and Sancho are continually subjected. Replacing the rather crude efforts at manipulation carried out by the Barber, the Curate, and Dorotea in Part I, Sansón Carrasco, the Duke and Duchess, and Altisidora introduce highly complicated inventions in Part II. The number of characters who engage in deception increases in Part II, as does the complexity and mastery of their art. If the mechanics of deception are made more obvious in Part II than in Part I, so is the controlling hand of the author. Cide Hamete becomes much more evident in Part II and speaks to the reader much more confidently and frequently.[8]

The author also shows less interest in discussing literary precepts in Part II. Outside of Sansón Carrasco's discourse in chapter 3, almost nothing is explicitly said about literary problems. Instead, literary problems are actualized. In place of theorizing about the theater, we see Maese Pedro in action; the poet-son of Don Diego de Miranda replaces a dis-

---

[7] "En 1605, se presentaba el misterio de la vida. En 1615 la vida es un enredo, y el novelista tiene que explicarlo" [In 1605 the mystery of life is presented. In 1615 life is a confusion, and the novelist has to explain it."] (*Sentido y forma del "Quijote"* [1966], p. 212).

[8] Ruth S. El Saffar, *Distance and Control in "Don Quixote": A Study in Narrative Technique* (to be published in Studies in the Romance Languages and Literature Series, University of North Carolina Press). Here it is explained that the loss of depth provided by the juxtaposition of a character's lived reality and his fictional role, coupled with the increased sophistication of the character's deceptions in Part II, makes the reader much more dependent on the author for clarification: "The reader has no way of telling when the characters are being "authors" and when they are being characters controlled by an author outside the story. Because of this possible confusion, an author outside the story is the reader's only point of reference. Cide Hamete, only briefly and infrequently mentioned in Part I, becomes a much more salient figure in Part II as a result of the need for distancing and clarification. He appears at least a hundred times in the course of Part II to comment, to explain, or to be commented upon."

cussion about poetry; Basilio and the allegorical play at Camacho's wedding demonstrate the role of controlled deception in art; the false Arcadia reveals the bankruptcy of the pastoral novels discussed in Part I.[9]

Don Quixote, for his part, is more introspective in Part II, less active, more victim than aggressor. If in Part I his goal was so abstract as to be ultimately unattainable, and therefore also indestructible, in Part II the goal has become concrete. In Part I love for Dulcinea and the search for knightly adventures were means to the end of creating a new and heroic image for himself in the world. In Part II the seemingly impossible goal of Part I has been miraculously achieved: Don Quixote has become famous and universally recognized as knight-errant. Now the relation between means and end is reversed: fame and knight-errantry have become the concrete data which determine his relation to others, while Dulcinea and the adventures become the goals after which Don Quixote seeks in vain. Dulcinea, who was never actively sought in Part I, becomes the major focus for Don Quixote in Part II as he sets out first to find her and then to disenchant her. As elusive as Dulcinea are the adventures that Don Quixote seeks. The lion who turns tail on him or the Moorish pursuers who are nothing but puppets are far more disconcerting than the actual blows he receives in Part I from resisting reality. The obdurate reality of Part I almost entirely disappears in Part II.

In Part I Don Quixote could only be defined negatively with regard to his flight from surrounding reality. In Part II he is accepted—at least apparently—by everyone he meets as the fictional character that he himself created. In contrast to Part I Don Quixote finds himself in Part II surrounded, not with his old friends from home who know him and recognize him as Alonso Quijano, but with strangers who know him only as a character from a book. Having been robbed of the springboard from which his rejection of his surroundings was made possible, the Don Quixote of Part II finds himself in limbo, having neither his old self as Alonso Quijano nor his dream of becoming another Amadís left to clarify his position. He therefore appears to retire within himself, and to show signs of boredom, irritation, weariness, and melancholy. All impulse to self-creation has disappeared, leaving in its place the necessity for self-discovery.

What this means for the relationship between narrator and character is that the narrator has asserted full control over the novelistic environment in Part II. Like Maese Pedro, Cide Hamete is supreme manipulator, pulling the strings—no longer sparring with characters who threaten his

---

[9] Canavaggio, ". . . parece como si los mismos problemas se transformaron en seres de carne y hueso" [It seems as if the same problems were transformed into flesh and blood beings.] ("Pinciano y estética literaria" pp. 18–19).

autonomy.[10] The narrator's confidence contributes to an atmosphere in general less charged with moral ambiguity. The characters in Part II stand out more clearly as good or bad, and their various claims to importance within the novel are less imperative. Our sympathy toward Don Quixote in Part II is more developed; our antipathy toward his surrounding characters is greater. The Duke and Duchess, whose gratuitous manipulation of Don Quixote easily turns from diversion for its own sake to cruelty, replace the benign Barber and Curate of Part I. While we could share, in Part I, in Andrés's anger with Don Quixote and understand why the muleteer or the Toledan merchants reacted to Don Quixote as they did, we cannot be sympathetic with the people who ridicule Don Quixote, unbidden, in Part II.[11]

In Part II there are no false starts, as in Part I, and no changes in direction.[12] The narrator clearly conceives of the second part of his novel as a unity the beginning and end of which are planned from the start. The parallelisms and oppositions through which the episodes are balanced against each other are well discussed by Casalduero.[13] In place of a strictly chronological disposition of events, there are, in Part II, actions which are carried on simultaneously (e.g., when Don Quixote and Sancho separate between chapters 44 and 55) and events which are nar-

[10] This analogy comes from George Haley's justifiably renown article ("The narrator in *Don Quijote*: Maese Pedro's Puppet Show" [1966]: 145–65). It might be worth pointing out, however, that I see the relationship between narrator and character as different in Part I from Part II. Symptomatic of the difference is the fact that both Cide Hamete and Cervantes appear within the novelistic world they are presenting in Part I (in chapter 16, when Cide Hamete is said to be the cousin of the muleteer in the inn; in chapter 6, where Cervantes is said to be a friend of the Curate, in the Captive's tale, when "un tal de Saavedra" is referred to, and in chapter 47 where the author of *Rinconete y Cortadillo* is said to have stayed in Juan Palomeque's inn). No such existence by the author and narrator within the tale is alluded to in Part II.

[11] John J. Allen develops the distinction between the two parts of *Don Quixote* on the basis of the changed relationship between Don Quixote and his friends and the increased sense of reader sympathy with Don Quixote against his tormentors in Part II, in *Don Quixote: Hero or Fool?* (1969).

[12] For a discussion of some aspects of this, see Goeffrey Stagg's "Sobre el plan primitivo del *Quijote*" (1964), pp. 218–25.

[13] *Sentido y forma del "Quijote,"* pp. 213–14. See also Enrique Moreno Baez, *Reflexiones sobre el "Quijote"* (1968): "Si ahora comparamos con la primera la segunda parte del *Quijote*, vemos que desde este punto de vista presenta un aspecto muy diferente, ya que en ella Cervantes ha seguido un plan que nos anuncia desde el principio y que determina su desenlace" (pp. 14–15). ["If now we compare the second part of *Don Quixote* with the first, we see that from this point of view it presents a very different picture, since in it [Part II] Cervantes has followed a plan which he announces to us from the beginning and which determines its outcome."]

rated out of their chronological order (as when the details of the plan Sansón Carrasco discusses with the housekeeper and the niece in chapter 6 are kept from the reader until much later; or when, in chapter 24, Cide Hamete refers ahead to Don Quixote's death and recantation). The narrator shows his confidence in this over-all structure in the consistency with which he keeps Don Quixote and Sancho in the forefront of the action, in the way he keeps the reader informed about the tricks and deceptions intended to beguile Don Quixote and Sancho, and in the weakened character of Don Quixote himself. He has replaced mystery with manipulation, and equivocal moral situations with clear-cut instances of cruelty on the part of Don Quixote's acquaintances and goodness on the part of Don Quixote. The author appears to be teaching not only the reader but his main character a lesson about the nature of appearances.

Don Quixote escapes from fiction at the end of Part II as from a bad dream. His renunciation of his self-created image corresponds with his acceptance of death and the reality of a truth that transcends human understanding. In the ending to *Don Quixote* Part II, Don Quixote rejects his fictional role and embraces death in full acceptance of his home, his family, his religion, and the transcendent truth that hides behind all appearances. He achieves, in that final moment of lucidity, the knowledge that makes him clearly superior to all the characters who had assumed his madness, by understanding that all human actions are equally fallacious and that true reality will always elude the seeker, who is, after all, chained by words and social customs and literary models to the automatic actions and thoughts which inevitably distort reality.

Don Quixote, having rejected the chimeras of chivalric and pastoral works of fiction, sees everything in true perspective and becomes one with the narrator who lays down his pen when Don Quixote dies. He and the artist are truly one, from the perspective of the end, for both have collaborated in vain in the task—impossible as much for the author as for the character—of capturing reality. Reality captured automatically becomes, like Don Quixote's giants and enchanters, what it is not.[14]

Don Quixote's rejection of his enterprise is not only coterminous with Cide Hamete's but is its exact equivalent. All the romantic efforts to

[14] Although Cervantes certainly felt intimately drawn to the written word, he appears to have discovered in it finally only a negative validity. That is, that the written word is necessarily that which is not, but it is at the same time the only means by which one can discover that which is. It is surely this final intuition which leads Cervantes, in his later fiction, back into tales of more fantastic content—tales which stretch the concept of verisimilitude to its extreme. This may be the underpinning for what Forcione has so convincingly found to be Cervantes's continued anti-Aristotelianism even in his most studiously precept-oriented work.

identify Cervantes with his hero are, though in quite a different way, substantiated in the simultaneous rejection by character and author of what is now seen to be their identical passion. When this is understood, we can see, with René Girard,[15] that the ending is not defeat, as so many have interpreted Don Quixote's death, but victory. The narrator has in fact liberated himself from the confusions both he and his character underwent, confusions which were the reason for the book. The author does not reject fiction, however, as the existence of the *Persiles* proves. He rejects the illusion that fiction can capture reality. The end of illusion, as we shall see in the analysis of some of the *Novelas ejemplares*, is not necessarily an end to life or to fiction, but an end to a way of understanding life or fiction. The quality of both life and fiction changes, once the validity of individual perspective has been undermined.

An analysis of the *Novelas ejemplares* will show that the changes in outlook illustrated in *Don Quixote* Part II antedate by some time the 1615 publication of that work. The very conscious unity of Part II and the control revealed by the narrator attest to a prior understanding by Cervantes of a new role of the narrator in a work of fiction. This change, reflected in the differences in narrative technique and character presentation found in Parts I and II of *Don Quixote*, occurs after the publication of *Don Quixote* I and before the publication of *Don Quixote* II, for it can be clearly detected in the *Novelas ejemplares*, published in 1613.

The simultaneous end of the book and of the life of Don Quixote shows how much Cervantes had come to see fiction as exemplary in his later works. The narrator and character are engaged in a new kind of dialectic in the later works and achieve a new kind of identity. The character is now charged by Cervantes with the undertaking of an arduous task in an alien milieu, such that he must draw on resources of his character which reveal his courage and stability. The narrator, because he is conscious of the testing involved in this process, becomes the apparently cruel hand of fortune who presents a series of obstacles for his character to overcome. In this sense, Maese Pedro, the Duke and Duchess, and Altisidora are accurate representatives of the narrator's new position in Part II. They are shown as masterful in the art of contrivance and insensitive to the subtleties of character of the ones whom they manipulate.

The much closer involvement of narrator with character in Part I is represented in the efforts of the Curate, the Barber, and Dorotea to control Don Quixote. These manipulators within the story are shown as

---

[15] *Mensonge romantique et vérité romanesque* (1961), pp. 290–91. See also Jorge Guillén, "Vida y muerte de Alonso Quijano" (1952): 102–13.

amateurs, unsure of their craft, feeling at the same time a bit foolish and rather amused by the task they have undertaken. Their attitude toward Don Quixote is one of benevolence, and their interest in fooling him is far outweighed by their concern for his well-being. In making this analogy, however, it must be remembered that Cervantes cannot be fully identified with the author-characters within the story any more than he can be with Don Quixote. The author-characters are nonetheless representative of an aspect—exaggerated, just as Don Quixote is—of the creative process engaged in by the author himself.

Both narrator and character are represented in Part II as being forced to play roles with which they are uncomfortable. Cide Hamete shows his feelings of constraint in the well-known passage in chapter 44 of Part II and Don Quixote reveals his not fully conscious sense of dissatisfaction in the "Cueva de Montesinos" episode. Neither Don Quixote nor Cide Hamete sees himself as a free agent in Part II. Yet it is only through these abnormal roles that the "normal" roles can be seen in true perspective. When, at a distance from his given position in life, it becomes clear that the character is greater than any role he plays, he is able to return to his normal situation with a sense of self-transcendence.

In both parts of *Don Quixote*, Cervantes shows a concern for distinguishing between history and poetry, fiction and reality. From the discussion in Part I, chapter 47, as well as from the very conception of the novel, it is obvious that Cervantes was familiar with neo-Aristotelian esthetics before writing *Don Quixote* I. The rejection of the chivalric novel, along with the correlative search for an acceptable prose epic, discussion about variety and unity, and a consideration of verisimilitude and the role of the marvelous all appear in Part I and reveal Cervantes's familiarity with neo-Aristotelian precepts.[16] In Part II these concerns have certainly not been abandoned: in some cases they appear to have intensified. Cervantes now holds more rigorously to the principle of diversity within unity and deals more explicitly with the role of the marvelous. As E. C. Riley says of the *Persiles,* Cervantes takes great care in Part II of *Don Quixote* to show the physical plausibility of every apparently miraculous event.[17]

Because on the level of literary precepts the distinctions between the two parts cannot be made manifest, it is now evident why commentators who limit their concern to this area of Cervantes's thought have not generally engaged in the question of chronology or with the *Novelas*

[16] For a summary of Cervantes's use of neo-Aristotelian themes in *Don Quixote,* see Canavaggio, "Pinciano y estética literaria," pp. 48–49; Forcione, *Cervantes, Aristotle, Persiles,* chaps. 1 and 2; and E. C. Riley, *Cervantes's Theory of the Novel* (1962), chap. 1.

[17] *Cervantes's Theory,* pp. 190–91.

ejemplares. Riley says at the beginning of his book that from the point of view of literary precepts, there is no significant development in Cervantes's literary thought from *Don Quixote* I to the *Persiles*. There is, however, an undeniable change of attitude and technique which must be accounted for if we are to be able to deal effectively with the disparate nature of the short novels published together in 1613 under the title *Novelas ejemplares*.

Although some controversy still surrounds the question of when the *Persiles* was written, a word might be added here about many characteristics it shares with *Don Quixote* II. In the *Persiles*, especially after Book II, the narrator maintains an intrusive and manipulative role reminiscent of Cide Hamete in Part II of *Don Quixote*. As in *Don Quixote* II, Cervantes clearly marks off the major characters in the *Persiles* and sends them wandering through a maze of adventures and temptations. Like Don Quixote, they are accepted everywhere by strangers who believe that what are actually their fictitious names are their real names, and that what is actually a fictitious relationship—brother and sister—is their real relationship. Like Don Quixote, they must live out their fiction in alien territory, surrounded by people ignorant of their true origins. And, like Don Quixote, they prove to be exemplary—greater than the trials presented them.

The emphasis on religion in the denouement of the *Persiles* also recalls the ending to *Don Quixote*. The only real difference is that whereas Persiles and Sigismunda join in marriage after they have overcome their trials, reached their destination, and revealed their true selves, Don Quixote must die. But in the religious context of the end of *Don Quixote* Part II, death becomes not annihilation but fulfillment. In death Don Quixote discovers himself in the other—for he fully embraces his nonfictional self and dies surrounded by his family and friends.

Determining circumstances of Part I, coupled with the fortuitous appearance of Avellaneda's spurious second part, make death the only possible ending for *Don Quixote*.[18] Don Quixote is, at the beginning of his adventures, already defined as old and unmarried. Dulcinea is already defined as unattainable. There would have been no way, within the context established in Part I, to remain faithful to its outlines and give *Don Quixote* a "happy ending." Avellaneda settled the matter once and for all by showing that, if left alive or with progeny, the Don Quixote of Cervantes's masterpiece could easily become the plaything of scores of imitators. This provides the overt excuse for Don Quixote's death at the

---

[18] For a discussion of the role of Avellaneda's work in the ending of *Don Quixote* II, see Carlos Blanco Aguinaga, "Cervantes y la picaresca. Notas sobre dos tipos de realismo" (1957): 336, n. 44; and E. C. Riley, "Three Versions of *Don Quixote*" (1973): 807–19.

end of Part II.[19] But both death and marriage represent the acceptance by a formerly imperfect and alienated individual of a reality beyond his understanding. In this sense the end of *Don Quixote* II is similar to that of the *Persiles*. Death and marriage are transformed from unwilling acts of acquiescence and loss of freedom to acts of willed acceptance. The new stance allows for the union of the formerly opposing concepts of authority and freedom.

In the emergence of religion as a theme in Cervantes's works, the author perceives clearly a positive goal toward which to lead his characters. The goal is a self-transcendence which emerges out of the dialectic established between the "normal" and the fictionalized self. The two selves are pulled so far apart that the fictionalized self can no longer be deluded about the possibilities for fulfillment within this role. The character is held totally isolated from his original self. In Part I the periodical appearance of Don Quixote's former friends and family provided the excuse, in their pursuit of him, for his continued flight. When in Part II Alonso Quijano disappears almost completely from the context in which Don Quixote lives, the emptiness and loneliness he feels reveals his dependence on his rejected self and proves the sham of his self-creation. It was not the creation in itself that had attracted Don Quixote, but the opposition it established to a lived situation which he felt he must reject. Cervantes's characters in his late fiction identify their self-created roles so much with misery and suffering that they exert all their energies toward regaining their original state. Since the departure from the original state is associated with evil or error, the return is made with the character purged. The novelized state becomes punishment and purgatory in the later works.[20]

Through this analysis of the differences between Part I and Part II of *Don Quixote*, and the similarities between Part II of *Don Quixote* and the *Persiles*, certain guidelines have been established on the basis of which the various stories within the *Novelas ejemplares* can be meaningfully distinguished. Within this framework the first steps toward distinguishing early from late novelistic tendencies in Cervantes's work can be made. The presence, in *Don Quixote* II, of a more passive and more exemplary Don Quixote, a more assertive Cide Hamete, and of a plot

---

[19] In the prologue to *Don Quixote* II, Cervantes ends by saying: "In this book I give you Don Quixote continued and, finally, dead and buried, in order that no one may dare testify any further concerning him, for there has been quite enough evidence as it is." [. . . te doy a Don Quijote dilatado, y, finalmente, muerto y sepultado, porque ninguno se atreva a levantarle nuevos testimonios, pues bastan los pasados" (VP, 1273)].

[20] Rafael Lapesa, "En torno a *La española inglesa y El Persiles*" (1950), pp. 356–88, discusses the religious tone of Cervantes's late works and the testing which Recaredo must undergo. This will be taken up in a later chapter.

more carefully structured, suggests tendencies clearly developed in the *Persiles* and the idealistic novelas. The obvious differences that divide Cervantes's work into two distinct types are the result of a development through time and not of the author's schizophrenia, hypocrisy, or senility. In the section to follow, the distinctions discussed with regard to the two parts of *Don Quixote* and the *Persiles* will be applied to the *Novelas ejemplares*.[21]

General Distinctions between Early and Late Works

A basic thread that runs through all of Cervantes's fiction from *Don Quixote* Part I to the *Persiles* is the notion that the world is bigger than any single view of it by a protagonist in his works. The difference between the early and the late works in their treatment of this common theme is that in the late works the central protagonists are exemplary in their acceptance of their given role in life and in their devotion to a transcendent reality. In the early works, on the other hand, the main characters try to remake their lives. They reject the circumstances into which they have been born and show no faith in any reality beyond the one they perceive. From this single difference, a number of corollary distinctions between early and late works can be derived. The main characters' faith, in the late works, allows them to persevere through great hardship and suffering without yielding to the many pressures and temptations to which they are exposed. Since the character, in his exemplarity, remains unchanged, his development and his perceptions are no longer the central focus of the story. The scenes in the later works are richly described by a narrator who appears to be most preoccupied with the tasteful arrangement of incidents and an author who sees all earthly events as abstract representations of a reality which stands in changeless, timeless perfection against the chaos of existence in time. Opposing the serenity of the transcendent reality toward which the later characters aspire is the agitation and confusion they are forced to suffer. The later stories are filled with high adventure. The dizzying movement and action portrayed devalues the importance of the lived moment by the sheer quantity of its representation.

[21] Although it remains to be conclusively proved, I will be using in subsequent discussions the terms "early" to refer to the works whose elements reflect *Don Quixote* Part I and "late" to refer to the works more similar in style and content to *Don Quixote* Part II and the *Persiles*.

The fixation on a transcendent reality also affects the structure of the story. Rather than allowing the reader to move with the character, sharing his uncertainties, toward an undefined end, the characters' submission to a higher reality causes the reader's attention to focus in the later stories, on the plot construction itself. We are asked to admire the author's skill in inventing new and different twists and surprises; to watch him begin the story in the middle and then work back toward the beginning before finally bringing the threads of the plot into perfect resolution. Since the characters' reactions are predictable, it is now the author's skill that must draw our attention.[22]

Emphasis on the plot and the way in which it is developed also supposes that the story will have an ending. Since the main characters are exemplary, the ending will be happy. In all of the late stories the main characters are moved out of their normal circumstances, placed in situations in which their lives and honor are threatened, and then returned, through recognition and peripety, to a settled state within society in reward for their faith and dedication.

The early stories appear to have a much less planned development. The characters, while also living their lives in fiction outside the bounds of society, do so not because they are forced but because they choose to escape what they feel to be society's oppressive nature. In their escape they are constrained to start, in fiction, out of nothing: to recreate themselves and the society they are rejecting. Because the story builds from an initial choice by a character to recreate himself, it appears to have only the design developed by the character himself. In the early stories the narrator's role is severely restricted. He introduces the main protagonist with a brief statement of his prehistory, often omitting even the most rudimentary information concerning his character. The character then seizes upon some plan of his own devising and proceeds to impose that plan on himself and the others in the story. The early characters convert themselves, within a few paragraphs, from characters in someone else's story to authors of their own stories. Since the stories which they create are, from their point of view, unique and unrelated to their pasts, the ending to the early stories remains uncertain.

The prehistory outlined by the narrator at the beginning of the early stories reveals in every case a character whose escape into self-creation is

[22] The Russian formalists' distinction between plot and story (see, for example, Boris Tomashevsky's article, "Thematics" in *Russian Formalist Criticism* [1965], esp. pp. 66–78) might be useful in understanding the change in time disposition in the later works. The dominance of plot, the author's ordering, over story, the order in which the events would occur in life, may be another indication of Cervantes's changed attitude toward himself as author. Tzvetan Todorov (*Poétique de la prose* [1971], p. 39) refines the distinction, opposing *discours* and *histoire* and linking the differences to the various ways the author is related to the character.

instigated by a sense of alienation and lack of fulfillment in the normal
context of his life. His invention must be unique because it must offer
him a new route, an escape from everyday life. And because his existence
depends upon it, ĩ. will seek to perpetuate the fiction into which he has
cast himself.

The later characters, on the other hand, endure their fictional state.
They neither choose it nor invent it. Though a flaw in their own person-
alities, or a mistaken choice, may have participated in causing their subsequent alienation, their prehistory is desirable and peaceful, and the
later characters do not consciously seek escape from it. They work for
and wait for the end of their trials. They seek a way out of fiction. The
story leads the character through a maze of circumstances which interrupt
the fulfillment of his wishes for peace and marriage and return to
society.

Of the early stories, all end either with the destruction of the central
character or with no conclusion at all. Anselmo, in the *Curioso impertinente*, Carrizales, in *El celoso extremeño*, and the Licenciate, in *El
licenciado Vidriera*, all die after having seen their dreams shattered. All,
having planned to create their futures by the force of their ingenuity,
must face the absolute disintegration of their plans, recognize their folly
in having tried to control reality, and die. In *Rinconete y Cortadillo*, *El
coloquio de los perros*, and *Don Quixote* I, the ending is suspended. By
the end of *Rinconete y Cortadillo* the two young protagonists have
achieved a certain distance on the thieves' life they have chosen, but, we
are told at the end, they remain in Monipodio's confraternity for several
months beyond the end of the story. The promised continuation will
deal, according to the narrator, with Rinconete and Cortadillo's subsequent adventures with Monipodio's gang, not with their life beyond
Monipodio's world. The ending, therefore, is no ending. The story simply
dissolves into the continuing reality beyond its fiction. *Rinconete y
Cortadillo* is nearly static, a copy of a moment of reality which, because
the copy must reflect the reality exactly, has no right even to impose the
arbitrary limitations of beginnings and ends.[23] For such limitations be-

---

[23] Cervantes's early concept of imitation may reflect a dilemma discussed with
respect to Tasso by Robert Durling in *The Figure of the Poet in Renaissance Epic*
(1965): "It has been pointed out before that the ambiguity in Tasso's position rests
in part upon a confusion of historicity with truth, by which he is put in the paradoxical position of identifying the universal with the false. . . . One fact that may
give us pause is that the universal and the verisimilar are not at all identical; a
poetic representation may approach the universal as a limit, but the very act of imitation, as Tasso conceived it, means representing events as concrete particulars, especially since it seeks an effect of vividness" (pp. 194–95). (See also Riley, *Cervantes's
Theory*, chap. 5; and for a good general statement, Hazard Adams, *The Interests of
Criticism* [1969], chap. 2.)

long to the imagination of the writer and not to the reality which he is reproducing. The absence of ending in *Don Quixote* I is identical to that in *Rinconete*. In both cases the narrator anticipates a final end: Rinconete and Cortadillo will eventually leave Monipodio; Don Quixote will eventually die. But in both cases the narrator emphasizes that the second part will deal not with that ultimate end, but rather with the continued adventures that connect the present moment with the end. In other words, the continuation promised in each case would be a repetition in structure of the present story, not a conclusion. The *Coloquio de los perros* also ends in the middle, the two talking dogs anticipating another night in which they will be able to enjoy conversing with one another.

A picture begins to emerge regarding all the characters who appear in Cervantes's pre-1606 fiction.[24] All are in flight from a reality with which they cannot successfully deal. All are cerebral in that they rely on their intelligence, ingenuity, or understanding to fill up the emptiness of their lives; all fail in fact to understand their past or to control their future; and all find that the present state of suspension in which they have willfully sustained themselves is an illusion from which all—some happily and some tragically—must fall before their story ends.

The irony in the early characters' apparent autonomy and voluntarism is that their reliance on their mental constructs—their faith in their own understanding—actually immobilizes them. Monipodio's world threatens to absorb Rinconete and Cortadillo entirely. The Licenciate's wisdom is swallowed up in his madness; and Don Quixote's reforming zeal is rendered useless by those who, having been rejected by Don Quixote, reject him in return. Cardenio and Dorotea (*Don Quixote* I), each wrongly convinced that their love and honor have been permanently destroyed, decide to give up even trying and are found, semi-wild, living alone in the mountains. Anselmo (*El curioso impertinente*) and Carrizales (*El celoso extremeño*), having established the outlines of their stories, drop out of the picture, only to be overwhelmed by real forces which are in fact beyond their grasp.

The later characters, in contrast, are far more successful in their life projects, despite their apparent passivity. Though many major characters in the later stories (i.e., Leocadia [*La fuerza de la sangre*], Teodosia [*Las dos doncellas*], Recaredo [*La española inglesa*]) face seemingly impossi-

---

[24] In the development of the distinctions between early and late novelas, it may be objected that the characteristics I am proposing as typical of the late works appear in some of the intercalated stories in Part I of *Don Quixote*. The main example is the similarity between the stories of Dorotea and Cardenio in the 1605 *Don Quixote* and *Las dos doncellas*. For a discussion of the differences that justify the assignment of a late dating for the latter, see chap. V, pp. 117–18.

ble situations, they do not base their actions upon any intellectual assessment of their chances to extricate themselves successfully from their problems. Because they do not conceptualize or invent for themselves a future in which present despair is justified, they maintain hope and act in every way to free themselves from their suffering and alienation. As a result, many of the later characters are highly active. Recaredo and Ricardo (*El amante liberal*) exert their energies strenuously, despite repeated failures and disappointments. They are shown engaged in a constant struggle against an unacceptable present circumstance, but never worried about understanding or reinterpreting the past or predicting the future.

The series of distinctions between early and late stories began with a comparison of the characters who appear in each type of story. Whereas the characters in the early stories were captured in fiction because of their flight from reality and were unsuccessful in recreating themselves because of their insistence on self-reliance and their belief in their own apprehensions regarding their past, present, and future, the characters in the late stories were shown to be in fiction not out of choice but because of circumstances beyond their control. Rather than running from society, they are shown constantly seeking release from their alienation from it, constantly striving to reintegrate themselves with society. The attitude of the early characters results in stories which appear autonomous, moving forward toward an undefined goal by the actions and reactions of the characters. In the later stories, the controlling hand of the author is so evident that the characters appear almost as puppets, victims rather than creators of the plot that complicates their lives.

Any change involves all the basic elements of the story. The differences in character attitude cannot truly be separated from the way the plot develops, the way the narrator presents himself with respect to his characters, or the way the major characters are related to the minor characters. Even such questions as the organization of the events narrated and the setting of the stories cannot be divorced from the other elements. It is surely no accident that historical detail is much more evident in the early than in the later stories. It is significant that the story's development in the early works follows a more or less chronological pattern, with the narrator rarely anticipating the story's outcome or rearranging the events in his presentation, while in the later works the chronology is destroyed by the controlling organization of the narrator. To determine, among the intertwining elements of fiction, which one caused the others to change would be a hopeless task. The story is an organic unit. The conventions of criticism which separate it into plot, characterizations, setting, diction, etc. are useful for discussing the way the story is designed, but they do not suggest a causal relationship between them. For causes we must look behind the changes.

In the later works, as they have been described here, Cervantes appears to have adopted a view of society greatly at variance with the one reflected in such works as *El licenciado Vidriera* and *El coloquio de los perros.* The problem that must be resolved, if we are to avoid the conclusion that the idealistic tales represent Cervantes's capitulation to the dominant forces of society, is why marriage, nobility, and happy endings become persistent elements in Cervantes's post-1606 novelas, while the early works tend to champion rebellious heroes whose exertions lead only to failure. The change that mutes social criticism and exalts social conformity cannot be explained by Cervantes's personal recovery from ill-fortune after 1606. From the prologue to *Don Quixote* II, as well as from the *Viaje del parnaso*, we know that Cervantes still suffered from attacks on his character, poverty, and personal troubles at the end of his life.[25] What appears to have changed, as a result of the fame and literary recognition he finally achieved after 1606, is his own perspective on his personal fortunes.

It is well known that *Don Quixote* I poses questions concerning the nature of reality and the relation of reality to fiction. From the way authors become readers and readers become authors and characters become alternately authors and readers; from the way basins become helmets and nags become steeds, it is likely that not only Don Quixote, but Cervantes, is challenging the commonly accepted meanings of words and suggesting that words are actually independent of the things they represent. Don Quixote's devotion to words and his blind faith in their truth; the attention he gives, as author of his life as knight-errant, to naming; his love for poetry; and his concern that Sancho and the others whom he meets speak properly, is only humorous because the words and names he believes in so fully are not in accord with those commonly accepted by everyone else he meets in the novel. The more verbally careless and illiterate Sancho and the more skeptical Barber, Curate, and Canon appear closer to an understanding of truth than Don Quixote. Lotario, in *El curioso impertinente,* speaks out most eloquently against empiricism as a source of knowledge,[26] and Anselmo's total delusion after Camila's pretended state-

---

[25] A good discussion of the *Viaje del parnaso* and Cervantes's social position at the time of its composition can be found in Elias River's "Cervantes' Journey to Parnassus" (1970): 244–48.

[26] ". . . supposing that Heaven or good fortune had made you the master . . . of a very fine diamond to whose quality and purity all the lapidaries who had seen it had testified; . . . and supposing, further, that you yourself believed all this to be true, without knowing anything that would cause you to believe otherwise, would

ment of her fidelity reveals the fallacy of reliance on sense impressions for true information. In *Don Quixote* I no one, including the original narrator, the "second author," Cide Hamete, Don Quixote, Sancho, the Curate, or the Canon, has a privileged position of greater knowledge within the novel. All are shown as limited and struggling, through language and their own understandings of each other, to maintain their autonomy and independence. Cervantes does not choose between them because he includes himself within their confusions, being as uncertain as they about reality and truth.

At the base of that confusion lies a nihilism and an individualism which threaten to destroy art and communication. The only way out of chaos and uncertainty is the affirmation of a truth that transcends language, society, everyday experience, social customs, and sense impressions. Human hardships lose their intensity when viewed as temporary, as unreal in comparison with a reality of greater meaning beyond life. Cervantes appears, for reasons on which we can only speculate, to have achieved such a faith sometime after 1606.

The novelistic expression of this position in Cervantes's works appears as an abrupt break from the earlier individualism and character autonomy. The early works represent an intense exploration of the consequences of individualism. Cervantes's alienated and cerebral characters, no matter how sympathetic the author may be with them, fail in their projects, doing damage to themselves and to those around them. The later works, starting with *La ilustre fregona* and *La gitanilla*, and continuing through *El amante liberal, La fuerza de la sangre, La española inglesa, Don Quixote* II, and the *Persiles* show a detachment from everyday reality and an increasing effort by the narrator to distance himself from the characters. Reality in Part II of *Don Quixote* becomes elusive rather than vindictive, as it had proved to be against *Don Quixote* in Part I. The minor characters in the *Persiles* who allow themselves to be beguiled by the world of reason or of sense perception are clearly presented as negative examples to be compared with Persiles and Sigismunda's chastity

---

it be right for you to wish to take that diamond and place it between a hammer and an anvil and then by force of blows and strength of arm endeavor to see whether or not it was as hard and fine as they had said it was?" (I, 33). [". . . si el Cielo, o la suerte buena, te hubiera hecho señor . . . de un finísimo diamante, de cuya bondad y quilates estuviesen satisfechos cuantos lapidarios le viesen, . . . y tú mismo lo creyeses así, sin saber otra cosa en contrario, ¿sería justo que te viniese en deseo de tomar aquel diamante, y ponerle entre un yunque y un martillo, y allí, a pura fuerza de golpes y brazos, probar si es tan duro y tan fino como dicen? (VP, 1177).] For a detailed discussion of the ways in which empiricism and other epistemological methods are discussed in Cervantes's works, see J. B. Avalle-Arce's "Conocimiento y vida," in *Deslindes cervantinos* (1961), pp. 15–80.

and single-minded devotion to their goal of reaching Rome in fulfillment of their pledge. The seven years Leocadia (*La fuerza de la sangre*) spends in pretense after her rape and the birth of her illegitimate child pass as nothing in the story which is devoted not to her suffering but to the nearly miraculous salvation of her honor. The evil characters in whose charge Ricardo and Leonisa find themselves in *El amante liberal* are, like the minor characters in the *Persiles*, to be regarded as symbolic of the evil passions which control men and women divested of a sense of transcendent truth. Recaredo, in *La española inglesa*, proves the emptiness of sense impressions in his pledge of love to Isabela when her face has lost all of its beauty after her poisoning by the jealous Arnesto's mother. As in *La fuerza de la sangre* and *El amante liberal*, years pass before the characters' desires are fulfilled in *La española inglesa*. Adventures become more variegated and fantastic, and the spatial and temporal distances covered by the characters are larger because the entire experience that makes up the work is understood by both the author and the major characters to be fiction. The vain search for truth in this life—the search that marked the project of characters and narrators alike in the early stories—gives way in the later stories to a conviction that life itself is inimical to truth—that all reality within the reach of human reason and human senses is, by virtue of that reason and sense perception, false. Life itself becomes a fiction. Cervantes's literary fiction then becomes a meta-fiction—a fiction whose truth resides in its exposure of both itself and the reality it is supposed to reflect as fiction.

Ironically, it is the stories which emerge out of this view of life's unreality and of man's inability to perceive it which appear to be structured most carefully and in a most ordered way. The narrator's voice is much more assured and authoritative in the later stories. In a reversal of the early relationship between narrator and character, the central characters in the later stories are made to rely on the narrator to unravel their entangled lives. In the early stories the narrator appeared to rely on the character to develop his own life and initiate his own adventures. The new relationship between narrator and character, however, accurately reflects Cervantes's changed metaphysical position. The later stories are teleological, presenting a fiction and an existence justified by its ending. The later stories enclose longer stretches of time and space and present disoriented characters because they reflect life viewed as a totality, as struggle and confusion relieved only by the faith that the struggle has a transcendent significance not apparent in time. In the later stories the narrator is sure of himself and of his craft because he reflects the author's view that God is also a reliable narrator weaving a fiction of infinite complexity in which the characters will be saved if only they trust in His mercy and act in accordance with their faith.

In the later works social criticism is not absent, but simply relegated to a position of lesser importance.[27] When Cervantes reworked *El celoso extremeño* for publication in the *Novelas ejemplares*, he omitted a long and bitter section criticizing the young rakes of Seville. The same type of character appears in *La fuerza de la sangre* in the figure of Rodolfo, Leocadia's abductor. However, in the later version of the *El celoso extremeño*, as in *La fuerza de la sangre*, the wrongs of these characters are individualized, not attributed to only one class or type of person. In *La fuerza de la sangre*, Leocadia's father does not notify the authorities about his daughter's rape because he does not trust their dedication to the cause of a poorer man against the very wealthy. Preciosa, in *La gitanilla*, sings and dances for a group of noble men and women who are too penurious to pay her anything. They are shown to be vain, selfish, and exploitive of Preciosa's talents.

The lessened importance of social criticism in the later stories should not be regarded as acceptance of social corruption or blindness to it. It is rather indicative of a change of perspective. From reform of society, from the hope of rediscovering truth in literature, Cervantes has moved in the later fiction toward a concern for personal salvation through faith in a truth not understandable in human life. All of life comes to be viewed as a fictional journey through which one must pass on his way to salvation. Social corruption is only one manifestation of life's delusive nature and deserves no special attention. Not only is the bailiff who colludes with the underworld in *El coloquio de los perros* corrupt because of the distance he establishes between appearance and reality, but all things that man sees and touches and experiences are corrupt. For appearance is antithetical to reality, and understanding is antithetical to truth. The particular examples of fraud and deception in social life have been generalized in Cervantes's later work. Social corruption is only the most obvious symbol of the unbridgeable separation in life between individual perspective and truth. By making this a universal condition, Cervantes undercuts his earlier suspicion of a particular group who specialize in deceiving others and his resentment of the wealth and prestige of some of his rivals.

The liberation this new perspective on human life offers does not, however, catapult Cervantes into the next world or make him privy to the

---

[27] For a catalogue of the appearance of social criticism in the novelas, see Armando Payás's "La crítica social en las *Novelas ejemplares* de Cervantes" (1970). His conclusion is that social criticism is less frequent and less bitter in what I am calling the later novelas.

truths he intuits as existing beyond life. If the nature of living and writing is to be caught up in a journey through life whose appearances are all snares and delusions for the unsuspecting, then Cervantes must still undergo those hazards. As a writer he must try to capture transcendent reality through symbols. Nobility and marriage become the social and literary correlatives of the elect of God who achieve union with Him after death. Marriage is represented as salvation and is achieved in the later works not automatically or easily, but only after long struggle and peregrination. Later characters—both male and female—face temptations and obstacles which they reject and overcome without losing faith in the achievability of their ultimate goal. All the later stories, as the specific analyses in subsequent chapters will show, force the major characters to break down their sense of uniqueness and individuality and to accept the other—the loved one—as independent of himself, as having a meaning and a reality that transcends and enriches his own. This process is most clearly evident in *El amante liberal*, but is essential to all the stories of love and marriage. This sense of the other's reality, this breaking out of selfishness and isolation as a precondition of marriage, is symbolic of the type of conversion necessary for faith and true belief in God.

In all the late stories, the chaos and uncertainty in which the characters live end at the point when marriage is achieved and the main characters return to stability within the social order. This again is a symbolic, necessarily earth-bound representation of the chaos and uncertainty which is life's fiction and the ending in death and salvation which marks the return to reality.

A story without an end is inconceivable in the later works. Both early and late works express a relationship between fiction and reality. The open-endedness of many of the early works—of *Rinconete y Cortadillo*, *Don Quixote* I, and *El coloquio de los perros*—suggests that only the particular point of view of each individual can determine whether an event is true or only imagined. Fiction flows into reality and reality flows into fiction, but there is no truly distanced vantage point from which an absolute determination can be made. Just as Cide Hamete is, for Don Quixote, the "real" author—the scribe and enchanter who alternately records Don Quixote's deeds and befuddles his intentions—he is, for the reader, fictitious. The books which for the Canon are fictitious are real for Don Quixote. Don Quixote slashes the wine skin which he says is the head of the giant whom Dorotea had commissioned him to kill in order to free her for marriage. The others wink (or, in the case of the owner of the wine skin, get angry), yet the reader has another laugh when he sees that it is precisely after Don Quixote has slain the imaginary giant that the real Dorotea is released from her predicament and the way is in fact opened for her marriage.[28] At the end of Part I, Don Quixote remains essentially unchanged. In the struggle for self-assertion that marks all of the interrelationships of Part I, Don Quixote neither wins nor loses. He is returned home in a cage, but still refuses to give in to Alonso Quijano and prosaic, everyday reality. The world view that produced *Don Quixote* I could not resolve the struggle. For the author is no more an authority than anyone else. Each character is equally right. Don Quixote is not juxtaposed against his essence in Part I, but against a society which, like him, is a mixture of pretense and reality. It is only when Cervantes conceives of his characters' struggles as oriented toward the problems of salvation and transcendent truth rather than toward society that resolution becomes possible. In Part II, Don Quixote comes to see all of reality as appearance and finally recognizes that he himself is another appearance —a mask that must be shed before reality can be glimpsed. His return to Alonso Quijano, like the characters' return to society, in the idealistic stories, is not capitulation. It is, rather, symbolic of a rejection of pretense and self-invention, a return to origin which within life means society and one's given name and circumstances, but in religious terms means eternity and God's will. In the later stories the characters end where they began. Only for the span of the story—which symbolizes the span of their lives—are they alienated from their origins. The main characters are pilgrims of life whose story ends when their goal of salvation is achieved.

Not only the characters and milieu, but the disposition of the story elements undergoes change in the later works. In the early works the stories develop chronologically. Because time is seen as endless movement along a continuum which has neither a beginning nor an end, the narrator does not anticipate the fate of the characters. It is this time orientation that permits many of the works to remain without an ending. For endings, like beginnings, are arbitrary in a world seen as continual flux. The conventions of beginning and ending are just as false as the conventions of author, reader, and character, or of naming, or of any of the processes by which man breaks up, for his own convenience, a con-

[28] Many critics have analyzed in detail the way fiction and reality are intertwined in *Don Quixote* I. See especially, Bruce Wardropper's "The Pertinence of *El Curioso impertinente*" (1957): 587–600, and "*Don Quixote*: Story or History?" (1965): 1–11; Manuel Durán, *La ambigüedad en el "Quijote"* (1961); Avalle-Arce, "El curioso y el capitán," in *Deslindes*, pp. 121–61; Richard Predmore, *El Mundo del "Quijote"* (1958), pp. 13–31; and Mia I. Gerhardt, "*Don Quijote*": *La vie et les livres* (1955). My purpose here is not to reveal again that characteristic but to relate it to the phenomenon of endless stories, a phenomenon I find only in the early works. Raymond Willis's (*The Phantom Chapters* [1953]) discussion of the "restless ending" as a characteristic of some chapter endings in *Don Quixote* and as epitomized at the end of Part I is most interesting in this regard. See especially pages 44–47.

tinuum that permits any subdivision, but substantiates none of them. In the *Coloquio de los perros* Cervantes chooses arbitrarily the duration of a single night to limit Berganza's discourse, though presumably Berganza could continue to speak indefinitely if such an external limit were not imposed on him. Don Quixote's defeats in Part I become part of the stimulus for his next effort, tracing a pattern of alternations: of defeat and victory, of rest and struggle, of discourse and action, leading nowhere.[29] There is no indication at the end of Part I that a development has taken place.

In the late works, the narrator, clearly separated from the characters, does not present the story of their lives in the order in which they experience it. The *in medias res* beginning, characteristic of the Greek novel and present in the *Persiles*, is more than just a literary convention.[30] It is part of the new metaphysical orientation reflected in the later works. By beginning in the middle of the story and working simultaneously toward the beginning and the end, the narrator further distinguishes himself from the character about whom he is writing. For the character, as a creature in fiction, like man in life, must experience events through time, chronologically. But the narrator is free, since he already knows the character's history as well as his destiny, to present the story to the readers in any way he chooses. This disjunction between

[29] J. J. Allen discusses this pattern of victory and defeat in Part I in *Hero or Fool?*, chap. 2. For a more theoretical analysis of the relationship between defeat and victory in *Don Quixote*, see Marthe Robert, *L'Ancien et le nouveau (De "Don Quichotte" à Franz Kafka)* (1963), pp. 125–35.

[30] As Avalle-Arce points out so succinctly ("Introducción," *Los trabajos de Persiles y Sigismunda*, pp. 24–26), the literary vogue of Heliodorus in the early seventeenth century was not entirely fortuitous. It responded to the image of man's pilgrimage on earth characteristic of the Spanish Counter Reformation. Vilanova ("El peregrino andante" [1949]: 97–159) also discusses at length the adaptability of the Greek novel to the esthetic and metaphysical needs of the Counter Reformation. He says the Greek novel is a "novela educativa y moralizadora, inspirada por una intención trascendente y por un contenido humano, que une al deleite de lo maravilloso la enseñanza de una norma moral, su afinidad con los ideales cristianos la convierte en el género novelesco predilecto del humanismo de la Contrarreforma" (p. 124). [". . . didactic and moralizing novel, inspired by a transcendent intention and a human content, which unites delight in the marvelous with the teaching of a moral norm. Its affinity with christian ideals converts it into the favorite novelistic genre of the humanism of the Counter Reformation."] Finally, Albinio Martín Gabriel makes the same point in "Heliodoro y la novela española," pp. 215–34: "Creemos que no solamente se imita a los bizantinos porque cronológicamente coinciden sus traducciones, sino por cierta afinidad espiritual y circunstancias concomitantes de las dos épocas" (p. 215). ["We believe that the Byzantines are imitated not only because their translations coincide chronologically with this period, but because there are certain spiritual affinities and concomitant circumstances between the two periods."]

the character's time and the time of the work further emphasizes the character's fiction, and the arbitrariness of the events which affect him. Finally, the story's organization suggests the eternity beyond human time and offers a perspective on chronology that reveals its ultimate unimportance. The character must save himself by his ability to intuit a pattern beyond the one apparent to him in his experience. He must be able to detect an essentiality in the present that undermines his sense of sequence and determinism. Adherence to this unseen essence will save him from both corruption and despair.

Another indication of the changelessness that the later works seek to express within change is the pattern of naming characters. All Cervantes's major characters in early and late works appear in fiction in disguise. Alonso Quijano truly enters fiction when he recreates himself as Don Quixote. Tomás Rodaja at the beginning of *El licenciado Vidriera* marks his progress through life by a constant change of names: from Tomás Rodaja to the Licenciado Vidriera to Tomás Rueda. Rincón and Cortado become Rinconete and Cortadillo according to Monipodio's wishes, and the once libertine Carrizales becomes "the jealous" upon entering the fictional world of *El celoso extremeño*. In all early stories, the main protagonists continue within their fictional roles until the end. Anselmo and Carrizales repent of their folly, but die without returning to their prefictional state. Tomás Rueda dies in a new role, his original one long since forgotten, and Don Quixote's and Rinconete and Cortadillo's stories end with them still suspended within their fictional roles and names.

In the later works the characters also live out their lives in disguise. Preciosa turns out to be Doña Constanza de Meneses at the end of *La gitanilla*, and Costanza, in *La ilustre fregona*, discovers herself to be the daughter of Don Diego de Carriazo. Tomás de Avendaño and Diego de Carriazo, in the same work, become Tomás Pedro and Lope Asturiano during the course of their adventures, only to return to their original names at the end. Teodosia and Leocadia adopt men's names in *Las dos doncellas* during their struggles and return to their correct names when they have succeeded in their efforts. In *La fuerza de la sangre,* Leocadia must pretend to be Luisico's cousin until the moment when she finally marries Rodolfo. Sometimes, as in *La fuerza de la sangre* and *Las dos doncellas*, the disguise is conscious, while other times, as in *La gitanilla* and *La ilustre fregona*, it is unconscious. But in all cases the main protagonists feel a disparity between the roles they are playing and their essential selves. While Preciosa and Costanza do not know they are of noble birth, they do know that they do not belong fully to the situation in which they find themselves. The disparity between the existential situation of the main characters in the late works and their true being constitutes the tension which marks their lives. Their struggles are in all cases directed toward relieving this tension not by yielding to the existential situation, which is always known to be false, but by striving to bring that situation into harmony with their true selves. Therefore, since the major characters are exemplary, when their stories end they find themselves rejoined to their original selves. "Teodoro" becomes Teodosia again; Costanza and Preciosa find their true parents. The late stories end when the protagonists are free to cast off their disguises and return to the destiny promised by their birth.

The circular pattern of the late stories, the search for and achievement of return, does not suggest changelessness, however. The infant Constanza de Meneses, whom the gypsies robbed, was born only potentially noble. Her noble birth was no guarantee of her nobility of character. When, at the end of the novel, she returns to adopt her original name, it is with a sense of fulfilled promise. The Constanza at the end is truly noble, for her actions during the period of her disguise brought her external faith into accord with her internal worth. That nobility is not a condition of blood, as many have wrongly interpreted *La gitanilla* as saying, can be seen in the vapidity of the noblemen for whom Preciosa performs at the beginning of the story. Nobility is the label Cervantes applies to a condition achieved only *a posteriori* through, and as a result of, struggle. This is true for all of the characters in the later works. Marriage, after the trials of Isabela and Recaredo in *La española inglesa,* is not the same as their marriage would have been prior to the struggles. This point is important because it reveals the role of existence within essence. It is through time, through living and struggle, that the essence is both proved and made possible. Though time and human life may be fiction when viewed from the standpoint of eternity, just as the character's chronology is meaningless when viewed from the point of view of the novelist, or the character's name is false from the point of view of the reader and often of the character himself, chronology and deception are absolutely essential to the character's salvation. The character must take seriously his deception. Leocadia must hide from others the fact she is Luisico's mother or lose all chance actually to regain her proper status; Recaredo must hide his Catholicism from the Queen of England in order to be given the opportunity later to express it fully; Mahmut, in *El amante liberal,* must pretend loyalty to Alí Baja in order to survive to return to Christianity and to save Ricardo and Leonisa. The late characters engage in a dialectic of a most delicate nature. From the perspective of existence, the dialectic is established between a pretense that keeps a character within the appearances demanded by society and the truth which, because it is apparently impossible to find, may be abandoned or forgotten. Too much giving in to either the pretense or to the absolute truth would destroy the ultimate goal of uniting the two publicly. In the context of Cervantes's fiction the dialectic is established between the character in chronological time and the author outside it. The character must act according to the immediate demands of his situation and at the same time believe, often against appearances, that the immediate situation belongs to a larger plan that will ultimately lead to his salvation. Recaredo's release of the captured Spanish sailor in *La española inglesa* is a most dramatic example of the delicacy of the characters' position. Despite the urging of his men that he kill the Spanish captives so that they would not be able to alert the Armada and pursue them, Recaredo lets the captives go, because as a Catholic he could not kill other Catholics. His action threatens to reveal that he is a covert Catholic and exposes the entire ship to attack by the Spanish navy. His courageous taking of the right choice, however, was rewarded by the author's plan for his success.

All life, in the later works, is seen as fiction. Perceived reality, when measured against transcendent reality, is as a fiction. The fiction, however, is not devoid of meaning, for it is part of a dialectical process through which transcendent reality is finally achieved. The return to origins, the circular pattern suggested by the joining of ending to beginning, is not antithetical to growth and progress through time. For only through time can the end be rejoined to the beginning. The ending is at the same time a transcendence of time and a fulfillment of the beginning. The circle is an earth-bound representation of eternity. But since eternity is beyond human grasp, existing on a higher plane than temporality, the circularity suggested involves a vertical component. The movement through time produces a vertical trajectory which is expressed novelistically by completion. Time conceived of horizontally, as the early stories showed, has no beginning or end. When, in a story, beginning and end meet beyond fiction, time can be viewed as having both horizontal and vertical components: horizontal within the space of fiction and vertical in the ultimate ceding of fiction to a reality beyond it. The difficulty is in seeing that, rather than being isolated and disjoined, the horizontal and vertical components are interconnected.[31] The origin provides for the possibility of

---

[31] In nearly identical language, Michel Déguy discusses the symbolizing aspect of reality that gives depth to succession and the banal and that permits artistic expression: "C'est en lui-même avec lui-même que le spectacle présent *symbolise*; la *platitude* s'échange contre la profondeur. La platitude est longitudinale, horizontale; il s'agit avec elle, pour nous qui ne cessons d'être retenus en elle, de la logique linéaire de l'affairement, de la concaténation des instants-de-passage qui passent en vue d'un

chronological time. Proper understanding of chronological time in turn provides for the possibility of an ending which fulfills the promise of the origin by transcending chronology.

Just as he does in the early works, in the later works Cervantes builds an implied interchange between character and narrator, between truth and fiction. The difference is that in the later works the character and narrator exist on two clearly distinguished planes. The narrator no longer confuses himself with his characters and no longer pretends to be victim of the same uncertainties as they. This distance, clearly defined, between narrator and character does not, however, obviate their interaction. The characters appear to be on trial in the later works, yet free to choose their actions. Each proper choice by a character appears to be rewarded by the narrator by the presentation of a new circumstance which will make his ultimate goal more possible. Works like the *Persiles* are filled with minor characters who, having made the wrong choices, are left unfulfilled. The plot, then, is not so much an abstract pattern as a collaborative effort of an autonomous character oriented toward salvation and a benevolent narrator who both tests and rewards the character at each juncture. The way this happens will become clear in the analyses of the idealistic tales.

Fiction has a role in the later works. The role is to define the province of illusion and to reveal the dual nature of reality and time. Truth, salvation, and peace are not the province of fiction. But they are the realities toward which fiction can point and which the chaos of fiction can create as desirable. The wild adventures, the shipwrecks, the pilgrimages, the peripeties and changes of fortune, the recognition scenes, the presentation of an elaborately deceptive reality, and the creation of rhetorical pirouettes become the hallmark of Cervantes's later fiction because he no longer believes in words or temporal reality as truth. The exaggerated invention of the later stories emphasizes his lack of concern with everyday reality and reveals his vision of all of life as chaotic deception. But this highly imaginative literature can be exemplary because it represents not

---

but; lequel est un *moyen* à son tour dans l'ajournement indéfini de la fin le long de la série infinie cause-effet, où Kierkegaard voyait la résidence même du mal.

"La profondeur est transversale, radiale, verticale; elle rompt la chronique; elle est ce qui s'ouvre quand la chronique est rompue" ["It is in itself and with itself that the present spectacle *symbolizes*; platitude is exchanged for depth. Platitude is longitudinal, horizontal; for us, who never cease to be held back in it, the important thing is the linear logic of daily activity, the linking of brief encounters which happen with a goal in mind; the goal is a *means* in its turn in the unending postponement of the end all along the infinite series of cause and effect, in which Kierkegaard saw the very seat of evil.

"Depth is transversal, radial, vertical; it breaks the chronicle; it is that which opens when the chronicle is broken."] *Actes* (1966), p. 259.

the author's madness (a point fully explored in the analysis of the *Casamiento engañoso* and the *Coloquio de los perros* in chap. III), but the essential confusion and diversity, the empty plentitude of human existence. The calm which surrounds the late stories, the social order serenely confident of itself, suggests that beyond fiction, beyond alienation, struggle, and disappointment, is order, an order which fiction cannot, by its very nature, depict. In the same way, we are led to see by analogy that beyond the chaos and struggle there is peace. The struggle is meaningful only because it makes one desire an end, and the end is possible only because an intuition of it in the struggle keeps life and fiction going.

Time enters into a dialectic with eternity, and fiction enters into a dialectic with life. In the resultant totality life is identified with fiction. Neither, in itself, is true, and both, being limited by time and individual perspective, are equally imaginary. A study of the liberation of the imagination in Cervantes's late fiction cannot be divorced from its metaphysical implications. For that liberation does not suggest divorce from life, but rather a new way of relating to it. Cervantes's late work reflects both his sense of the chaotic multiplicity on the surface of life and the promise of its invisible underlying and overriding truth.

II. ANALYSIS OF THE EARLY NOVELAS

Rinconete y Cortadillo

I n *Rinconete y Cortadillo* an examination of the relationship
between character and narrator reveals many of the fundamental qualities of Cervantes's early works. *Rinconete y Cortadillo* appeared first in manuscript form around 1604[1] and then,
slightly modified, in 1613 in the published collection of the *Novelas
ejemplares*. Criado del Val has discussed stylistic differences between the
two versions to show Cervantes's tendency especially to alter verb forms
and to reduce redundancies when polishing the work for publication.[2]
The few changes in the substance of the story do manifest later tendencies
and will be taken up in this analysis. It is sufficient here to point out only
that *Rinconete y Cortadillo* is a work essentially reflective of the early
period of composition of the novelas.

The story combines two planes: one temporal, suggesting the question
of the development and transformation of Rinconete and Cortadillo
within the work; the other static, spatial, and descriptive of Sevillian
society as seen from the perspective of the underworld confraternity of
Monipodio. These two aspects of the story appear to be so unintegrated
as to be almost independent of one another. The work, however cannot
be properly identified as either a picaresque story or a *cuadro de
costumbres*.[3] Nor is it fair to say that the work has no unity. Unity can
be found if we trace the evolution of Rinconete and Cortadillo as they

---

[1] The mention of the work in *Don Quixote* (I, 47) pushes the date of composition
back to 1604 at the latest.

[2] "De estilística cervantina; correcciones, interpolaciones y variantes en el *Rinconete
y Cortadillo* y en el *Zeloso extremeño*" (1953): pp. 233–48.

[3] While the two positions are not always clearly opposed in a critic's commentary,
in general, it can be said that the following studies tend to emphasize the picaresque
aspects of the work: Frank Wadleigh Chandler, *Romances of Roguery* (1899), 1:10;
Adolfo Bonilla y San Martín, *Cervantes y su obra* (1916), p. 140; Angel Valbuena
Prat (ed.), *La novela picaresca española* (1946); A. A. Parker, *Literature and the
Delinquent* (1967); and José Luís Valera, "Sobre el realismo cervantino en *Rinconete*"
(1968). The next group of critics, on the other hand, tends to resist associating the
work with the picaresque, preferring instead to see it as a felicitous example of
Cervantes's gift of description: Paolo Savj-López, *Cervantes* (1917), p. 151; Américo
Castro, *El pensamiento de Cervantes* (1925), pp. 235–37; Francisco Rodríguez
Marín, "*Rinconete y Cortadillo*" (1920), p. 187; and Agustín G. de Amezúa y
Mayo, *Cervantes, creador de la novela corta española* (1956–58), 1:369.

become transformed, like so many of the early characters of Cervantes, from creators to observers of the reality in which they find themselves. The type of development traced by Rinconete and Cortadillo follows a pattern much more typical of other early works of Cervantes than of the picaresque. The third-person narrator who introduces the boys at the beginning of the story opposes their temporal vision of themselves at the beginning with an atemporal one, just as the narrator of Don Quixote in the first chapters of Part I opposes Don Quixote's self-vision with his own more detached view of the character. When Rincón and Cortado propose to tell each other their life stories, they begin, like true picaresque characters, at the beginning, stating name, parentage, and place of origin: "I . . . am a native of Fuenfrida, ... My name is Pedro del Rincón, and my father is a person of quality, being an agent of the Holy Crusade."[4] Cortado follows with his account: "I was born in the pious village that lies between Salamanca and Medina del Campo. My father is a tailor and taught me his trade."[5] Each goes on to describe his subsequent life of crime and the circumstances which led up to his present state of exile. The narrator, on the other hand, begins the story at a moment of temporal and spatial indefinition. He begins the story at noon when everyone is taking a rest from the preoccupations of the day. The place is an inn on the border between Castile and Andalusia. Haziness of time and place, escape from routine, and the fortuitous meeting of strangers form the background against which the two would-be pícaros tell each other the story of their lives. The narrator's description of the scene undermines the sense of temporal and hereditary determinism characteristic of the pícaro's view of the world.[6]

In a fashion characteristic of Cervantes's early works, the narrator's introduction of the boys remains brief and noncommittal. He does not give the reader any information about his characters beyond the appearance they offer. It is the boys who discover each other and give the reader their names, histories, and ideas. Their self-naming, like that of other

---

[4] "Yo, señor hidalgo, soy natural de la Fuenfrida; . . . mi nombre es Pedro del Rincón; mi padre es persona de calidad, porque es ministro de la Santa Cruzada" (Cervantes Saavedra, *Novelas ejemplares*, 2 vols. [1915–17], 1:138; edited by Francisco Rodríguez Marín. Hereafter referred to in footnotes as RM, with pertinent volume number and page). This and all subsequent translations of *Rinconete y Cortadillo* come from *Three Exemplary Novels*, translated by Samuel Putnam (1950), pp. 9–71. Other pages on which translations from this source occur are pp. 32, 33, 34, 35, 36, 37, and 38.

[5] "Yo nací en el piadoso lugar puesto entre Salamanca y Medina del Campo: mi padre es sastre; enseñóme su oficio" (RM 1:141).

[6] For an excellent discussion of this and other aspects of the picaresque, see Carlos Blanco Aguinaga's "Cervantes y la picaresca. Notas sobre dos tipos de realismo" (1957): esp. 316–28.

early characters, comes after they have discovered their independent identities. The naming suggests that they are autonomous and free from the control of the narrator.

In the opening dialogue, the boys achieve independence not only from their narrator, but from the past and from the self-image they project in their initially picaresque accounting of themselves. The dialogue begins with Rincón, the one whom the narrator calls the "older boy." Through his efforts, the narrator remaining outside of the time of the story, the younger boy, Cortado, is led from isolation, hostility, and a tragic view of life, to companionship, self-confidence, and the playful attitude which characterizes the boys' subsequent contacts with the world. Rincón's first efforts to discover something about his chance companion are met with temporizing: " 'Sir Gentleman,' said the older to the smaller boy, 'What is your Grace's country and in what direction are you traveling?' " " 'Sir Cavalier,' replied the one to whom the question had been put, 'I do not know the name of my country, nor where I am bound.' "[7] After more prodding he adds, ". . . for my land is not my land, seeing that all I have in it is a father who does not look upon me as a son and a stepmother who treats me the way one does a stepchild. I go where chance may take me until I find someone who will provide me with what I need to get through this wretched life of mine."[8] Here, in the words of this yet unnamed boy, is the expression of the classic picaresque sense of solitude, evasion, and distrust. The younger boy refuses to expose himself to even the friendly questioning of one who is, from an outsider's point of view, nearly his double. He describes himself as alienated, unwanted, and miserable. Even in the area of his talent he finds himself unappreciated: "My father . . . is a tailor and hose maker, and he taught me to cut leggings. . . . I cut them so well, really, that I could pass my examination as a master of the craft. The only thing is, my luck is so short that my talents go unrecognized."[9] Despite the older boy's continued sympathy, the younger one

---

[7] "—¿De qué tierra es vuesa merced, señor gentilhombre, y para adónde bueno camina? —Mi tierra, señor caballero,—respondió el preguntado—, no la sé, ni para dónde camino tampoco" (RM 1:136).

[8] ". . . porque mi tierra no es mía, pues no tengo en ella más de un padre que no me tiene por hijo y una madrastra que me trata como alnado; el camino que llevo es a la ventura, y allí le daría fin donde hallase quien me diese lo necesario para pasar esta miserable vida." (RM 1:136).

[9] "Mi padre, por la misericordia del cielo, es sastre y calcetero, y me enseñó a *cortar* antiparas, . . . y *córto*las tan bien, que en verdad que me podría examinar de maestro, sino que la *corta* suerte me tiene arrinconado." ([RM 1:137], italics mine). The play on the word "cortar" prefigures Cortado's verbal dexterity and suggests that the name he later gives himself, "Diego Cortado," is truly, like Don Quixote's, of his own invention.

still remains sealed within himself: "If I am not mistaken . . . you have other accomplishments, which you prefer to keep secret. 'That I have,' the small boy admitted, 'but they are not for the public gaze, as your Grace has very well remarked.' "[10]

The younger boy, who will eventually emerge as Cortado, finds himself cut off from the mainstream of life, unappreciated, directionless, and unable to break out of the circle of his self-imprisonment. Only through the mediation of his garrulous and self-confident friend is he dislodged from the impasse of solitude and uncommunicativeness. Rincón forces him to recognize outside himself the situation which he fears is his alone: ". . . in order that your Grace may feel free to unbosom yourself and confide in me, I will first tell you all about my own life."[11] Cortado finally agrees to do the same and the two seal their friendship with a formal embrace. Rincón's role in the opening pages is to externalize Cortado's vision of himself.

Close analysis of the stories narrated first by Rincón and then by Cortado reveals that they are already, by their very articulation, distortions of the picaresque tale. The boys have not been forced into a life of crime nor have they been rejected by their families. "I learned the trade [of *bulero*] so well that when it comes to dispensing bulls, I would not take second place to any man no matter how good at it he might be. But one day I came to love the money from the bulls more than the bulls themselves, and having embraced a bag of it, I made off for Madrid."[12] Cortado admits, "My father is a tailor and taught me his trade; and with my ability, from cutting with shears I went on to cutting purses. I became tired of the cramped life in a small town and the lack of affection my stepmother showed me, and so I left and went to Toledo to practice my calling there."[13] Both boys have fathers, a trade, and legitimate skills.[14] Boredom and the desire for instant wealth, more than poverty, drove them from

[10] "Si yo no me engaño y el ojo no me miente, otras gracias tiene vuesa merced secretas, y no las quiere manifestar." "Si tengo,—respondió el pequeño—pero no son para en público, como vuesa merced ha muy bien apuntado" (RM 1:138).

[11] ". . . y para obligar a vuesa merced que descubra su pecho y descanse conmigo, le quiero obligar con descubrirle el mío primero" (RM 1:138).

[12] "Y le aprendí de manera, que no daría ventaja en echar las bulas al que más presumiese en ello; pero habiéndome un día aficionado más al dinero de las bulas que a las mismas bulas, me abracé con un talego, y di conmigo y con él en Madrid" (RM 1:139).

[13] "Mi padre es sastre; enseñóme su oficio, y de corte de tisera, con mi buen ingenio, salté a cortar bolsas. Enfadóme la vida estrecha del aldea y el desamorado trato de mi madrastra; dejé mi pueblo, vine a Toledo a ejercitar mi oficio" (RM 1:141–42).

[14] It must be noted that the jobs of *bulero* and tailor were regularly satirized by writers of the Golden Age, including Cervantes.

home. As they emerge at the end of their stories, the boys more resemble Don Quixote than Guzmán de Alfarache, for like Don Quixote, they have chosen a life of adventure in imitation of literary models in the hope of escaping the drudgery of everyday life. The danger that Cortado is forced by Rincón to overcome is that of becoming so submerged within his adopted identity that he loses a sense of its unreality. By forcing him to confront his image, Rincón releases Cortado from its control over him.

One need only contrast Cortado's first statement of his situation with his final narration to see how the process of articulation converts the speaker from victim to controller. At first he had said, ". . . for my land is not my land, . . . all I have in it is a father who does not look at me as a son." The victim relies on fortune to give him direction and sees himself as dependent on others and miserable: "I go where chance may take me until I find someone who will provide me with what I need." Later he admits that it is he who has rejected his father and shows that he has confidence in his ability to survive. "In that city [Toledo] I did wonders; for there was not a reliquary dangling from a hood or a pocket so well hidden that my fingers did not find it out or my scissors clip it, even though it might have been guarded by the eyes of Argus."[15]

From the point when Rincón and Cortado seal their friendship until the end of the story, they control the action entirely. They have transcended their sense of alienation by accepting one another; and they have escaped their picaresque self-image by transforming it into words. From here on the two operate as a single character. The two were distinguished at the beginning of the story to reveal the almost miraculous process by which the self escapes the confines of its isolation and sense of dependency.[16] The fortuity of the meeting of the boys not only serves to contrast with the predetermined atmosphere of the picaresque novel, but to reveal the mys-

---

[15] "Y en él he hecho maravillas; porque no pende relicario de toca, ni hay faldriquera tan escondida, que mis dedos no visiten, ni mis tiseras no corten, aunque le estén guardando con los ojos de Argos" (RM 1:142).

[16] An interesting article by E. J. Brehm ("El mitologema de la sombra en Pedro Schlemihl, Cortadillo y Berganza" [1961–62]: 29–44) discusses at length the importance of Cortado's discovery of himself in the image of Rincón. He sees the two as a single character, Rincón being the shadow or depth which provides Cortado the distance which marks the story of his adventures. His argument, though useful in its implications for Cervantes's art, is weakened by the prominence given Rinconete at the end of the work and the mistake Cervantes makes in having Monipodio call Cortadillo "the good" and then later conferring the same title on Rinconete. As both boys appear equally involved in the story, it is difficult to agree with Brehm that Cervantes intended to subordinate Rinconete to Cortadillo. Joaquín Casalduero (*Sentido y forma de las "Novelas ejemplares"* [1969], p. 108) is perhaps more accurate in seeing the boys simply as doubles.

tery of friendship and communication. Rincón remarks, "I think it is not without some hidden purpose that fate has brought us together."[17] The mystery that the two characters feel is that of the power of the word, a power that renders the weak strong, the dependent independent, the miserable and despondent carefree and joyful. In the presence of a sympathetic other, the self can shed its determining past by the simple yet nearly miraculous ability to recount it.

The liberated Rincón and Cortado immediately begin playing their tricks on the people around them. In reversal of the normal relationship between young boys and the corrupt adult world depicted in picaresque novels, it is Rincón and Cortado who exploit the innocence and kindheartedness of the adults they meet. The muleteer at the inn not only loses at cards with the young boys, but is unable to overpower them physically when he attempts to take his money back from them. The travelers who offered them the ride to Seville and who had defended them in their fight with the muleteer fare no better, since the boys take the opportunity, upon arriving in Seville, to steal from them whatever they can easily get. Finally, the student who entrusts Cortado with the goods transported from the market place loses first his purse and then his handkerchief to his young employee.

Rincón and Cortado distinguish themselves from the pícaros they had originally appeared to emulate not only in their invulnerability and consummate skill in sleight of hand but in the gratuitousness of their activities. Not necessity, but the pleasure they derive from duping others motivates the series of tricks they play before being recruited for Monipodio's confraternity. The culminating trick is Cortado's robbery of the student's handkerchief, having already relieved him of his purse. The act is a true *tour de force*, designed to prove his dexterity and to underscore the student's stupidity. Whereas the pícaro may steal to get food, the tricks he uses being subsidiary to the goal of possession, in *Rinconete y Cortadillo*, as revealed especially in the handkerchief episode, it is the dexterity, the ability to fool, that is elevated to central importance, the object attained being of indifferent value.

In Cervantes's world as it is depicted in the early works, the issue repeatedly becomes a struggle of wills, a struggle by characters within the world to assert their control over others. Rincón and Cortado had apparently hoped to achieve freedom and control by thievery. This explains their surprise upon hearing that thieves must pay tribute to Monipodio. " 'I thought,' remarked Cortado, 'that thieving was a trade that was free of tax or duty. . . .' 'Why, Sir Gallant,' said Rincón, 'can it be that thieves in

[17] ". . . imagino que no sin misterio nos ha juntado aquí la suerte" (RM 1:138).

this country have to pay a duty?' "[18] Like Alonso Quijano, Rincón and Cortado have sought evasion of routine through the self-appropriation of fictional models.

The role of pícaro was chosen by Rincón and Cortado because it promised freedom from social customs and material encumbrances and a foreshortening of the distance between actions and the goals toward which they are directed. The pícaro offers, in short, a combination of involvement and distance which allows him to subsist in society without belonging to it. Differing from the real pícaro, however, Rincón and Cortado have chosen the mask of pícaro as a disguise. Since the mask itself represents evasion, Rincón and Cortado have engaged in a double distancing from society: they hold themselves removed from a role which is itself removed from society. This is the importance, within the series of the boys' adventures, of the discovery of Monipodio's confraternity. For in the previous adventures they could pretend to be poor boys or porters while actually being thieves. Monipodio's fraternity, however, identifies them immediately as thieves. Just as Monipodio confers on Rincón and Cortado the names Rinconete and Cortadillo, he threatens to circumscribe them entirely by incorporating them into his society and subjecting them to a new set of rules, not so very different, after all, from the ones from which they were escaping.[19] Monipodio strips off one layer of pretense. In his presence, the boys must keep their independence by seeing clearly that their new appearance before the world—their appearance as thieves—is also a pretense behind which there is another reality. The role of observer and critic which the boys adopt when in the company of Monipodio reveals their capacity for distance. When Monipodio insists that they tell him their parents' names Rinconete manages both to mimic Monipodio's verbal errors, and to slide out of revealing to him anything of his past.

From the beginning of the story the boys have revealed a great capacity for verbal gymnastics. That this is associated with self-protection and evasion can be seen immediately in Cortado's play on the word "cortado" and "corte," when he is still distrustful of Rincón in their opening dialogue. Cortado's theft of the handkerchief is almost as much a feat of verbal guile as of manual dexterity. When they meet the noviciate of Monipodio's order of thieves, much of their interest in him will center around the words he uses. Their easy mastery of the new vocabulary will be a source of pride when they finally meet Monipodio himself.

[18] "—Yo pensé—dijo Cortado—que el hurtar era oficio libre, horro de pecho y alcabala. . . .";—Págase en esta tierra almojarifazgo de ladrones, señor galán?—dijo Rincón" (RM 1:156).

[19] The identification of Monipodio's society with other social orders is made by G. Hainsworth, *Les "Novelas ejemplares" de Cervantes en France au XVII*[e] *Siècle* (1933), p. 11.

The continuous word play by which the boys deal with the others in the novel shows how they maintain their delicate position as both observers and participants. Their interest in the word deformations of Monipodio and his company inspires them to corrections and verbal parodies which draw the reader's interest away from the words' meaning toward a focus on their surface.[20] The verbal play also makes Monipodio's world appear less real—more like an artistic creation to be judged and criticized on the basis of its surface flaws. The horror that an unmediated introduction into Monipodio's society would evoke is diluted by a distancing factor that replaces fear with laughter.

The Monipodio episode, in the Porras manuscript, was separated from the earlier portion of the story by a subtitle.[21] The omission of the subtitle in the published manuscript suggests that in his later view of the work Cervantes was more interested in Rinconete and Cortadillo's developing role within the story than in depicting the life of the underworld in Seville. When the story is not subdivided, the movement of the two boys from pure physical presence to almost complete transparency and distance continues uninterrupted. Seen in this light, the story falls into several discernible periods which the early subtitling distorted.

In the first and shortest period, the boys are separate, unconscious, unnamed, and described only by their general external appearance. In the second period, slightly longer, the boys awaken from solitude by discovering each other, naming themselves, and, in the process, establishing an identity which frees them from dependence on others and determination by their past. Thus liberated, the boys embark on a third stage in which they demonstrate on a physical level their ability to control their environment while not being controlled by it. In the final stage, their powers are put to a greater test by their entrance into a defined social system. The success the boys have in continuing to escape its obligations results from a refinement of their skills. From manual skills on the streets, they revert to verbal skills in their relations with Monipodio. With each step in this progression, the boys cede more and more of their visibility to the reality which surrounds them.

In Monipodio's house, the mediating role of the two boys is carefully maintained. The narrator makes it clear that everything the reader sees goes first through the eyes of the two main protagonists. The boys are shown carefully observing the house, which gives the narrator the opportunity to describe it in some detail: "As they waited for Señor Monipodio to come down, the two lads attentively eyed the furnishings of the

[20] For example, see RM 1:156, 161, 168–70, 216.
[21] *Casa de Monipodio, padre de los ladrones de Sevilla.*

house."[22] Description of another room is preceded by the explanation that Rincón has gone in there: "Rincón ventured into one of the two low rooms that opened upon the patio."[23] Later, when Monipodio has called for a conference with some of his men, the reader is allowed in on the conversation only after it has been explained that Rinconete and Cortadillo have overheard it: "Bringing the newcomers into the courtyard, Monipodio called for Chiquiznaque, Maniferro, Repolido, and ordered the rest to remain above. Since they were in the patio, Rinconete and Cortadillo were able to overhear the conversation that took place between the new arrival and his host."[24]

The care with which Cervantes handles the mediating role of Rinconete and Cortadillo engages him in what may be an inconsistency. It is by Monipodio's request that Rinconete read him his book that a fuller picture of the activities in which Monipodio and his company engage is placed before the reader. "He took out a memorandum book, which he carried in the hood of his cape, and gave it to Rinconete, as he himself did not know how to read."[25] Several pages earlier, however, Monipodio was boasting of his skills as a poet. La Gananciosa had suggested to La Cariharta that if Repolido does not repent soon, she should compose some verses about him to make him angry. Monipodio says: "I will be the scribe, if necessary; for although I am not a poet by any means, if a man but roll up his sleeves to it he can turn out a couple of thousand couplets in no time at all."[26] It is possible that Monipodio is contemplating oral composition, but the use of the word "scribe" (*secretario*) suggests that written composition is what he has in mind. Perhaps, also, it is consistent with Monipodio's personality to boast of skills he does not possess. In any event, the later request that Rinconete read his book is a clear example of the importance Cervantes attaches to the boys' mediating roles. For it must be through them that we know whatever we know about Monipodio's life.

The story is built on several levels: the narrator who introduces the

[22] "Miraban los mozos atentamente las alhajas de la casa en tanto que bajaba el señor Monipodio" (RM 1:162–63).

[23] ". . . se atrevió Rincón a entrar en una sala baja, de las pequeñas que en el patio estaban" (RM 1:163).

[24] "Monipodio le entró consigo, y mandó llamar a Chiquiznaque, a Maniferro y al Repolido, y que de los demás no bajase alguno. Como se habían quedado en el patio Rinconete y Cortadillo, pudieron oir toda la plática que pasó Monipodio con el caballero recién venido." (RM 1:204).

[25] ". . . sacó un libro de memoria que traía en la capilla de la capa, y dióselo a Rinconete que leyese, porque él no sabía leer" (RM 1:208).

[26] "Yo seré el secretario cuando sea menester . . . y aunque no soy nada poeta, todavía, si el hombre se arremanga, se atreverá a hacer dos millares de coplas en daca las pajas" (RM 1:191).

work retires to the background, allowing Rincón to represent him in inviting Cortado to emerge from his solitude; Rincón and Cortado subsequently shed their separate identities and fuse into a single character who represents a thief. When the thief is recognized as such, the character again sheds the role. In all cases an identity is first presented and then superseded by a character who always measures the distance between the role he is playing and his actual nonfictional identity. The movement is toward greater and greater skill in manipulating the mask and hiding the true self. *Rinconete y Cortadillo* is an allegory of the author's role: from embittered solitude to self-discovery, to a conscious playing of roles, to a transparency through which the surrounding world is observed.

The ending is a strange mixture of attraction to and rejection of the world of thieves, an ambivalence shared by Rinconete and Cortadillo and their narrator. The boys plan to leave, but not now; the narrator insists that the society is an "infamous academy" whose evil ways should serve as an "example and a warning to those who read," and yet he seems to feel that the reader would be most pleased by a sequel which continues to describe Monipodio's way of life. Both Casalduero and Predmore have referred to aspects of Monipodio which "de-villainize" him.[27] In fact, Repolido, for all his brutality, and Cariharta, for all her dissolution, are not unsympathetic characters. Rinconete and Cortadillo, on the other hand, for all their good humor, have taken rather pitiless advantage of people who did them no harm.

The ambiguities in the work appear to be based on Cervantes's struggle with the roles of time, social obligation, and morality in art. Rinconete and Cortadillo's will to escape social obligations lands them in a playful but amoral position through which they eventually emerge as authors by virtue of their powers of self-distancing, critical observation, and word-play. Yet they cannot escape the world altogether. They are in the story, not outside of it. They resolve to leave Monipodio's society, but remain within it, even in the projected continuation. For all that they laugh at Monipodio's inept verbal expression, it is his name for them that the narrator carries over into the title of the work. The boys appear not to develop, and yet they evolve significantly through the course of the story. They appear not to be influenced by moral considerations, and yet they are convinced that Monipodio's way of life is evil. The boys had hoped for a life of absolute freedom through exercise of their skills, but found instead that thieves, just like the travelers whom they accompanied to the Customhouse Gate, must pay taxes and obey laws. The hypocrisy of the above-ground society

[27] "De-villainize" is a translation of Richard Predmore's word ("*Rinconete y Cortadillo*: realismo, carácter picaresco, alegría" [January 1969]: 18), correctly invented to avoid the more lofty but inapplicable connotations of "ennoble."

is mirrored in the underworld. Clear vision, a highly developed sense of the distance between the self and the other, and a mastery of verbal skills permits art to be developed but rejects life. The conflict between seeing art and life severed from the demands of time and morality, and art and life as purposeful, remains unresolved in Cervantes's early novels. Rinconete and Cortadillo cannot make the leap from thieves outside of society to authors within it, although they move in that direction, just as Don Quixote cannot, in 1605, escape the alienated role as his self-creator. It is only in works written after 1606 that Cervantes introduces author-characters who both affect and are affected by society—author-characters who achieve both mastery over themselves and acceptance by others.

El celoso extremeño

L ike *Rinconete y Cortadillo, El celoso extremeño* is a story which appeared in manuscript form sometime before 1606, but was reworked and substantially changed before being published in the *Novelas ejemplares*.[28] The story thus combines characteristics of both periods in Cervantes's writing. The particularly startling revision of the denouement has resulted in considerable debate over the various merits of the two versions of *El celoso extremeño*.[29]

[28] The conjecture that the story was written before 1606 is based on the discovery of *El celoso extremeño* in the Porras manuscript, presumed to have been compiled before that date. The flavor of Seville, especially in the description of the young men about town (the "gente de barrio"), has suggested to some critics that the *Celoso* was written during Cervantes's stay in Seville (e.g., Eugenio Mele, "La novella *El celoso extremeño* del Cervantes" [1906]: 475–90; and Francisco A. de Icaza, *Las "Novelas ejemplares" de Cervantes . . .* [1916], p. 167). Casalduero (*"Novelas ejemplares"* [1969], p. 149) sees similarities with the spirit of *Don Quixote* I that make him suggest that it was written around 1605. Amezúa (*Cervantes, creador* [1956–58], 2:276) finds significant the absence of reference to the *Celoso* in chapter 47 of *Don Quixote* I, where *Rinconete y Cortadillo* is mentioned. He suggests that Cervantes probably wrote the *Celoso* shortly after writing the *Curioso* and *Rinconete*, around 1604 and 1605.

[29] Earlier twentieth-century critics tended, in general, to view less favorably the 1613 ending than more recent critics. Icaza (*Las "Novelas ejemplares,"* p. 167), Rodríguez Marín (*Novelas ejemplares* [1915–17], 2:158, n. 15), and Amezúa (*Cervantes, creador,* 2:255–63), for example, criticize the later version as unrealistic. Amezúa suggests that the change was motivated by sincere religious concerns. Américo Castro (*"El celoso extremeño,* de Cervantes" [1967], pp. 420–50), on the other hand, insists that Cervantes was being hypocritical in removing adultery from the 1613 version. Leo Spitzer, in two articles ("Das Gefuge einer cervantischen Novelle"

Since we are concerned with the question of development in Cervantes's work, both the original manuscript and the changes Cervantes made for the published version are worthy of attention.

The central figure is Felipe Carrizales, who, like all the early main characters, is a solitary man inspired to action by imaginative constructs through which he determines his own identity and that of those around him. Carrizales, as the story begins, identifies jealousy as his chief characteristic and allows this trait to control his choices in the course of the story. As in other early stories, the action revolves around the main character's unsuccessful effort to dominate the secondary characters. Carrizales's abstract, intellectualized rules for living are confronted by the vital impulses of the less cerebral characters, just as Don Quixote's fixed vision of the world is challenged by empirical realities.

Carrizales's dominant characteristic is his solipsism, a trait perceptible not only in the house he constructs in his old age, but in his earlier role as wasteful womanizer.[30] Everything the narrator says contributes to the picture of Carrizales as isolated and self-absorbed. His controlled accumulation of wealth while in America, his lack of friends and family upon his return to Spain, and his inability to share his wealth with the poor, of whom he is expressly conscious, all reveal a man who has retreated into himself. Carrizales's choice of a wife further reiterates the point. Her youth and inexperience, while ostensibly guaranteeing her chastity, offer in fact the possibility that she can be assimilated by him. The liberality which he shows with respect to her—the dowry, the dresses, the sweets, the gifts—is a reassertion of the earlier trait of free-spending, for Carrizales gives to Leonora because he has converted her into a version of himself.

This solipsism in Carrizales's character joins together the two halves of his life, in many ways so apparently opposite. The wandering, free-living Carrizales is, after all, the same as the diligent, wealthy "indiano" who carefully built up a fortune over twenty years of work in America. The change in life style reveals the underlying characteristic, proving its constancy in the most diverse situations and circumstances. The conversion

---

[1931]: 194–225; and "Die Frage der Heuchelei des Cervantes" [1936]: 138–78), compares *El celoso extremeño* with *El viejo celoso* and supports the altered 1613 version of the former as more consistent with the exigencies of the short novel. He discounts Castro's charge of Cervantes's hypocrisy. Casalduero ("*Novelas ejemplares*," pp. 184–88), also defends the later version as fairer to the characterization of Leonora, who was conceived of as a mere child, innocent, and not to be sullied by the role of adultress ascribed to her in the early version. Other recent critics who support the 1613 version are: Francisco Ayala, "El arte nuevo de hacer novelas" (1958): 81–90; Luís Rosales, *Cervantes y la libertad* (1959–60), 2:409–35; and Marcel Bataillon, "Cervantes et le 'Mariage chrétien'" (1947): 129–44.

[30] This point is emphasized by Castro in "'*El celoso extremeño*'" (1967).

from poverty to wealth failed to prove calming to Carrizales: "If then he had been unable to rest because he was poor, now he could not sleep because he was rich."[31] Carrizales suffers anxiety in all circumstances. His attitude toward his money parallels that toward his wife. The bars of gold and silver brought back from America are "an invitation to the greedy and a bait for thieves."

Only after the presentation of this prehistory is the word "jealous" selected as descriptive of Carrizales. The word appears to be exact, for all the insecurity, self-doubt, and sense of exposure to assault shown to be characteristic of Carrizales are present in this trait. Like the robbers envisioned in his bars of gold, Carrizales sees the imprint of the seducer on the face of his wife, even before he has picked her out. The narrator describes Carrizales's reaction on thinking of marriage: ". . . no sooner had this idea occurred to him than he was assaulted by a fear that rent and unraveled it like mist in the wind."[32] Carrizales barely exists; his ideas are no more substantial than mist. In his solipsism he harbors a sense of identity so weak that awareness of his own reality comes only from imagined assaults upon it. The pursuer, then, is integral to his concept of himself, for only under assault will his own reality be affirmed.

Like Don Quixote, Carrizales created the protagonists of his imagined world. The characters who emerge out of the monomania of his jealousy are embodiments of Carrizales himself. For the jealous man has been created by the womanizer, just as the wealthy man was created by the free-spender, and the searcher after calm and a settled existence by the restless wanderer. The total character is a composite of all these roles, each of which is linked to its opposite. It is because Carrizales spent too much money that he determined to start saving it; and because he knew so many loose women that he was apprehensive about the propriety of his wife. Hidden beneath Carrizales's present rectitude is the seducer of his youthful days. When Carrizales considers marriage, the vision of the handsome seducer presents itself before him simultaneously with the vision of the wife. Leonora and Loaysa were born simultaneously in Carrizales's imagination.

Carrizales's passivity and scant ability to communicate vitally give the narrator a free hand to describe him. *El celoso extremeño* is the only early

[31] ". . . si entonces no dormía por pobre, ahora no podía sosegar de rico" (RM 2:91). This and all subsequent translations of *El celoso extremeño* come from "The Jealous Hidalgo" in *Six Exemplary Novels*, translated by Harriet de Onís (1961), pp. 202–39. Other pages on which translations from this source occur are pp. 44, 45, 46, 47, and 48.

[32] ". . . y en viniéndole este pensamiento, le sobresaltaba un tan gran miedo, que así se le desbarataba y deshacía como hace a la niebla el viento" (RM 2:93).

story by Cervantes in which the narrator, rather than the character himself, reveals the main character's name. The narrator's control of his character is consistent not only with Carrizales's taciturnity and solitude, but with the pattern of narrator to character relationships established within the story. Carrizales's character is Leonora. He has chosen her so that he might mold her according to his wishes. She is silent, submissive, and passive, much like Carrizales with respect to the narrator. Leonora accepts Carrizales's will to retire from the world and find peace in his escape from its noise and struggles. It is in this relationship between narrator and character that an identity between the young girl and the old man can be perceived. The experienced old man and the innocent young girl are equally passive— equally undefined and self-absorbed. Leonora submits without rebellion to Carrizales's construct for her, just as Carrizales submits to the narrator's construct.

If Carrizales can be identified with Leonora in his passivity and lack of established self-identity, he can also be identified with Loaysa. Loaysa represents precisely the young man out of whom Carrizales has grown. Loaysa embodies the youthful Carrizales: wasteful, irresponsible, woman-chasing. Like Carrizales, Loaysa does not seek women out of a desire for communication, but for the gossip value or for the honor it may give him among his peers. Leonora is unimportant. She is as much a non-person for Loaysa as she is for Carrizales. Carrizales is simultaneously Leonora and Loaysa: he is passive and self-absorbed and at the same time aggressive and abusive. The marriage he imposes on Leonora, the house he builds for her, and the restrictions he places on her reveal his need to dominate her, while his desire for peace and silence and his implied impotence reveal his identity to her. The imbalance in self-concept which makes Carrizales unable to find peace with himself is expressed externally in his simultaneous identity with the opposing characters of Leonora and Loaysa.

Like the Ensign Campuzano, or Anselmo, or Rinconete and Cortadillo, Carrizales, once having been introduced, ceases to be the central focus of the story's unfolding. Having awakened from the narrator's description to present himself and create a new situation on the basis of the definition he wrongly establishes for himself, he retires to sleep, while the consequences of imbalances in his view of himself and the world work themselves out in the lives of characters who embody his internal conflict. Both his belief in his ability to control reality by excluding it and his entrapment within the oppositions which tear away at his sense of his being reveal the solipsism and lack of contact with reality that have characterized Carrizales.

Loaysa, active, aggressive, and restless, appears in the story on his own terms. He talks, sings, and charms his way through innumerable barriers and takes control from the narrator in the presentation of his being. Only on Loaysa's appearance does dialogue enter the story. Loaysa's role enriches our understanding of the deceptive nature of words and stories and appearances. While Carrizales was unconsciously inviting Loaysa to take his wife by creating an elaborately protective structure for her, Loaysa, active and controlling by definition, consciously constructs appearances at odds with desired ends. In Loaysa's hand, the excision between the construct and its true meaning is intentional.

Whether the deceptive nature of appearance is consciously exploited or not, it is clear that communication involves to a greater or lesser extent a disjunction between the intent of the creator and the understanding of the receiver. The creator may believe that his words or actions express the entirety of his intention. Don Quixote, Anselmo, and Carrizales all make this mistake. The receiver may believe that the creation embodies externally the sum of its meanings. The innkeeper in *Don Quixote* Part I, the Duke and Duchess in Part II, and Luís and Leonora in this story make this mistake. The creation, however, once externalized, becomes nothing more nor nothing less than an object, open to many interpretations and always more expressive than the feelings motivating it.

The vital characters—Loaysa, Leonora's duenna Marialonso, and the maids—are less cautious about their words and deeds than the more introspective Leonora and Carrizales. Before being allowed to enter Carrizales's house Loaysa is made to swear three times that he will obey the wishes of the women inside.[33] Only Leonora cares about these formalities, the others clearly discounting their importance. Each of Loaysa's promises is more elaborate than the one before. Yet all the assembled women, except Leonora, clearly recognize the promises as ritual, as a tool for entry, unimportant in content. Several maids would as soon dispense altogether with the promises, but their over-all reaction is summed up in the praise not of their meaning but of the beauty of their articulation: "That is a promise that would melt a stone. A murrain on me if I want him to swear any more, for with what you have already sworn you could go down the gorge of Cabra!"[34] Only Leonora accepts the words at their face value: "Well, if he has sworn, then he is in our power. Oh, how wise I was to make him swear!"[35]

The maids are skeptical not only of Loaysa's words, but of the social conventions of honor and marriage that hamper Leonora's discovery of her-

---

[33] See Leo Spitzer's article " 'Y así juro por la intemerata eficacia' " [1954]: 483–84.

[34] "¡Este sí que es juramento para enternecer las piedras! Mal haya yo si más quiero que jures; pues con sólo lo jurado podías entrar en la misma sima de cabra!" (RM 2:147).

[35] "Pues si ha jurado . . . asido le tenemos. ¡Oh, qué avisada que anduve en hacelle que jurase!" (RM 2:147).

self. " 'What honor?' asked the duenna. 'The King has enough for us all. Let your ladyship stay locked up with your Methuselah, and let us amuse ourselves as best we can.' "[36] Marialonso's inconsequence, even her failure in seducing the seducer reveals, however, that Cervantes is not proposing the abolition of social conventions, or story conventions, or character stereotypes, or words. For total formlessness destroys identity as much as total acceptance of form. Silence is only meaningful in the context of words. Transgression of social customs is a powerful means of self-expression only in the context of those social customs. Leonora and Carrizales are central figures in the story because they are struggling between forms and structures which, far from being meaningless to them, constitute the core of their being.

Leonora is perhaps the character most neglected in the critical commentary on this story. Most discussion centers around whether or not it is realistic for her to have resisted Loaysa, as the 1613 version has it. Leonora is shown as timid, docile, and more or less content with her lot, despite its disagreeable aspects from the point of view of her parents, the maids, the reader, and the author. When the opportunity for inviting in Loaysa presents itself, however, Leonora's complicity is essential. She joins (with considerable enthusiasm) in the plan to get the key to the house from Carrizales and to administer the sleeping ointment. She is genuinely excited to find the ointment working so well. "Congratulate me, sister," she exclaims, "Carrizales is sleeping like the dead."[37] At the same time she fears Loaysa's covert intentions and cries as she is led off by Marialonso to the bed chamber where Loaysa is waiting. The mixture of shame and rebellion makes it impossible to predict the outcome of the ensuing encounter. Américo Castro objects to the compromising position in which Leonora remains (fast asleep in the arms of Loaysa) while having, according to the later version, successfully defended her virtue. Still the compromise might be exactly expressive of the Leonora in whom neither licentiousness nor its opposite has been firmly established. Just as she neither invited nor rejected Loaysa, she may have achieved a similar balance with Loaysa in Marialonso's bed. For until the point when Leonora acts independently of the promptings of Carrizales or Marialonso,

---

[36] "—¿Qué honra?—dijo la dueña—. El Rey tiene harta. Estése vuesa merced encerrada con su Matusalén, y déjenos a nostras holgar como pudiéremos" (RM 2:133–34).

[37] "—Dame albricias, hermana; que Carrizales duerme más que un muerto" (RM 2:141). Leo Spitzer ("Das Gefüge einer cervantischen Novelle," pp. 194–225) sees in this statement a subconscious expression of her wish for Carrizales's death. It is not necessary to have recourse to the subconscious, however, to see in Leonora's actions and words an excitement that belies her docility and loyalty to Carrizales (RM 2:141).

her own character remains undefined. Like Carrizales, her imagination contains unassimilated aspects of herself, aspects which make her incapable of self-awareness and action. In order for Leonora to emerge as a credible character, she must make a fundamental choice on her own.

To understand the enrichment in the conception of both Leonora and Carrizales that the second ending provides, we must focus not on the possibility or probability of a young girl's successful resistance of a handsome seducer, but rather on what takes place afterward between Leonora and Carrizales. After the night spent by Loaysa in Carrizales's house, Carrizales and Leonora are shown engaging each other for the first time directly. Leonora hugs and caresses Carrizales and shows concern for him. Carrizales, for his part, looks at Leonora, seeing her as if for the first time: "The unfortunate old man slowly opened his eyes, and like one bemused and spellbound, he fixed them on her, and remained gazing at her for a long time."[38] As for Leonora, the narrator says, "putting her arms around her husband, she fondled him as she never had before, asking him what it was he felt, with such tender and loving words as though he were the thing she loved best in the whole world."[39]

When Leonora's parents arrive, they find Carrizales "with his eyes fixed on his wife, her hands in his, and the two of them weeping profusely; she, because she saw the tears her husband shed; he, to see how feigned hers were."[40] The expressions of tenderness continue throughout the denouement. Because of the changed ending, Leonora also emerges from her passivity after her experience in bed with Loaysa. When she arrives at Carrizales's room, she finds her husband unconscious and has no reason to suspect that he has witnessed her transgression. His misery and apparent illness awaken Leonora's concern for him and inspire the caresses which provoke such ambiguous happiness in the old man.

The underlying assumption in this discussion of Carrizales's and Leonora's solipsism is that only a clear sense of his own identity permits a character to communicate with others. Leonora and Carrizales remained locked up within themselves during most of the story because their lack of

[38] ". . . y abriendo los ojos desencasadamente [sic], como atónito y embelesado, los puso en ella, y con gran ahinco, sin mover pestaña, la estuvo mirando una gran pieza" (RM 2:161).

[39] "Abrazándose con su esposo, le hacía las mayores caricias que jamás le había hecho, preguntándole qué era lo que sentía, con tan tiernas y amorosas palabras, como si fuera la cosa del mundo que más amaba" (RM 2:162). Openly interpretive comments of the narrator do not alter the fact that the two are communicating. They only serve to reveal his incomprehension of his characters once they have escaped his stereotype. The narrator's final statement makes this clear.

[40] ". . . siempre clavados los ojos en su esposa, a la cual tenía asida de las manos, derramando los dos muchas lágrimas; ella, con no más ocasión de verlas derramar a su esposo; él, por ver cuán fingidamente ella las derramaba" (RM 2:163).

true self-awareness gave them no perspective from which to view anyone else.[41] Leonora, captured for the first time in the story in outgoing gestures of concern for her husband, has emerged from her experience with Loaysa more clearly self-defined. To choose to accept Loaysa's adulterous advances would not be self-defining, since both Marialonso and Loaysa have predetermined that path. The only nondetermined choice is rejection of Loaysa. For Carrizales has, along with Marialonso and Loaysa, anticipated Leonora's acceptance of Loaysa. Carrizales justified his extreme caution in protecting Leonora because he believed that she had no will of her own and that she would be unfaithful if the opportunity for adultery presented itself. Rejection of Loaysa and maintenance of her own honor under the most adverse and unlikely circumstances is therefore the only truly liberating step Leonora can take. Her freedom is found not in yielding to Loaysa—for that would only confirm Carrizales's version of her—but in showing through her resistance that the prison surrounding her was unwarranted.

The first true communication between Leonora and Carrizales takes place at a moment when their particular interpretations of the events of the preceding night are most radically at odds. Carrizales's discovery of Leonora is based on his interpretation of what he sees. Since Leonora is unable to disabuse him, he dies believing that he has been dishonored. But since the central issue is the escape both characters have made from the limitations of their own self-construct, the misunderstanding between them does not matter. The perception of a world wider than the prison in which both were self-enclosed permits each for the first time to discover the other as real. Loaysa is a tool for the self-discovery of Carrizales and Leonora. Like Loaysa's own words, his actions are, in their content, unimportant. What is important is the way in which each of the other two characters responds to the challenge Loaysa offers.

Carrizales discovers the error in his behavior at the same time that he discovers his wife's being: " 'Like the silkworm, I myself fabricated the house in which I shall die, and I do not blame you, misguided child'—and saying this, he leaned over and kissed the senseless cheek of Leonora."[42] The intensity of the moment finally overcomes Carrizales as well: ". . . he sank into a deep swoon and fell down at Leonora's side, their faces resting against each other."[43]

[41] See section on *Rinconete y Cortadillo* in this chapter (pp. 34–35) for a discussion of the way Cervantes reveals the opposite situations: where characters through a firm acceptance of themselves are able to control the world around them.

[42] "—Yo fuí el que, como el gusano de seda, me fabriqué la casa donde muriese, y a ti no te culpo, ¡oh niña mal aconsejada!—y diciendo esto se inclinó y besó en el rostro de la desmayada Leonora" (RM 2:167).

[43] ". . . le sobrevino un terrible desmayo, y se dejó caer tan junto de Leonora, que se juntaron los rostros" (RM 2:168).

Carrizales's eloquence, his generosity, his lucidity, and his tenderness toward Leonora reveal his emergence from the stereotype of the jealous husband. Had he reacted automatically, according to prescription, he would have avenged the dishonor. When he rejects the prescribed role, Carrizales escapes his solipsism. He looks at Leonora and thinks about her for the first time.

Essential to Carrizales's subsequent self-transcendence is the sight of the sleeping Leonora and Loaysa. For that sight releases Carrizales from the internal struggle which was expressed externally in his nearly maniacal efforts to keep them apart. When he sees them outside himself, he discovers his own reality as distinct from and above either of the two with whom he had formerly identified himself. Carrizales is now able to transcend that dichotomy and to identify himself as more than the miserable product of its opposition. The new Carrizales has discovered himself beyond the cartoon-like single dimension of "jealous husband."

The emergence of Carrizales and Leonora from their solipsism has another effect. As characters having transcended their stereotypes, they are no longer controlled by the narrator. The narrator who appears in the last paragraph expresses his perplexity with the way the story has ended: "The one thing I do not know is why Leonora did not make more of an effort to excuse herself and convince her jealous husband how guiltless she had been in that whole affair."[44] This doubt, coming as it does at the very end of the story, shows the narrator's awareness of the character's independence. The narrator becomes mere interpreter at the point when the characters begin to speak and act for themselves. This establishes another dimension of the character's freedom and involves the narrator and the reader in a new way with the work of art.

When the narrator becomes interpreter, his fallibility becomes apparent. Just as Loaysa's words and Leonora's deeds are unimportant as isolated facts, the changed ending allows us to see that the very words which make up the story do not entirely contain its meaning. No facts are possible isolated from a perceiver and interpreter of them. The narrator simply provides another interpretation for the actions of characters who are suddenly as real as he is. The narrator cannot control his characters or his reader any more than Carrizales can control Leonora.

Although the sense of the narrator's powerlessness is characteristic of the early works, it coexists with an opposing impulse toward total control, producing an atmosphere of conflict and irresolution. In later works the air of self-confidence does not necessarily imply dominion over his characters on the part of the narrator. The author also presents himself as partici-

---

[44] "Sólo no sé qué fué la causa que Leonora no puso más ahinco en desculparse y dar a entender a su celoso marido cuán limpia y sin ofensa había quedado en aquel suceso" (RM 2:171).

pant in the failings to which all living beings are subject, as will be shown in the discussion of the *Casamiento engañoso* and the *Coloquio de los perros* (chap. III). The narrator in the later works both transcends and identifies with his characters. A consideration of the change in Cide Hamete's role with respect to Don Quixote in Parts I and II reveals this distinction. The emergence of the narrator as man and story-teller at the end of the work is typical of the later stories, as will be seen.

El celoso extremeño resembles the early works of Cervantes in its presentation of a solitary, cerebral central character who seeks to control life and to define himself by means of mental constructs and faith in fixed forms. In this case the disparity between the character's actual situation and the formal means by which he seeks to define it is represented by the misapplication of the convention of marriage to the lives of a man in his seventies and a girl no older than fourteen. In the early version, the natural result of such a misalliance comes about when a handsome young man interposes himself between the old man and his child bride and succeeds, though not in such a brazen way as in the comic interlude *El viejo celoso*, in seducing her.

The changes Cervantes made in the work before including it in his collection of exemplary novels are consonant with a change in his perspective with regard to social, ideological, and literary matters in later life. Since in the published version Leonora resists Loaysa's efforts to seduce her, the obvious conclusion is that Cervantes no longer considers the central question to revolve around the conflict between life and abstract forms, or reality and fiction. For in the version of the story published in 1613, Leonora does not do what would have been expected of her had this been the central question. The marriage, however misused the institution appears to have been in Leonora's and Carrizales's case, survives the challenge of life, of natural impulses.

The criticism that the resistance to Loaysa is inverisimilar depends on a naturalistic interpretation of verisimilitude which Cervantes appears to have rejected in his later writings. Cervantes is concerned with verisimilitude in the later works only as a check on his impulse to allow his characters to perform impossible acts, such as those performed by the heroes of chivalric novels. Cervantes clearly did not find impossible the sort of moral heroism displayed not only by Leonora, but by Leocadia (in *La fuerza de la sangre*), or by Persiles and Sigismunda. Leonora's last-minute salvation of her honor saves Carrizales from ignominy, gives religious, rather than simply social meaning to her entrance into the convent after Carrizales's death, and reveals Cervantes's interest in his major character's moral development.

The removal of the section describing the young man about town whose representative in the story is Loaysa, the less grave fate assigned to Loaysa, and the overt identification of Loaysa with Carrizales reveal Cervantes's less partisan attitude toward his characters. Loaysa is seen not as an example of a class of society hated by Cervantes, but as part of the inevitably repetitious struggle in life to possess what belongs to another. Carrizales, equally selfish and possessive, suggests Loaysa's destiny, just as Loaysa reveals Carrizales's past. And Carrizales's self-transcendence offers hope for Loaysa's ultimate salvation.

Because any social form which replaces true human interaction is seen as bad in Cervantes's late work, a marriage between an old man and a young girl becomes symbolic of any marriage in which the partners have not escaped their own self-absorption. When two people have done this, when they have discovered a truth which reaches beyond their stock roles in life and in fiction, their marriage is meaningful no matter what their ages. Carrizales and Leonora, in the published version of the story, both confront and transcend the limitations they have imposed on themselves and have had imposed on them. The final scenes of tenderness reveal the true communication made possible not because they understand each other's words but because they have been released from the preoccupation with a formal concept of themselves and can see the essential humanity of the other.

An early story of social criticism and the failure of an old man to control his young wife is transformed, by a change in Leonora's final actions, into one in which moral strength and self-transcendence are highlighted. Like *Rinconete y Cortadillo*, *El celoso extremeño* is interesting for the alterations which reveal the shift in Cervantes's thinking in the later works. Though characteristic of the earlier works in general outline, later modifications provide interesting insight into the thinking which is more fully revealed in stories conceived later.

El licenciado Vidriera

With very few exceptions, the critics who have concerned themselves with the date of composition of *El licenciado Vidriera* agree that it was written in Valladolid between 1604 and 1606.[45] In the character of the mad Licenciate can be seen the most extended representation in Cervantes's work both of his need for literature and of his sense of its futility. The work reveals his unreconciled ambivalence toward the word, abstraction, and literature itself.

[45] Of the critics who comment on the chronology of the *Novelas ejemplares*, William J. Entwistle (*Cervantes* [1940], p. 95), Francisco Rodríguez Marín (*El Loaysa de "El Celoso Extremeño"* [1901], p. 219) and M. A. Buchanan ("The

Tomás Rodaja, the boy who later becomes the mad Licenciate, begins his life within the pages of the novela consumed by the ambition to give glory to his family and himself by his successful accumulation of knowledge. As the work develops, however, it becomes clear that the desire for fame and the means chosen for the fulfillment of that desire are not complementary, but mutually exclusive. Tomás's early success at the University of Salamanca comes about in relative obscurity. The fame he later achieves derives not from his wisdom but from the madness that impells him to rail against society with bitter denunciations, for when his sanity is restored to him, he finds no market for his wit and intelligence. Apparently, having to choose between fame and a career in letters, he decides on the former and dies in battle.

The madness into which Tomás falls upon graduating from the University of Salamanca was caused ostensibly by poison. The poisoning unites the early, successful, charming, and happy Tomás Rodaja with the later Licenciate Vidriera, consumed by the fear of others and violent in his denunciation of all stations in society. The frailty of the link has caused many critics to deny any connection at all between the mad Licenciate and his prehistory as Tomás Rodaja.[46] This peculiar disjunction is compounded by another. More than one-half of the work is nothing but a series of apothegms delivered by the mad Licenciate and scarcely attached to the plot through which they are presented.[47] The disjunction between

---

Works of Cervantes and Their Dates of Composition" [1938]: 39) consider the *Licenciado* to have been written in Madrid. Fitzmaurice-Kelly (*The Exemplary Novels* [1902], p. xxv) cautiously suggests that the work was written sometime after 1606. While he offers no explanation for his conjecture, Entwistle bases his date (1610) on the "unflattering references" to Madrid in the work. Narciso Alonso Cortés, however, (*Cervantes en Valladolid* [1918], p. 102), explains these references as growing out of the rivalry between Madrid and Valladolid that was current during the years that the court of Philip III was in Valladolid. Icaza ("Algo más sobre *El licenciado Vidriera*" [1916]: 38–44); Apraiz (*Estudio histórico-crítico* [1901], p. 70); Luís Rosales ("La evasión del prójimo o el hombre de cristal" [1956]: 260); and Schevill and Bonilla ("Introducción," *Novelas ejemplares*, [1925], 3:401), all agree on an early dating for *El licenciado Vidriera*, or between 1604 and 1606.

[46] Armand Singer makes the most radical statement of this position: "What precedes Rodaja's answers is but an introduction, clearly divorced from the body proper of the text, and not particularly important to it" ("Cervantes' *Licenciado Vidriera*: Its Form and Substance" [1951]: 13).

[47] Again it is Singer who states this position in its most extreme form: "There is no organic connection between the nature of the apothegms and the illness; the framework of the story bears no relation to its content" ("The Sources, Meaning, and Use of the Madness Theme in Cervantes' *Licenciado Vidriera*," p. 45). It must be pointed out that Singer's position has been criticized by Frank Casa ("The Structural Unity of *El licenciado Vidriera*" [1964]: 242–46) in an article which seeks to establish an understanding for the work as a unity. Other efforts to unify

the mad Licenciate and his prehistory, and between the work as story and the work as a collection of apothegms suggests on a deeper level the confusion of an author too much bound up with his character to be able either to understand him fully or to control the story of which the character is a part.

Several issues link *El licenciado Vidriera* with the other early short stories being studied here. As in *El celoso extremeño, El curioso impertinente,* and *Don Quixote* Part I, the narrator in *El licenciado Vidriera* appears only briefly to trace the external outlines of the major character, who will then take over the development of his own personality. Like other major characters of the early works, Tomás Rodaja is obsessed by unexpressed impulses which drive him radically out of his past and into a future which he will, through his intellect, attempt to control. The drive of the character to create himself anew is reflected structurally in the apparent insignificance of the narrator in the development of the story.

The intense voluntarism, so often discussed as characteristic of Don Quixote, is found in its most extreme form in the character of Tomás Rodaja. Unlike Don Quixote, about whose background the reader knows something, and whose friends and family are never entirely absent in Part I, Tomás Rodaja emerges totally severed from his past and determined to be totally in control of his future. In both cases where he accepts companionship—first, as servant to the gentlemen-scholars, and later as Captain Valdivia's guest—it is always stressed that the acceptance will result in advancement for himself along his pre-chosen course of self-education. For Tomás has decided that he will honor his family through his learning. All his activities are subordinated to that end. He has naive faith that his learning will be applicable and appreciated. His belief that "out of men bishops are made" is reminiscent of Don Quixote's often-stated allegation that a man is the son of his works, and expresses the only hope for the low-born in a society strangled by privilege and narrow-mindedness.

What distinguishes Tomás from Don Quixote and from all the other early characters, however, is the general favor with which not only the narrator but the other characters view him. Tomás Rodaja's project at the beginning of the story about him is praised by all who hear it. The gentlemen-scholars are so impressed with the boy and so touched by his desire to learn that they quickly convert him from their servant to their companion. Captain Valdivia is also charmed by Tomás and offers him all sorts of

---

the disparate elements of *El licenciado Vidriera* can be found in the work of Casalduero ("*Novelas ejemplares,*" pp. 141, 147–49); Otis Green ("*El licenciado Vidriera:* Its Relation to the *Viaje del parnaso* and the *Examen de ingenios* of Huarte" [1964]: 213–20); and J. B. Avalle-Arce ("Introduction," *Three Exemplary Novels* [1964]).

inducements in order to get him to join his military company on its way to Italy and Flanders.

The sympathy accorded Tomás by characters within the work is echoed by the narrator. Although he remains in the background during the period of Tomás's youth and service to the students at Salamanca, he intervenes during Tomás's encounter with the Captain to introduce bitter invective arguments against soldiering. The Captain has painted the charms of the soldier's life in order to persuade Tomás to accompany him to Italy and the Netherlands with the new company being assembled near Salamanca. The narrator adds passionately, ". . . but he said nothing about the cold of sentry duty, the danger that lay in an attack, the terror of battles, the hunger endured in a siege, the destruction wrought by mines, or other things of that sort, although there are some who look upon these as burdensome accompaniments of the military life, while in fact they constitute its chief characteristic."[48] A subsequent comment suggests that he feels that the Captain has led Tomás astray: "In short, he talked so long and so well that Tomás Rodaja's judgment began to waver, and the lad came to feel an attraction for this way of life which is always so near to death."[49]

While Tomás is clearly free to do as he chooses—the narrator, as in all the early stories, apparently having no direct control over the protagonist's life—the narrator comments on Tomás's decision to go to Italy with the Captain: "And as if everything were to happen to the measure of his desires, he told the captain that he would be glad to accompany him to Italy."[50] Exemplary behavior, rather than the need to escape entanglement,

[48] ". . . pero no le dijo nada del frío de las centinelas, del peligro de los asaltos, del espanto de las batallas, de la hambre de los cercos, de la ruina de las minas, con otras cosas deste jaez, que algunos las toman y tienen por añadiduras del peso de la soldadesca, y son la carga principal della" (RM 2:15–16).

This and all subsequent translations of *El licenciado Vidriera* come from "Man of Glass" in *Three Exemplary Novels*, translated by Samuel Putnam (1950), pp. 75–121. In this quotation I have altered Mr. Putnam's translation. His phrase "although there are some who look upon these burdensome accompaniments of the military life as constituting its chief characteristic," does not render the narrator's obvious concurrence with the idea. Other uses of Mr. Putnam's translation appear on pp. 54 and 56.

[49] "En resolución, tantas cosas le dijo, y tan bien dichas, que la discreción de nuestro Tomás Rodaja comenzó a titubear, y la voluntad a aficionarse a aquella vida, que tan cerca tiene la muerte" (RM 2:16). It is these two passages (here and in footnote 48) that lead me to reject the idea, expressed by Avalle-Arce (*Three Exemplary Novels*), that Tomás's final joining of the army at the end represents completion rather than defeat.

[50] "Y como si todo hubiera de suceder a la medida de su gusto, dijo al capitán que era contento de irse con él a Italia" (RM 2:17). Again here I have altered Mr. Putnam's translation. He says, "He appeared bent, however, upon having everything to suit his own wishes." This does not accurately reflect the attitude of the narrator implicit in "como si. . . ."

is clearly what the narrator sees in Tomás's early action. When Tomás refuses special favors offered by the Captain, he explains: "That would go against my conscience . . . I would rather go as a free man than be under any obligations." The Captain answers, "So scrupulous a conscience as yours is the sort one would expect to find in a monk rather than a soldier; but have it your way, for we are comrades in any event."[51] Each rejection of involvement is explained in such a way as to make the young man's actions not only defensible but laudatory.

Tomás's solitude, which the narrator presents as indicative of his character's independence and incorruptibility, becomes structurally significant during the presentation of Tomás's observations while traveling in Italy. The absence of companiòns undercuts the distance Cervantes generally establishes between narrator and characters in his stories. Since Tomás's impressions cannot be played off against those of other characters, the narrator must transmit them to the reader directly. Tomás's trip through Italy becomes a travelogue in which his personality becomes totally insignificant. He becomes pure transparency, simply conveying reactions and impressions. His role as traveler doubles that of the narrator, and the two fuse as they limit themselves to mediating between the reader and the various scenes afforded by the trip. Nothing like hunger, or the various mishaps that may befall the traveler, intervene to individualize the commentary. The sympathy detected in Cervantes's presentation of his character affects not only the content of the story, but its structure, allowing the character so to take over the story as to be confused with the narrator.

The lack of criticism of the main character either through ironic statements by the narrator or through ridicule by his companions, and the absence of distance established between narrator and protagonist during the travels in Italy suggests an unusual closeness and sympathy between the narrator and the character. This feeling is heightened with the appearance of the woman who is to poison Tomás. The woman whose passionate advances Tomás rejects is presented as repugnant, thus justifying his response. If the narrator were trying to present a rounded picture of Tomás, he would have made his actions more problematic by making the woman more attractive. In the same way, the narrator's statements against war had made Tomás's evasion of participation look more like wisdom than cowardice. A more sympathetic presentation of Tomás's alternatives would have emphasized his reactions and encouraged the reader's closer examination of

---

[51] "—Eso sería . . . ir contra mi conciencia; . . . y así, más quiero ir suelto que obligado." "—Conciencia tan escrupulosa . . . más es de religioso que de soldado; pero como quiera que sea, ya somos camaradas" (RM 2:18).

his motives. As it is, the narrator's presentation makes it appear that Tomás is both reasonable and admirable.

The unusually close character-narrator relationship established in the first section of the work remains unchanged in the second section, where Tomás, now mad, unleashes a steady stream of acerbic judgments against society. The *vulgo* has replaced the cities in Italy as the touchstone for Tomás's commentary. The only difference is that while the cities in Italy provided a pleasing atmosphere for his observations, the crowds that follow him everywhere in Salamanca and Valladolid provide an irritant. Nothing in the narrator's presentation of either set of observations suggests an error of perception on the part of the observer. For, as in the descriptions of Italy, the observer is as of glass, his own personality intervening only minimally in his perceptions. This gives further insight into the metaphor of glass with which Tomás chooses to represent his state. For, while it qualifies him for madness, it also declares his absolute lucidity. Tomás, through the image of glass, merges with the narrator to mediate between the reader and the environment. He protects Cervantes from censure, as the madness protects him, in his unmitigated attack on the variety of pretentions and misrepresentations that make life in the city and in the court impossible for the literate man.

The only truly anecdotal presentation of the Licenciate takes place when the narrator describes the particular things which made the madman fearful and the details of his strange actions upon recovery from the poison. In this brief interlude the Licenciate becomes a character in the story and an object of the narrator's description. Shortly thereafter, however, when he is transported to the court, the Licenciate again becomes pure observer, tending to merge once again with the narrator. Both the madness and the anecdotal description of its external manifestation reveal an effort by Cervantes to distinguish the character from the narrator within the work, an effort which betrays not only his fear that he be associated with the bitter criticisms made by his character, but his awareness that unity in a work of fiction depends upon the continued distance between author and character—a distance that can only be maintained if the character is clearly delineated and circumscribed. The threatened collapse of the work's pretense as a story is remedied artificially by the interjection of a description of a madman.

The absence of a clearly drawn distinction between the character's voice and the narrator's explains why this story has caused so much confusion among critics. For although this analysis is focused on the major character, little space in the story is devoted to him. The far larger part is taken up with the travel impressions of Tomás and the aphorisms he produces in his mad state. The part devoted to delineation of Tomás's character must be seen as ancillary to the novel's main project. His intellectual failure, his inability to gain the distance required to formulate a total system out of the perspicacious criticism of everything he sees, is paralleled by Cervantes's failure to grasp his character as a whole and his inability fully to distinguish narrator and character within the work. In both cases the result is a fragmented production whose parts, though individually interesting, fail to cohere into a convincing whole.

In addition to introducing the young Tomás as faultless and emphasizing the criticisms against society rather than the madness that inspired them, Cervantes reveals his misunderstanding of his character by having recourse to poison to explain the madness which afflicts Tomás. There is an underlying unity between the young Tomás and the crazed Licenciate which Cervantes appears to obscure by introducing poison to explain the transformation. In order to study this identification of Cervantes with the Licenciate it is necessary to see a consistent pattern of behavior in the Licenciate—a pattern which is responsible both for Tomás's early success and for his later madness—and then to see the ways in which the author reveals his blindness to that pattern.

The principal characteristic of the mad Licenciate and the young Tomás Rodaja is fear of the other. In the early part of the story that fear expresses itself in Tomás's apparently salutory unwillingness to engage in actions that would commit him to someone else. The poison administered to Tomás by his lady friend accelerates the crisis of identity indicated in his portrayal up to the point of his illness. Tomás had always rejected the efforts of others or of circumstances to determine his destiny or to control him. His refusal to give his family's name or his place of origin, the fear and repugnance contact with soldiers and a sea voyage inspired in him, his solitary and restless travels, and his avoidance of love and marriage trace a pattern of escape. The poisoning condemns Tomás to six months of mortal illness after which he declares that he is made of glass. The narrator makes it clear that the mental illness emerges from the physical illness: "For six months Tomás was in bed, and in the course of that time he withered away and became, as the saying goes, nothing but skin and bones, while all his senses gave evidence of being deranged."[52] The conclusion to be drawn is that it was the experience of illness itself and not the poison which weakened the Licenciate's brain. The illness simply induced the crisis that all the other activities of Tomás's life had been designed to avoid, for the illness brought him forcibly, and for the first time, into confrontation

---

[52] "Seis meses estuvo en la cama Tomás, en los cuales se secó y se puso, como suele decirse, en los huesos, y mostraba tener turbados todos los sentidos" (RM 2:36).

with his contingency, his dependence on time and chance occurrences, his limited position in life, and his necessary recognition of death. In study Tomás had sought to escape not only his past and the obscurity to which it threatened to condemn him, but all of life's conflict and, implicitly, death itself. Tomás's apotheosis of the intellect reflects a struggle to efface the demands of time and death. The illness and near-death imposed on him by the poisoning activated the previously submerged anxiety of a body after all vulnerable and of a mind destructible despite its wit and intellectual achievement. The madness exaggerates an aspect of a personality never really at ease with itself, but which, until the crisis of illness, is never in full confrontation with its contradictions. Knowledge, for the Licenciate, like words for Rincón and Cortado or literature for Don Quixote, is a means by which one seeks to disarm reality of its persistent corrosion of life and health and personal integrity. In the course of his prehistory Tomás is shown fending off first the compromises of soldiering and then the compromises of marriage. Only when he is actually caught in the trap of illness and directly threatened by death, however, does it become clear that the earlier enticements represented the same assault on his integrity, but in lesser degree, that death represents as the most extreme case.

The madness follows the logic of Tomás's personality and grows more out of his fear of death than out of an externally administered potion. The Licenciate expresses the anguish that awareness of his vulnerability causes him by declaring himself to be made of glass. Glass is a particularly appropriate image, for it captures not only the Licenciate's sense of his fragility, but his clarity of thought and his need for distance. The fear of physical suffering, the will to isolate himself from others, and the exaggerated importance ascribed to mental acuity are elements of the Licenciate's personality present from the beginning. In the mad state, they crystallize in a single image of glass. In its simplicity, the image projects a false unity. Beneath the image, two impulses, no longer controllable within the scope of normal behavior, race in opposite directions, unconnected except for the metaphor which holds them together. The Licenciate's retreat into madness reveals his inability to assimilate his sense of contingency with his desire for intellectual transcendence. The resultant opposition allows the same man who astonishes university dignitaries with his wisdom to quake during thunderstorms, fear for falling bricks, scream when approached or touched, dress in a baggy suit, and sleep the winter nights in a hay stack. The fear of death has been released and runs rampant in a man whose energy has been directed toward transcending that fear through abstraction.

The effect of the Licenciate's ingenious identification of himself as a man of glass is, in exchange for his credibility, to grant him both increased protection and increased audience for his intelligence. His fame pushes into ever-widening circles from the beginning of the novel to the end. After his madness, even, he cannot be hidden long within the circle of his friends. And, consonant with his ambition, he does not want to be hidden: "His friends kept him shut up much of the time; but when they saw that he was getting no better, they decided to yield to his wishes and let him go about freely."[53] The achievement of patronage in the court of Phillip III represents the culmination of his ambitions at the same time that it exaggerates their failure. For while patronage liberates him from fear of recrimination and permits his intelligence to aim at any target, however sacrosanct and off-limits to ordinary men, it liberates him only within the context of the glass box. Like visitors to the zoo, the crowds who follow him everywhere can thrill to the roars and snarls of his wit safe with the knowledge that the space between them is filled with a glass barrier which they from their side call madness. The Licenciate's sharp-tongued capsulization of urban and courtly society is neutralized by the counter thrust which locks him up inside the word "madman" and renders him harmless.

One of the principal differences between *El licenciado Vidriera* and Cervantes's other stories rests in the relationship established between the main protagonist and the others who surround him. With the exception of the Captain, none of the people with whom Tomás has contact are even named. All appear generically: gentlemen-scholars, soldiers, shopkeepers, noblemen. They remain unspecified by their speech, dress, or other peculiarities of character. Unlike all of Cervantes's other major characters, Tomás is never shown telling stories to other characters, or engaging them in some way in an effort to control or fool them. Although his friendship with the student gentlemen, the Captain, and the group at Salamanca is referred to, its secondary importance is suggested by the absence of scenes or dialogues in which it is developed. During the period when the Licenciate is denouncing society through his aphorisms, he is constantly surrounded by people, but still without dialogue or companionship.[54]

The Licenciate is so thoroughly bound up in words and abstractions that he is incapable of confronting the concrete and particular. When

---

[53] "Tuviéronle encerrado sus amigos mucho tiempo; pero viendo que su desgracia pasaba adelante, determinaron de condecender con lo que él les pedía, que era le dejasen andar libre, y así, le dejaron" (RM 2:38–39).

[54] Luís Rosales, who makes such a sensitive study of the Licenciate's alienation in his article ("La evasión" [1956]), entitles one subsection: "El mundo del Licenciado es el mundo de la evasión del 'tú'."

confronted with a particular tailor, for example, he pronounces on the tailor in general, uninterested in the individuating characteristics which may make this tailor different from others. Don Quixote exhibited similar characteristics when he was involved in the process of creating his chivalric world. Empirical data provided only the briefest springboard for his rapid assimilation of things into his own preestablished naming system. Two things at once distinguish the Licenciate from Don Quixote and make his case more desperate. First, the Licenciate, in his mad state, has no friends. Thus, there is no period of relaxation available to him—no respite from his task of converting the concrete into an abstract form in which it can be controlled. And second, the scope of the Licenciate's madness is not circumscribed. Don Quixote limited himself to chivalric novels. Outside their scope, he was free to discuss intelligently such questions as the various merits of careers in arms and letters, poetry, or the art of governing. Both the companionship of Sancho and the limited nature of his need to transform his surroundings gives a dimension of sanity to Don Quixote not permitted to the Licenciate. The Licenciate's field is the whole of human knowledge. He must transform every bit of concrete data into an abstract, generalized formula.

The aphorism expresses both the Licenciate's will to succeed as an intellectual and his utter failure. Each aphorism traces a movement from the particular to the general. The ceaseless application of this trajectory to everything the Licenciate sees betrays his will to transform the entirety of experience into a generalized form. Yet the aphorisms themselves remain particular. That is, their very fragmentation denies the totality to which they aspire. His constant, restless, and harried confrontation with a hostile world offers him no resting place from which to organize the angry fragments of thought which he strews about so compulsively. The crowd has disarmed him both by identifying him as mad and by engaging him so mercilessly that it undermines him even at his own game by forcing him to release his over-all knowledge in bits and pieces which never find their way into a coherent and potentially dangerous alternate system.

Don Quixote engaged the world and challenged its assumptions by the presentation of an alternate system which was harmless because of its inapplicability to the society he was confronting. The Licenciate, however, confronts society at its heart: in the city, at the court. His challenge is rendered harmless by its fragmentation, its potential for a comprehensive program for change being reduced to the complaints of a crank. Neither Don Quixote nor the Licenciate, through literature or abstraction, can challenge successfully the society to which they object. The intellectual, these works seem to be saying, is an alienated being whose will to make direct contact with the society from which he has at the same time wished to escape is condemned to failure.[55] The Licenciate fails both in life and in letters. In life he cannot make meaningful contact with society. He has no friends outside of the intellectual community and finds only sickness and death in alternative roles. But in letters he fails also, for he cannot transform his surroundings into meaningful abstract forms. His intellectual creativity is reduced to the production of only occasionally witty aphorisms. His is an unrelieved story of estrangement in which the main protagonist is shown only in roles of conflict with his environment.

Tomás's entire life is wrapped up in learning, in concepts, in abstractions and words which appear as opposed, within his own life, to the concrete commitments involved in love and war. The constant press of life represented by the woman and Tomas's illness finally awakens in him the need to protect himself. The words, the abstractions, become not just vehicles of escape but weapons. As weapons, however, the words lose their power, exposing the user, as much as the object which the words seek to capture, to ridicule. Tomás fails as an author because he does not communicate by his words nor does he transform.

Yet Tomás clearly desires communication: his friends cannot keep him home, and even after his cure he seeks the chance to share his knowledge with others. But when he is with people, he feels the need for protection and shows his aggressiveness through constant verbal attack. Tomás seems to represent the opposite pole from Ginés de Pasamonte—another in Cervantes's gallery of authors who have failed. While Ginés is too bound up in life, too much a participant in its shifts and changes, Tomás is too removed from it. Neither the perpetual actor nor the perpetual bystander can communicate with others. The author, like every man, must alternate between roles of distance and roles of involvement, in order to be successful in mediating between himself and the people around him. The selec-

---

[55] One is tempted to find in this lesson a hint of the "New Christian's" desperation. Cervantes himself has made the equation illiteracy = "Old Christian" often enough (with Sancho, *El retablo de las maravillas*, and *La elección de los alcaldes*) to suggest his awareness of the other half of the proportion. For more on this point, see Américo Castro, *Cervantes y los casticismos españoles* (1966), pp. 84–92, and Stephen Gilman's "Los inquisidores literarios de Cervantes" (1970): 9. For a study of the way the question of literacy figured in the acrimony between "new" and "old" Christians, see Albert A. Sicroff, *Les controverses des statuts de "pureté de sang" en Espagne du XVe au XVIIe Siècle* (1960). (It might be noted in passing that the importance of this theme in Spanish studies of the fifteenth to seventeenth centuries has come under considerable recent criticism, especially from Eugenio Asenio. See his "En torno a Américo Castro. Polémica con Albert A. Sicroff" (1972): 365–85, for the presentation of an opposing view and bibliography of articles on the subject.)

tion of glass as a representation of Tomás's state suggests his fear, his unapproachability, his inability to change, and his fragility. All of these life-negating characteristics disqualify him for successful communication.

The closeness of narrator and character in *El licenciado Vidriera* is a function of the Licenciate's failure to become truly a character. He threatens at any moment to disappear from the narration and to be seen only in his words. He exaggerates the faults of the narrator, while the narrator shows no critical distance on his character. The result is a partial fusion in which no complete picture, either of the character or the narrator's attitude toward him, can be developed. The work represents the nadir of Cervantes's confidence in both his possibility for success and the possibility that wisdom and intelligence have any meaning in a world governed by ignorance and prejudice. The choice he offers his characters is between death in military service and madness, in which the effort to abstract and discover the truths behind appearance becomes a machine-gun fire of hateful statements lacking all cohesion and order.

III. TRANSITION I: *EL CASAMIENTO ENGAÑOSO* AND *EL COLOQUIO DE LOS PERROS*

E
l coloquio de los perros, if not *El casamiento engañoso,* was probably written before 1606.[1] Though both stories present author-characters alienated from the mainstream of society, the style of the frame story suggests a later dating.[2] Taken together, the series of author-characters in the two works reveals an increasing movement away from degradation, deception, and failure toward the self-confident and creative stance with respect to reality and art more typical of Cervantes's later work. The significances of the *Casamiento* and the

[1] A great deal of evidence has led to general agreement on an early dating for the *Coloquio.* Francisco A. de Icaza, *Las "Novelas ejemplares" de Cervantes . . .* (1916), pronounces most firmly on the datability of the *Coloquio:* ". . . y cabalmente no hay en las *Novelas ejemplares* otras cuya fecha pueda determinarse con más probabilidades de acierto" (p. 208). Agustín A. de Amezúa y Mayo (*Cervantes, creador de la novela corta española* [1956–58]) is equally affirmative about the dating of the *Coloquio:* "Tengo para mí que después de su resonante éxito editorial [del *Quijote*], éxito que Cervantes no pudo sospechar, o no se hubiera escrito el *Coloquio,* o su espíritu y tono hubieran sido muy distintos" (p. 399). Narciso Alonso Cortés (*Cervantes en Valladolid* [1918]) demonstrates convincingly that Cervantes must have been in Valladolid when he wrote the *Coloquio.* All the above-mentioned critics draw on references made within the work to place the date of its composition at around 1604–05. Other critics such as Américo Castro concur for the reason, mentioned above by Amezúa as well, that the work could not be a product of Cervantes's success and must, therefore, antedate the publication of *Don Quixote* I ("La ejemplaridad de las *Novelas ejemplares*" [1967], pp. 466–67). The lone dissenting voice in this catalogue of concurring opinion is that of William Entwistle (*Cervantes* [1940], p. 95) who, for reasons easily disputed, dates the composition of both the *Casamiento* and the *Coloquio* as 1609. Joaquín Casalduero, who in any case had disavowed concern with the chronology of the novelas in his introduction (*Sentido y forma de las "Novelas ejemplares"* [1969]) suggests a late dating for the *Coloquio,* but without great conviction: "El *Coloquio* pudo ser una de las últimas al escribirse, pero es arriesgado hacer ninguna afirmación" (p. 11).

[2] Maurice Molho's speculations about the dating of the double novela are interesting (in his "Remarques sur le *Mariage trompeur* et *Colloque des chiens,*" [1970]). All the evidence he presents for a 1605–06 dating applies to the *Coloquio* (pp. 89–90), while the considerable discussion relating the Ensign Campuzano to Don Quixote refers to the character and mentality of *Don Quixote* Part II (pp. 91–93). While Molho's analysis appears to take for granted a single plan of composition for the two novelas, his speculations regarding their dating would tend to support, rather than to render invalid, my supposition that the two works were written separately and joined toward the time when the collection was published.

Coloquio become apparent when the works are studied in combination and when they are considered in the light of their place within the whole of the *Novelas ejemplares*.

In the *Casamiento* and the *Coloquio* can be found some of the most significant artistic expressions of the literary problems which are known to have concerned authors of fiction in Cervantes's day. Such well known problems as the relationship between illusion and reality, fiction and truth, and goodness and evil find expression throughout both works. Underlying these oppositions, for which no apparent resolution is offered, are the oppositions between author and critic which are built into both stories. The problem here is to analyze the presence of the oppositions which appear in each story and in both stories and in the whole of the *Novelas ejemplares* in an effort to discover the source of not only the conflicting but also the reintegrating impulses within the works. The analysis depends on a study of the interrelation of a series of first-person narrations which appear in the double novela. There are three—not two—first-person narrations to be considered, their order of presentation in the works representing an exact reversal of the order in which they occurred in the lives of the narrating characters.

Because of the complexity of the works, a brief summary of each must precede further consideration of their interrelation. The *Coloquio de los perros* deals with the dog Berganza's narration of his life to his friend Cipión. But because the gift of speech is so unexpected for the two dogs, Berganza's narration is as concerned with solving the riddle of his present garrulity as with recounting the events of his past. For this reason, Berganza skips lightly over the question of his natural origin as a dog, while sowing hints, throughout the narration of the first five episodes of his life, which produce in his listener anticipation of a supernatural explanation for his present ability to speak. Because of this anticipation, the linear, chronological ordering of Berganza's tale is opposed by a sense of crescendo, a sense that all the episodes do not have equal value. Anxiety and uncertainty about the present disrupt the apparent picaresque nature of Berganza's narration. They undercut the determinism that makes the explanation of naturalistic origins important and challenge the chronological ordering of events, replacing the idea of succession, of past leading inexorably to the present, with an idea of hierarchy, some events having greater importance within the succession than others.

The supernatural explanation finally comes when Berganza relates his experience in Montilla with the witch Cañizares. The central importance of the witch's episode can be seen in the patterning of the episodes which surround it. Numerically, the episode falls in dead center of Berganza's experiences with many masters. Before meeting Cañizares, Berganza had had contact with five masters. Afterward, Berganza serves five others. To these eleven situations is added the commentary by four madmen Berganza overhears—a poet, an alchemist, a mathematician, and a wild-eyed dreamer (*arbitrista*)—who have come to die in the hospital, as well as reference to Berganza's unsuccessful effort to tell the chief magistrate of Valladolid that prostitution should be kept under control.[3]

The witch's tale is the most fully developed of all the stories Berganza tells and the only one that mediates between his past as a dog and his present ability to speak. In addition, it is the only narration that duplicates the method of presentation of the story in which it is contained. The witch, like Berganza, gives a first-person account of her life. She recounts her past and reflects uncertainty about her present. Her words, "I pray but little, and only in public; in private, I still indulge in backbiting," and "it is better for me to be a hypocrite than an open sinner,"[4] capture the essence of Berganza's own struggle in his narration to avoid spitefulness and backbiting. The witch's problems, as well as the prophecy she has given Berganza, foreshorten Berganza's narrative, giving this single event in the linear chain of events Berganza had been narrating an immediacy that causes it to leap out of the chronological order in which it had been placed.

Berganza's first five masters are fully entrenched in established society. They represent fixed institutions—the butcher, the shepherds, the merchant, the bailiff, and the drummer—sure of themselves and surprisingly heartless and unconcerned about the deceptions by which they survive. The five masters whom Berganza serves after the witch's episode belong to the fringes of society—gypsies, moors, a poet, playwrights, and an alms collector. After entering into the service of the alms collector Mahudes, Berganza has contact, but with no ties of servitude to them, with characters totally alienated from society—men termed mad and put away in the hos-

---

[3] Maurice Molho's brilliant analysis of the double novela ("Remarques"), bound by his revelation of its binary structure, reduces the number of masters on either side of the witch episode to four, omitting thereby the drummer and the alms collector Mahudes. The former is assigned to the category "ensemble liminaire," forming a diptych with the witch Cañizares, while Mahudes exists beyond the spectacle portrayed as a signal of the dogs' renunciation of sin through charity. My count assumes that the *Coloquio* parodies the picaresque structure of service to many masters.

[4] ". . . rezo poco, y en público; murmuro mucho, y en secreto: vame mejor con ser hipócrita que con ser pecadora declarada" (Cervantes Saavedra, *Novelas ejemplares*, 2 vols. [1915–17], 2:297; edited by Francisco Rodríguez Marín. Hereafter referred to in footnotes as RM, with pertinent volume number and page). This and all subsequent translations of the *Coloquio de los perros* come from "The Colloquy of the Dogs," in *Three Exemplary Novels*, translated by Samuel Putnam (1950), pp. 125–217. Other uses of the Putnam translation appear on pp. 66, 67, 68, 73, 74, and 77.

pital. The increasing alienation is expressed not only by a movement from the heart of society to its fringes and ultimately beyond its borders, but by a movement from physical work to intellectual activity that finally becomes so rarefied as to have no practical application whatever. The madmen in the hospital are seeking perfection in the abstract, while the pillars of society have sacrificed both perfection and abstraction to a corrupt concrete reality.[5] As Berganza traces his history of alienation and increased awareness of society's failures, his bitterness and isolation continue unrelieved. There is no feeling that the difficulties have been transcended in the *Coloquio*. Cipión and Berganza enjoy a brief moment of shared experiences, but daylight returns them to a reality which condemns them to silence again. Cipión's wish for a second night's colloquy apparently remains unfulfilled. Without the *Casamiento*, the *Coloquio* remains unmediated, its mysteries unexplained.

A summary of the *Coloquio* would not be complete without a discussion of the way in which the dialogue affects and is affected by Berganza's monologue. The dialogue allows the question of the past and social injustice to be counterbalanced with questions of the present, and the proper role of the narrator in the face of the inequities and disappointments he is relating.[6] Cipión is Berganza's conscience on questions of morality and his arbitrer on stylistic matters. He insists that Berganza not allow himself to be carried away by the past either in his narration or in his commentary. He complains when Berganza begins to wander off the story line, or to develop to a tiresome degree side issues of little importance. And he objects when Berganza's bitterness allows him to draw hasty generalizations or to slander others. The two functions are, of course, interrelated. As critic of both style and content, Cipión is insisting that Berganza not let the present be determined by the past. The present dialogue is considered by Cipión to be not only recreation, but re-creation—a making anew of

[5] Again I refer the reader to Maurice Molho's stimulating discussion. His interpretation of the relationship between the first and the second group of episodes is quite different from mine ("Remarques," esp. pp. 78–82), but convincing in the context of his total analysis.

[6] L. A. Murillo, "Cervantes' *Coloquio de los perros*, a Novel-Dialogue" (1961): 174–85, stresses the importance of the monologue-within-a-dialogue structure of the *Coloquio*. Because of Cipión's presence, he sees the *Coloquio* not as a story of a servant with many masters, but as a dialogue in which life itself is taught: "The *Coloquio*, rather than a tale of a servant serving many masters, is, in fact, a story of apprenticeship in life, a pedagogy, in action" (p. 178). I also find this relationship extremely significant. Though Murillo does little with showing how the *Casamiento* relates to the *Coloquio*, the question of "pedagogy in action" is central to their interconnection, for it is from this lesson that Campuzano becomes capable first of copying the colloquy down, and second of telling his own story of disgrace.

the past. The task he sets before Berganza is to avoid being controlled by
that past by not becoming a product of the world of deception and irre-
sponsibility he has experienced.

In challenging Berganza's tendency toward slander, Cipión asks
Berganza to be better than the experiences that have shaped him. The
witch has linked decisively the concepts of *murmuración* and hypocrisy.
Hypocrisy is at the heart of all the experiences Berganza recounts: in the
beautiful woman who used her beauty to steal the meat Berganza was
carrying for the butcher, in the shepherds who killed and ate the sheep
and blamed it on the wolves, in the bailiff who arranged with the company
of thieves in Seville ways in which he could act with pretended bravery
while incurring no real danger to himself, and in the drummer who would
fool the credulous with his "wise dog." In all cases, what has been shown
to break down is the relationship between reality and the signs which are
used to represent it. In the bailiff's case, the words "honor" and "bravery"
have replaced his actual honor and bravery. Berganza expresses his horror
at this devaluation of systems of meaning and communication in words
that are paired with their opposites. "God help me!" he says of the discovery
of the shepherd's deception, "who can do anything about this evil? Who
is in a position to make it known that the *defenders* are the *offenders,* that
the *sentinels sleep,* the *watchman robs,* and the *guardians kill?*"[7] [*Italics
mine.*]

The only way that Berganza can show himself not to have been determined by the corruption in which he grew up is to avoid in his present
narrative the hypocrisy and slander of his masters. Berganza has agreed
with Cipión that he will bite his tongue if he ever engages in *murmuración,* though he admits that it is practically impossible to avoid it. "Upon
my word, Cipión," he says, "you have to be very wise and very much on
your toes if you want to keep up a conversation for a couple of hours
without slandering someone. I myself am but a brute beast, and yet every
three or four sentences I utter I find words swarming to my tongue as
mosquitoes do to wine, and all of them slanderous and malicious."[8] When
Cipión finally tells him to bite his tongue for having maligned the pedants
who pretend to know Latin and Greek, Berganza answers, "It is one thing

---

[7] "¡Válame Dios! —decía entre mí—. ¿Quién podrá remediar esta maldad? ¿Quién
será poderoso a dar a entender que la *defensa ofende,* que las *centinelas duermen,*
que la *confianza roba* y el que *os guarda os mata?*" (RM 2:232).

[8] "A la fe, Cipión, mucho ha de saber y muy sobre los estribos ha de andar el
que quisiere sustentar dos horas de conversación sin tocar los límites de la murmuración; porque yo veo en mí, que con ser un animal, como soy, a cuatro razones que
digo, me acuden palabras a la lengua como mosquitos al vino, y todas maliciosas y
murmurantes" (RM 2:240).

to praise self-discipline and another to practice it on oneself, for it is true that it is a long way from saying to doing. Leave tongue-biting to the devil; I don't intend to bite mine or make a point of any such scruples here on this mat where there is no one to see me and praise my noble resolve!" Cipión replies, "According to that, Berganza, if you were a human being you would be a hypocrite, and everything you did would obviously be false, a mere pretense covered by the cloak of virtue so that others might praise you, for that is the way with all hypocrites."[9] Within Berganza and Cipión's colloquy, appear the same words as those with which the witch described her own sinfulness.

At the beginning of the dogs' colloquy Cipión and Berganza remark in amazement on their ability to talk. Berganza admits that he has always wished to be able to talk. But they have spent life as dogs, and must therefore compare their nature as dogs with their new-found gifts of speech and reason. Cipión praises, as the ideal qualities of a dog, ". . . our remarkable memory, our gratitude, and our great loyalty, which has led to our being depicted as the symbol of friendship."[10] Berganza adds, "I am well aware that there have been dogs so affectionate as to throw themselves into the same grave with the bodies of their masters, while others have refused to leave the spot and, taking no food, have ended their own lives there."[11] It is against this ideal that the subsequent stories Berganza narrates must be judged. The very fact of a succession of masters undermines the ideal of loyalty of which the dogs have spoken. Berganza's narration is, from a dog's point of view, a confession. He has failed as a loyal servant. He ran away from the shepherd, attacked the Negro girl who had bribed him into silence for so long in her nightly trysts with her lover, turned on the bailiff, dragged the entranced witch out of her privacy into public view, and then savagely bit and shook her when she denounced him. Since a confession is as much an exposition of the faults of others as an admission of one's own transgression, Berganza justifies his disloyalty by

---

[9] "Una cosa es alabar la disciplina, y otra el darse con ella, y, en efeto, del dicho al hecho hay gran trecho. Muérdase el diablo; que yo no quiero morderme, ni hacer finezas detrás de una estera, donde de nadie soy visto que pueda alabar mi honrosa determinación. "*Cipión*—Según eso, Berganza, si tú fueras persona, fueras hipócrita, y todas las obras que hicieras fueran aparentes, fingidas y falsas, cubiertas con la capa de la virtud, sólo porque te alabaran, como todos los hipócritas hacen" (RM 2:255).

[10] ". . . nuestra mucha memoria, el agradecimiento y gran fidelidad nuestra; tanto, que nos suelen pintar por símbolo de la amistad" (RM 2:211).

[11] Bien sé que ha habido perros tan agradecidos, que se han arrojado con los cuerpos difuntos de sus amos en la misma sepultura. Otros han estado sobre las sepulturas donde estaban enterrados sus señores, sin apartarse dellas, sin comer, hasta que se les acababa la vida" (RM 2:211).

citing the hypocrisies and deceptions of men. Berganza had attacked the bailiff, because the Chief of Police had shouted, "Get the thief." Berganza explains, "Being tired of my master's evil-doings, I obeyed the Chief's order with a right good will and fell upon the runaway, who was my own master, and brought him to the ground without his being able to help himself."[12] By dragging the witch into the courtyard, he is similarly exposing hypocrisy. Berganza can only truly redeem himself if, in the narration of those breaches of loyalty that have divorced him from the dog's natural realm, he can prove faithful to the morality he says has prompted him to leave or attack his masters. This is why the discussion of *murmuración* is so important and why Berganza can be said to be recreating himself in his narration.

The *Coloquio* ends when the dogs' voices drift off into silence at sunrise. From their point of view, they remain locked within their silence, with nothing about their identity resolved and nothing about the future certain. The *Coloquio,* when taken alone, offers no internal explanation for its transmission beyond the room in which it was spoken. The reader must conclude that it represents a dream of Cervantes, a dream that had no satisfactory resolution and had, therefore, to be terminated artificially by externally controlling events. Neither the story's beginning, nor its ending, nor its transmission can be explained from within the story itself.

The *Casamiento engañoso,* when considered alone, presents aspects of society as unsavory as those in the *Coloquio.* The Ensign Campuzano who tells his story is shown on the first page of the *Casamiento* hobbling painfully out of the gates of the Hospital of the Resurrection into the streets of Valladolid where he meets his friend Peralta. Peralta, horrified to see the Ensign so deteriorated physically after only six months, offers him food and urges him to tell the story of his misfortunes. The story of the Ensign's marriage to the prostitute Estefanía is actually only an after-meal conversation within the *novela.* The Ensign relates to Peralta how he met Estefanía and how, believing her to be a wealthy lady, with a house, servants, and a considerable dowry, he sought to marry her. He tells how he promised her a chest of gold for his part. The marriage settled, the two spend a few leisurely weeks in Estefanía's house, only to be rousted out of bed one morning by the real owners, Estefanía proving to be nothing more than their servant. In the end, the Ensign finds himself robbed of his gold, abandoned by the girl, and suffering from syphilis. The loss of the gold, as it turns out, was of no consequence, since he had lied about its value. The syphilis, on the other hand, landed him in the hospital from which, on the day the story is being told, he has just emerged.

[12] "Yo, a quien ya tenían cansado las maldades de mi amo, por cumplir lo que el señor Asistente me mandaba sin discrepar en nada, arremetí con mi propio amo, y, sin que pudiese valerse, di con él en el suelo" (RM 2:277).

Despite the obviously detrimental effects the experience has had on the Ensign, he narrates his story with a sense of distance and artistry that belies the suffering he has undergone. He introduces his narration in typically Cervantine fashion, promising his friend Peralta that the story he is about to narrate is new and amazing. "Please excuse me," he says to his friend when they first meet in the street, "another day, with more leisure I will give you an account of my experiences, which are rarer and stranger than any you have heard in all the days of your life."[13] After further prodding and a good meal, however, the Ensign tells his story with pleasure, withholding until the end his part in the deception of Estefanía. Just when Peralta begins to commiserate with him about the lost gold, the Ensign replies that his whole trunk could not have been worth more than a few *escudos*. He offers two morals to his story: that truth cannot be found in appearances, and that he who wishes to deceive should expect to be deceived.

The lightness of tone, the sense on Campuzano's part that his narration is entertaining, his deft withholding of his own participation in order to keep his listener in suspense, and the facility with which he is able to admit, "I now see that I tried to cheat and ended up cheated," suggest that the narrator has achieved some distance on the story narrated. The type of distance is different from that displayed by Berganza, however. Campuzano is fully identified with the past he narrates. The actions he recounts are offered as the direct explanation for his physical condition at the time he is narrating. His declaration of guilt at the end, his admission that he wanted to deceive and was deceived, exposes him to his friend as concupiscent, untrustworthy, and foolish. Such a self-characterization is possible, however, because of an event in the hospital that changed the direction of the Ensign's life. He narrates the story of his failures and weaknesses only because he has gained a perspective which allows him to dissociate himself from them.

Many commentators have seen in Campuzano's story of his marriage an example of Cervantes's careful protection of verisimilitude.[14] By putting the story of the talking dogs into the mouth of a man already self-defined as untrustworthy, Cervantes dodges responsibility for the story's implausibility. Campuzano, according to this argument, would be trying to repre-

---

[13] ". . . vuesa merced me perdone; que otro día con más comodidad le daré cuenta de mis sucesos, que son los más nuevos y peregrinos que vuesa merced habrá oído en todos los días de su vida" (RM 2:178). All translations from the *Casamiento engañoso* are my own.

[14] E.g., Riley, *Theory of the Novel* (1962), pp. 195–97. "Whatever other reasons Cervantes may have had for doing this, there was one good motive. He needed a party other than himself to tell such an outrageously implausible story. The teller would also have preferably to be someone like Rutilio whose trustworthiness was questionable" (p. 196).

sent the story as having actually happened to win his friend's credulity in order to increase his enjoyment of the work, for neo-Aristotelian theory stresses the importance of credibility in the pleasure a work of fiction affords a reader.

The Ensign's introduction of the *Coloquio* and the confession of weakness and sin that precedes it could have another explanation, however. The lightness of tone that the Ensign achieves in the narration of his marriage to Estefanía, indeed, his very ability to confess so fully his participation in evil, suggests that he has overcome the weaknesses of the character who bears his name in the story he narrates. It is because he no longer identifies with him that he is able to characterize him so honestly and with such artistic mastery. There are several indications that the Ensign has transcended the version of himself that appears in the *Casamiento engañoso*. Though weak, he is represented as recovering from the illness that had confined him in the Hospital of the Resurrection. After recounting the story of what had forced him into the hospital, the Ensign says, "I have other things to tell you . . . suffice it to say that they are such, that I consider that all my troubles were worth it, since they helped to get me into the hospital where I saw what I will now relate."[15] The story is a marvel to the Ensign, and of such importance that it made everything else worthwhile. The past disgraces, because of the colloquy of the dogs he reports having overheard, have been transformed into blessings. Mahudes's dogs, well known in Valladolid at the time Cervantes was writing, are not only the material source of the Ensign's recovery in their daytime office as alms collectors, but the spiritual source, since, on the night before his physical recovery had been completed, they engaged in a night's dialogue which opened vistas to the Ensign for his spiritual recovery. It is this resurrection of the spirit that makes possible the Ensign's full confession of his faults in his narration to Peralta.

The Ensign appears to believe fully that the dogs actually held a conversation at the head of his bed, though he knows that his friend Peralta is not likely to accept this. He seems desperate to make Peralta believe that the dogs were really there: ". . . many times, after I heard them, I myself didn't want to believe it, and I wanted to take as dreamed that which, really being awake, with all my five senses just as our Lord saw fit to give them to me, I heard, listened to, noted, and finally wrote, without missing a word . . . so that, since I myself could not have invented them, despite myself, and against my own opinion, I have come to believe that I was not

---

[15] ". . . otros sucesos me quedan por decir: . . . no quiera vuesa merced saber más sino que son de suerte, que doy por bien empleadas todas mis desgracias, por haber sido parte de haberme puesto en el hospital donde vi lo que ahora diré" (RM 2:201).

dreaming and that the dogs were talking."[16] When Peralta objects that such nonsense has made him now doubt even the veracity of the Ensign's story of his marriage, Campuzano replies, "Don't consider me so ignorant, that I don't understand that if it is not by miracle, animals cannot talk."[17] But Peralta refuses to believe Campuzano. In one last effort, Campuzano reiterates his belief and concedes that Peralta, if he will only agree to read the manuscript, need not be convinced of its truth: "[I would be a fool] if I gave up believing what I heard, and what I saw, and what I will dare to swear with an oath that will oblige and even force incredulity itself to believe it. But supposing that I have deceived myself and that my truth is a dream, and my insisting on it is ridiculous, wouldn't you enjoy, Mr. Peralta, seeing written in a colloquy the things that these dogs, or whatever they were, said?"[18]

When once the Licenciate has agreed to read the manuscript, Campuzano explains the method he used in copying it down. He emphasizes the clarity of his own thoughts and his zealous concern that he transmit on paper the exact words the dogs spoke:

Since I was so attentive and had my mind so delicately tuned, my memory alert, subtle and unoccupied, (thanks to the many raisins and almonds I had eaten), I took everything by heart, and almost with the same words that I had heard I wrote it the next day, without looking for rhetorical colors to adorn it, nor things to add or take out to make it pleasurable. The conversation was not for one night only; there were two consecutive nights, although I have only one written, which is the life of Berganza. That of his companion Cipión I intend to write (which was the story that was told the second night) when I see if this one is believed, or at least, is not dismissed. I have the colloquy

---

[16] ". . . muchas veces, después que los oí, yo mismo no he querido dar crédito a mí mismo, y he querido tener por cosa soñada lo que realmente estando despierto, con todos mis cinco sentidos tales cuales nuestro Señor fué servido de dármelos, oí, escuché, noté, y finalmente, escribí, sin faltar palabra" (RM 2:204); ". . . así que, pues yo no las pude inventar de mío, a mi pesar y contra mi opinión vengo a creer que no soñaba y que los perros hablaban" (RM 2:205).

[17] "—No me tenga vuesa merced por tan ignorante—replicó Campuzano—, que no entienda que si no es por milagro no pueden hablar los animales" (RM 2:204).

[18] "Uno dellos sería yo, y el mayor . . . si creyese que ese tiempo ha vuelto, y aun también lo sería si dejase de creer lo que oí, y lo que vi, y lo que me atreveré a jurar con juramento que obligue, y aun fuerce, a que lo crea la misma incredulidad. Pero puesto caso que me haya engañado, y que mi verdad sea sueño, y el porfiarla disparate, ¿no se holgará vuesa merced, señor Peralta, de ver escritas en un coloquio las cosas que estos perros, o sean quien fueren, hablaron?" (RM 2:205). Maurice Molho ("Remarques," pp. 83–88) also stresses Campuzano's belief in the colloquy and its importance to him as a moral lesson.

tucked in my shirt; I put it in the form of a colloquy in order to avoid the "said Cipión, answered Berganza," which tends to lengthen the writing.[19]

Having given the manuscipt to Peralta, Campuzano goes to sleep while his friend reads the *Coloquio*.

Like Berganza, Campuzano finds himself in a netherland at the moment when he tells the story of the marriage to Peralta and offers to let him read the colloquy he has copied in the hospital. He is between illness and health, just beyond the hospital gates but still not reintegrated into the world outside. He sees in the story he carries in his shirt the salvation that allows him to confront the sordidness of his past, but has not enough confidence in it to write more without outside approval. He believes that he actually heard the dogs talking, but backs down in the face of the Licenciate's incredulity, allowing the question of the story's truth, like the question of its value as entertainment, to hang in balance. He has taken a step away from his past without being certain of the future.

The *Casamiento engañoso* is so clearly oriented toward the *Coloquio de los perros* that it is difficult to say much more about it in isolation from the story it appears designed to frame. For surrounding the *Coloquio* and the *Casamiento* is another story narrated in the third person. An unnamed narrator introduces the weak-legged and yellowed Ensign at the beginning of the *Casamiento*, and seals the *Coloquio* by telling of the Licenciate's approval of the story's artifice and invention. This unnamed narrator's presence adds yet another narrational layer to the double novela and makes a unity out of their separateness.

In the *Casamiento* a discussion between the fictional author and the fictional reader of the *Coloquio* raises the question of whether the manuscript reflects the fictional author's dream world or a real world in which miracles take place. Peralta, the reader, easily adopts the first explanation, while Campuzano, the author, for whom the experience was so intense and so immediate, is hard-pressed to give up the second. From the real reader's point of view, both stories, with their narrators and listeners, are encased within fiction, wrapped in paper and stamped with the name of Cervantes.

---

[19] ". . . que como yo estaba tan atento y tenía delicado el jucio, delicada, sotil y desocupada la memoria (merced a las muchas pasas y almendras que había comido), todo lo tomé de coro, y casi por las mismas palabras que había oído lo escribí otro día, sin buscar colores retóricas para adornarlo, ni qué añadir ni quitar para hacerle gustoso. No fué una noche sola la plática; que fueron dos consecutivamente, aunque yo no tengo escrita más de una, que es la vida de Berganza, y la del compañero Cipión pienso escribir (que fué la que se contó la noche segunda) cuando viere, o que ésta se crea, o, a lo menos, no se desprecie. El coloquio traigo en el seno; púselo en forma de coloquio por ahorrar de *dijo Cipión, respondió Berganza*, que suele alargar la escritura" (RM 2:206).

By insisting on presenting the fictional author's attitude toward his manuscript, Cervantes is asking the real reader to contemplate not only the
finished piece of work, but the process by which it was created. Since the
process involves the history of the artist and the chronology of events
through which the finished product finally emerged, we must look behind
the order in which the works are presented to the order in which the events
presented themselves, or appeared to present themselves, to the narrating
characters.

The witch's tale is told to Berganza while he is still a dog, apparently
unable to reflect upon the meaning of her words. When Berganza, in seem-
ing accordance with the witch's prophecy, later finds himself able to speak,
he incorporates her story into his own, offering it as an explanation for
the dog's colloquy and as a harbinger of their future as men. Campuzano
also sees in the colloquy he incorporates into his narrative an event that
would free him from his past. Through the witch's narration, Berganza
looks forward to his transformation from dog to man. Campuzano, for his
part, is transformed from man to artist through Berganza's narration. For
each succeeding narrator, the preceding narrative is both portentous and
mysterious.

After Berganza's repetition of the witch's narrative, Cipión, who has been
silent, interrupts to present a long critique of the story and its meaning
for the two dogs:

Before you go any further, Berganza, it would be well for us to pause and
consider what the witch told you and see if it is the truth to which you are
giving credence or if it is not rather a big hoax. Look here: it is utterly non-
sensical to believe that Camacha could change men into beasts. . . . These
things and others like them are nothing but humbuggery, lies, or illusions on
the part of the devil; and if it seems to us at this moment that we have some
little understanding and power of reason, whereas in reality we are but dogs
or at least appear to be such, we have already agreed that this is a portentous
and unheard-of case, and though it seems to us tangible enough, we should
not really believe it until the event has shown us where the truth lies.[20]

---

[20] "Antes, Berganza, que pases adelante, es bien que reparemos en lo que te dijo
la bruja, y averigüemos si puede ser verdad la grande mentira a quien das crédito.
Mira, Berganza: grandísimo disparate sería creer que la Camacha mudase los hombres
en bestias, y que el sacristán en forma de jumento la sirviese los años que dicen que
la sirvió: todas estas cosas y las semejantes son embelecos, mentiras, o apariencias del
demonio; y si a nosotros nos parece ahora que tenemos algún entendimiento y razón,
pues hablamos siendo verdaderamente perros, o estando en su figura, ya hemos dicho
que éste es caso portentoso y jamás visto, y que aunque le tocamos con las manos,
no le habemos de dar crédito, hasta tanto que el suceso dél nos muestre lo que
conviene que creamos" (RM 2:309–10).

Faced with Cipión's arguments Berganza makes a concession to this reasoning that sounds remarkably like the one Campuzano made to Peralta: "I admit that you are right, brother Cipión, and that you are wiser than I thought. From what you say I am led to believe that everything we have gone through and are going through now is a dream, and that we are but dogs, after all; but let us not for that reason fail to enjoy the blessing of speech that is ours and the invaluable faculty of being able to converse like human beings as long as we can."[21] In both cases the illogicality of an intensely experienced reality, when externalized for the benefit of a listener, must give over to the rationality that is necessary for shared experiences. The fantastic, when converted into words, is no longer credible and must find its justification not in its ability to reflect the natural world, but in the pleasure it offers its beholder. When Berganza and Campuzano fail to convince their respective listeners that their experiences actually happened, they must both fall back on the entertainment their words afford. The listener, in all three narrations, forces the narrator to view as independent of him the story which for him is so closely wedded to the experience that triggered it. The narrator finds himself caught between the reality which the past had been to him and the fiction into which he has transformed it for the benefit of his listener.

The dialectic established at every level of the story between speaker and listener is part of the dialectic between a past which is felt but remains unarticulated, and a present narrating moment through which that past slips away as it is converted into words and reason. Berganza expresses the difficulty of translating his experiences into coherent words just before having agreed to tell Cipión his life story: "Now that I find myself so unexpectedly enriched with this divine gift of speech, I wish to enjoy and take advantage of it all I can, being in haste to tell everything I can remember, even though it be confusedly and helter-skelter, since I do not know how soon I may be called upon to return this blessing that is but a loan."[22] It soon becomes clear that disorder threatens to sever the bonds between speaker and listener, destroying the possibility for speech.

The narrator, as Berganza's experience and Cipión's interruptions show, must impose a reason and an order on the past which was not a part of his

[21] "Digo que tienes razón, Cipión, hermano y que eres más discreto de lo que pensaba; y de lo que has dicho vengo a pensar y creer que todo lo que hasta aquí hemos pasado, y lo que estamos pasando, es sueño, y que somos perros; pero no por esto dejemos de gozar deste bien de la habla que tenemos y de la excelencia tan grande de tener discurso humano todo el tiempo que pudiéramos" (RM 2:312).

[22] "Empero ahora, que tan sin pensarlo me veo enriquecido deste divino don de la habla, pienso gozarle y aprovecharme dél lo más que pudiere, dándome priesa a decir todo aquello que se me acordare, aunque sea atropellada y confusamente, porque no sé cuándo me volverán a pedir este bien, que por prestado tengo" (RM 2:213).

original experience with it if he is to transmit it to someone else. On the other hand, he must not come to sense the narrated story as entirely separate from the reality it intends to capture. The narrator must engage in the intricate task of creating by means of words and reason an expression which is an accurate translation of physical reality and unreason. The central importance of this question in the last two stories of the *Novelas ejemplares* reflects the breakdown, in the world of letters, of faith in the word's power to represent the thing.[23] The split between the narrating self and the critical listener, between chaotic experience and reasoned narration, between the word and the thing, between dream and reality, is staged at every level in the *Casamiento* and the *Coloquio*. These antitheses point toward an ultimate resolution, however, but one which must remain unarticulated, beyond the boundaries of fiction.

Every story narrated in the first person in the double novela exposes both the literary and the moral problems confronted by the narrator. Cipión is as concerned with Berganza's attitude toward the past as he is with the style with which he presents his material. Campuzano's moral

---

[23] Michel Foucault, *Les mots et les choses* (1966), says of Don Quixote: "A lui de refaire l'épopée, mais en sens inverse: celle-ci racontait (prétendait raconter) des exploits réels, promis à la memoire; Don Quichotte, lui, doit combler de réalité les signes sans contenu du récit. Son aventure sera un déchiffrement du monde: un parcours minutieux pour reveler sur toute la surface de la terre les figures qui montrent que les livres disent vrai. L'exploit doit être preuve: il consiste non pas à triompher réellement—c'est pourquoi la victoire n'importe pas au fond—mais à transformer la réalité en signe. En signe que les signes du langage sont bien conformes aux choses elles-mêmes" (p. 61). ["It was for him to remake the epic, but in an inverse way: the epic recounted [pretended to recount] real exploits, promised to memory: Don Quixote, himself, must cover over with reality the empty signs of his tale. His adventure will be a deciphering of the world: a careful going-over to reveal along the whole surface of the earth the images which show that books tell the truth. The exploit must be a proof: it consists not in truly triumphing—which is why victory is not really important—but in transforming reality into signs. As evidence that the signs of language truly correspond to things themselves."] Although Foucault sees in *Don Quixote* the first modern novel "puisque le langage y rompt sa vieille parenté avec les choses" (p. 62) ["because language breaks there its old relationship with things"], he also points out that Cervantes has not rendered language completely impotent. He has built a construct of words in Part I which will represent reality in Part II. I quote Foucault because what he says here is highly relevant to the present discussion. For what is being contested by the Licenciate Peralta is the "reasonableness" of Campuzano's story. Campuzano shows that rationality and words belong to one order, while magic and experience belong to another. When a strange experience must be converted into words, the application of reason threatens to destroy the mystery of the original experience. Campuzano must resolve this impasse between his interior reality and its exteriorization by asking Peralta to enjoy the words without believing that they represent a real experience. As in *Don Quixote*, Cervantes shows here that words must build up reality out of their own alienation.

failures are as much a part of his story as is his stylistic success. The two threads of Cipión's commentary—his injunction against slander and his insistence that the story be told in an interesting manner—reveal the inter-dependence of social and literary integrity in the work. The narrator's concern accurately to reflect the reality he is transforming into words is as important as the bailiff's obligation to make the words "honor" and "brav-ery" reflect his actual condition. Berganza's narration is a testimony to the breakdown, in the social order, between appearance and reality: to a misuse of words that corrodes trust and threatens the viability not only of the social order but of literature as well. Berganza's is a story of inversions whose order he hopes to right by presenting in a verbally accurate and nondeceptive fashion the corruption and social breakdown which decep-tion and verbal inaccuracy foster. The task is extremely difficult. Berganza and Cipión fight a pitched battle with the urge to slander and malign, a battle sharpened by the feeling of hopelessness and isolation that surrounds them. Why should he bother to keep his narration free from slander, Berganza asks, why should he bother to be upright when there is no one listening, when no one is there to applaud or even to appreciate his efforts?

The implication of this double concern for artistic and social integrity is that the artist cannot be considered apart from the man, and that art can-not be separated from reality. And here another set of inversions is intro-duced into the stories. What emerges from the despair of corrupt society as seen in the *Coloquio*, and the degradation of a corrupted man, as seen in the *Casamiento,* is that art, generally considered a derivative of reality, reflecting it but less important than it, becomes the last bastion of truth and must undertake by itself society's restoration.[24] Art must recreate reality: set it straight by reestablishing the lost connections between words and things, between appearance and reality.

Each first-person narration within the *Casamiento* and the *Coloquio* duplicates the others with respect to the narrator's position, the role of the listener, and the basic questions each poses. But the series of first-person narrations does not simply present parallel cases of identical situations. The stories are interconnected, each one depending for its transmission on the one before it, in the order in which the narrator experiences it. The witch Cañizares, who only half-believes that the magic arts of Camacha, the chief witch of Montilla, can transform men into beasts, sees confirmation

[24] This is an entirely original contribution to the problem which is interestingly discussed by Alban Forcione in *Cervantes, Aristotle, and the "Persiles"* (1970), pp. 339–48. The question is how to value fiction as separate from reality—as a realm which justifies itself—and at the same time to allow for the moral edification which was one of literature's tasks. Cervantes makes the crisis of society into a verbal crisis and builds his story on the method by which words can be restored to reality.

of Camacha's skill when she meets Berganza. Cañizares's conversation with Berganza is held in a void: she has no certainty that the dog can understand her or that he is the transformed son of her friend Montiela. But she has kept the prophecy secret in the belief that she might eventually see a dog who would recognize Montiela's name and to whom she could transmit Camacha's message.

This is the first step in the conversion which will ultimately affect Campuzano, and beyond him, Cervantes: a half-believed prophecy uttered by a grotesque old witch is transmitted from the mouth of a dying sorceress to the ears of a dog who may be understanding nothing. The prophecy, which predicts that the dogs will become men again when social justice is restored, begins to be fulfilled when the witch implants in Berganza's head the idea that he is rational and the dog forces into exposure one of the worst of society's corruptions. Berganza's experiences after the one with the witch lead him increasingly away from society and toward masters who are both intelligent and ineffectual. When he finally chooses to take up charitable work in the Hospital of the Resurrection, the stories he recounts from his hospital experience deal exclusively with failed intellectuals and his own frustrated desire to speak out against the evils of society. The miracle which finally permits him to converse with Cipión, though of uncertain origin, is looked at by him as auspicious of his recovery of a man's shape.

The recovery, however, is not complete. The witch had said: ". . . it is with the greatest pleasure that I tell you these things together with what you must do to recover your original form. I only wish it were as easy as Apuleius makes it out to be in his *Golden Ass;* for, according to him, all you have to do is eat a rose. Your recovery depends not upon your own diligence but upon the actions of other persons. What you should do, my son, is commend yourself to God in your heart and wait for this prophecy, or better, this riddle, to be swiftly and happily fulfilled."[25] Berganza, with the help of Cipión, has no recourse but to keep his narrative as honest and as free from slander as possible. He must behave in an exemplary fashion even though no one is apparently listening. His narration, made possible, perhaps, by the witch's revelation to him of the original human shape to which he may someday return, must be made, like the witch's, in

[25] ". . . con grandísimo gusto doy noticia de tus sucesos y del modo con que has de cobrar tu forma primera; el cual modo quisiera yo que fuera tan fácil como el que se dice de Apuleyo en *El Asno de oro*, que consistía en solo comer una rosa; pero este tuyo va fundado en acciones ajenas, y no en tu diligencia. Lo que has de hacer, hijo, es encomendarte a Dios allá en tu corazón, y espera que estas, que no quiero llamarlas profecías, sino adivinanzas, han de suceder presto y prósperamente" (RM 2:294–95).

a void. Uncertain that he is even talking, or of the origin of his ability to speak, and without hope that any of the transformations he desires—of himself and of society—are possible or forthcoming, he creates his narrative. Like Montiela and Cañizares on hearing Camacha's dying words of prophecy, Campuzano memorizes and writes down every word of the dogs' colloquy. And like Cañizares and the dogs, he finds his rational mind very ill at ease with the phenomenon which he nonetheless feels himself so clearly to have experienced. So Campuzano, in a void, like the others, presents the written colloquy to Peralta, half fearing that his friend will take him to be mad, but depending on Peralta to remove the story from the realm of his fantasy and into the recognized world of human discourse and reason. Like Cañizares and Berganza, Campuzano is neither sure of the origin of the experience he has had, nor of its objective truth, nor of the reaction it is likely to receive from the one to whom it is offered. When Peralta finally reads the manuscript he says: "Although this colloquy may be invented and may never have happened, it seems to me that it is so well put together, that the honorable Ensign can go ahead with the second one."[26] And the Ensign replies, "With that opinion, I will work myself up to write it, without entering in any more disputes with you over whether the dogs talked or not."[27] By the time the obscure story that originated in the malice of the chief witch of Montilla reaches Peralta, by incremental steps based on belief in magic and portents and miracles, the conversion that her prophecy announced has been achieved. Peralta has pronounced the work a product of Campuzano's imagination, but has accepted it as valuable entertainment. Once Peralta allows Campuzano to see that the story need not be real to be good, he releases Campuzano from the necessity of understanding the origin of the work. He can now look at the witch and the dogs as transformations of his own mind, transformations of the "past actions and present disgraces" which he admits had been occupying him on the night he heard the dogs talk. Having once carried out that uncertain step and entrusted to Peralta for his judgment the written product of that sleepless night he can now admit that the dogs are a nightmarish projection of himself and that, having faith to believe in them and to tell his friend about them, he has been restored to himself. The man was transformed into a dog, figuratively, by his malice and the evil-doings of Estefanía. In the form of a dog, he reviews his past life and discovers the

[26] "Aunque este coloquio sea fingido y nunca haya pasado, paréceme que está bien compuesto, que puede el señor Alférez pasar adelante con el segundo" (RM 2:339).
[27] "—Con ese parecer —respondió el Alférez—, me animaré y disporné a escribirle, sin ponerme más en disputas con vuesa merced si hablaron los perros o no" (RM 2:340).

proper attitude to assume in the face of corruption and the devaluation of words and truth. The story at each level preserves intact the prophecy of his eventual return to human shape. This takes place when his work is approved, allowing him escape not only from the fear of madness and the vision of himself as trapped in silence and bitterness, but from his own corrupt past into a future full of possibility and creative opportunity.

The basic interaction in the story is between fiction and reality, which now appear to exist, like everything else, in dialectical interrelation. The dogs' colloquy depends for its transmission on its being experienced as reality by the one who will relate it, just as Camacha's prophecy depended on Cañizares's belief in order for it to be transmitted. But once transmitted, the reality becomes fiction. Cipión discounts the witch's power; Peralta discounts the dogs' colloquy. Only when the narrator can see his reality as fiction can the next step take place. At that point the reality turned fiction releases the author from his subservience to it and frees him for further work.

In the cases of all three first-person narrators—Cañizares, Berganza, and Campuzano—the transmission of someone else's words is accompanied by a narration of the past which involves confession and self-justification. The past becomes the subject of the narrator's interest through the awareness that the transmitted words have allowed him. This awareness allows him to dissociate himself from his past, making a dispassionate rendering of personal experiences possible. Berganza can tell with equanimity that he has not lived up to the standards set for the ideal dog because he feels that he may not be a dog anymore. Campuzano can reveal the ignominy of his marriage and illness because the dogs' colloquy has suggested to him that he can become more than that past. This is the sense in which the *Casamiento* can be said to be a product of the *Coloquio*. It is the experience of overhearing the dogs and of committing to paper the words they spoke that suggests to Campuzano a liberation from his past and therefore makes its telling possible. The liberation, however, is not completed until Peralta and Campuzano both see worth in the colloquy.

The fact that the process of speaking and writing is itself a part of one's experience in time and that the proper attitude revealed by the teller implicates the past being related as well as the personality of the teller himself can be seen in both the *Coloquio* and the *Casamiento*. Berganza's difficult task has been to cleanse himself of engagement in his past so as to avoid bitterness and *murmuración* in its retelling. He must recreate himself free from the bitterness which would otherwise be a natural consequence of the events experienced. In this way he can escape the automatism of mechanical reaction through the effort of retelling, so that retelling becomes truly re-creation—being both the cause and the result of his liberation. To escape enslavement by the past the teller must become a recorder, limiting himself to what he saw and what he did. The lesson implicates Campuzano as well as Berganza and is reflected in the way Campuzano introduces his story. For if the lesson of disengagement is really to be learned by Campuzano, then he must, like Berganza, avoid the engagement of his own passions in its transmission. Campuzano seeks to make the written word an exact reproduction of the spoken one, thus emphasizing once again the ideal identity of literature and reality. The effect of copying is to represent on another level Berganza's effort to speak words that capture his experience. The chain is then established which, if unbroken, leads directly from lived experience to the written word: from Berganza's past to his present dialectical recreation of it with Cipión, to Campuzano's copying it (from spoken to written form), to Peralta's reading it (from written to read form). This vertical chain from reality to the mind of the reader reveals along a different axis the difficulties Berganza and Cipión faced in honestly converting the raw material of life into acceptable patterns of expression. The affirmation of its possibility is also a statement of its difficulty. Its possibility becomes an issue of faith, like Cipión's and Berganza's hopes for human reform.

The story, taken as fiction, is a total denial of fixed points: neither the beginning controls the end, nor the end the beginning. The past does not control the present, nor the present the past. Even the witch Camacha, and Cañizares's demonic *cabrón* cannot pretend to circumscribe the future. For the future is pure possibility. The future which allows dogs to become human beings and syphilitic soldiers to become writers defines transcendence. The result cannot be confirmed within the terms of the constitutive elements. This is the importance of Berganza's narrative. Structured apparently on the picaresque model, it avoids its consequences by revealing through the dialogue the importance of the narrating process—that is, how the process of narration creates the past and is at the same time created out of the past. Campuzano, Berganza, and Cañizares, in their respective autobiographies, all trace histories of disorientation and deception. All search in vain for a stable sense of present, past, and future. But all unknowingly escape their indefinition by their efforts to convey it to another. When, in that effort, they speak and act in a void, unsupported by guarantees that they have communicated, they create the means by which they are not only understood but are transposed onto another level of existence in which they escape the limitations of time. That is, they transpose themselves from reality into fiction, from constant metamorphosis to stability in fixed time.

The autobiography is a process of redefinition of self which permits at its end a new beginning. The contiguity of beginning and end represents a circle and at the same time suggests a new definer who is capable of drawing it because he has escaped its confines. The ending of the *Coloquio* joins with its introduction in the *Casamiento* to complete Campuzano's self-portrait at the same time that it defines that self-portrait as radical past, discontinuous with a future which, because the past definition is now enclosed, has the freedom to be unknown. The process of recapitulation captures the past while releasing its narrator. This is the meaning of Campuzano's promise of another story. For this leaves the end of the story open and undefined at the same time that it is closed and completed. The story creates Campuzano and then ejects him beyond its bounds to a permanently undisclosed and undisclosable future. So the final antithesis in the work is the struggle between the known and defined and the unknown and undefined. Just as the first implies the second, so the known but fictional author and reader imply the real but unknown ones. And just as the known is, at the same time that it is defined, illusory and false by its very nature, so the known author is illusory, and Campuzano must ultimately give way to Cervantes, just as Berganza gave way to Campuzano, once the illusion of his independence has accomplished its purpose. As process, the work asks us to question whether dogs can talk, whether hallucinations are reality, whether Cipión is right or Berganza is right, whether Campuzano is mad or whether he is a liar. As finished product, the work declares itself invention, its realities words, its truths fiction. But we cannot be left off that easily. Campuzano, author, stands at the beginning of the work and within its unfolding to ask us to understand the intricacies and difficulties of its creation. Peralta stands at the end to call the whole thing very clever and a nice bit of entertainment. We, however, outside the novel, must see the work as process and product superimposed, as a cooperative effort of Campuzano and Peralta, who are characters in a work that encloses them both within fiction. Looking back now into the heart of the work, we rediscover pairs of characters separated at every level into distinct roles as narrators and listeners. The witch carries on her monologue because Berganza is there; Berganza, because Cipión is there; and Campuzano, because Peralta is there. Since each succeeding pair comments on the reality of the pair beneath them in this hierarchical scale out of the depths of fiction into a more and more familiar reality, and each pair judges as fictitious the words and deeds of the one below them, we find ourselves, as reader-critics, bound up in the fiction we have been reading. Our judgment establishes our role in a dialogue with Cervantes, the author, real like us, who claims to have written these stories.

When the hierarchical organization is superimposed on the dialectical one, we see that Cervantes has created a work which includes him in its analysis of human uncertainties and which at the same time he transcends, having a greater vision of its totality than any of the author-characters within it. Cervantes can create this double vision of himself and his relation to his work because he sees fiction as an aspect of reality. Inasmuch as the work is fiction he, like Campuzano with Peralta, can accept his reader's judgment concerning the work's invention and structure. But inasmuch as he, through the prologue, establishes a dialogue with us, his readers, and mentions death and the realities of the next life, he is placing us firmly within the hierarchy established in the last works of his collection of stories. Cervantes's work creates the impression of circularity and uncertainty. But the circularity and uncertainty exist not in isolation, but in relation to a transcendent goal which lends direction and meaning to what would otherwise be an empty construct.

These central issues, the relation of art to life, the salvation of the artist through his work, and the combined involvement of process and finished product—are woven into the work at every level. What is saved in the process is the author-character, and what is left is a work of art, which, like a cocoon, both represents the process of the artist's creation and the past whose confines he has escaped.

The Ordering of the Novelas ejemplares

*S*ince in this analysis we have had to deal not only with each story in isolation but with the problem of their interrelation, this may be the best place to introduce considerations regarding the interconnections between all twelve stories in the *Novelas ejemplares.* In the prologue to the *Novelas ejemplares,* Cervantes refers to the work as both a totality and a composite of separate stories. It is, in fact, Cervantes's reference to the "true benefits to be derived just as much from the whole collection as from each story by itself,"[28] in the prologue, that leads Casalduero to make his suggestive analysis of the pattern established by the entire work.[29] Implicit already, of course, in the title *Novelas ejemplares,* is the conjunction unity/diversity: twelve

---

[28] ". . . honesto fruto que se podría sacar, así de todas juntas como de cada una de por sí" (Cervantes Saavedra, *Obras Completas,* edited by Angel Valbuena Prat, 15th ed., 1967, p. 770. Hereafter referred to in footnotes as VP, with pertinent page number). All translations from the prologue to the *Novelas ejemplares* are my own.

[29] "*Novelas ejemplares,*" pp. 24–30. Casalduero quotes the remark translated above from the prologue to the *Novelas ejemplares* and adds: "Mi teoría podrá ser erronea, pero la manera de estudiar la obra es la única lícita" (p. 26). ["My theory could be wrong, but the means of studying the work is the only legitimate one."]

novelas, grouped under a single theme: 'I have given them the name *Exemplary*, and if you consider it carefully, there is not one from which you cannot draw some useful lesson."[30] This study has raised the question of chronology in an effort to discover a pattern through which the very different styles apparent in the totality of Cervantes's literary production can be explained. The *Novelas ejemplares* is a perfect work in which to carry out this examination, for the collection contains nearly equal numbers of realistic and idealistic stories. The chronology proposed here, which roughly places the realistic stories in the period 1596–1606 and the idealistic stories between 1606 and 1612, suggests a historical trajectory for the production of these works considerably at odds with the order in which Cervantes chose to present the works in his collection. Assuming, with Casalduero, that Cervantes's ordering of the tales was not haphazard, this chronological analysis of the works must at some point come to grips with the static, fixed, and totally nonspeculative fact of their given arrangement. It is through the last two works in the collection that this question can best be undertaken. For these two works not only pose the question of unity and separation inherent to the whole collection, but they suggest the question of chronological and artistic ordering—of diachrony and synchrony in a work of art.

The *Novelas ejemplares* itself is structured on the same dialectic as that established within the last two tales in the collection. Just as the end of the two stories points to the author and reader in conversation and to a sense of completion coupled with a sense of more to come, the end of the collection leads to the prologue—an epilogue, after all—in which the real author, Cervantes, talks to the real reader, "beloved reader," *lector amantísimo*. The prologue/epilogue completes the collection and at the same time points beyond it: "Following them [the novelas], if I'm still alive, I will offer you *Los trabajos de Persiles*, a book which dares to compete with Heliodorus . . . and first you will see, and very soon, extended the deeds of Don Quixote and the clever sayings of Sancho Panza, and after that the *Semanas del jardín*."[31] Two authors, then. The fictional author, the one, like the Ensign, who is temporal, weak, limited, struggling, and in search of salvation, both physical and spiritual, and Cervantes, the artisan, presenting with confidence one completed work while promising several others: "I am the first to have written short stories in the Spanish language,

---

[30] "Heles dado nombre de *Ejemplares*, y si bien lo miras, no hay ninguna de quien no se pueda sacar algún ejemplo provechoso" (VP, 769–70).

[31] "Tras ellas [las *novelas*], si la vida no me deja, te ofrezco los *Trabajos de Persiles*, libro que se atreve a competir con Heliodoro . . . y primero verás, y con brevedad, dilatadas las hazañas de Don Quijote y donaires de Sancho Panza, y luego las *Semanas del jardín*" (VP, 770).

for of the many short stories which are published in Spanish, all are translated from foreign languages, and these are my very own, neither imitated
nor stolen. My own genius engendered them and my pen gave them birth,
and they are flourishing in the embrace of the press."[32] This Cervantes,
artist, conscious of his literary powers, is only possible in the prologue
because of the temporal, physical one captured within the tales in his
several roles as fictional author. What we are tracing individually and collectively is precisely this dialectic between the man and the artist, between
the work of art as process and the work of art as finished product.

The collection, the *Novelas ejemplares*, is both a fixed unity with a meaning and ordering of its own and a collection of individual stories written
over a period of years and reflecting different moments in the actual life of
their author. The full meaning of the overall patterning, like the full meaning of the *Casamiento-Coloquio* in combination, can only be seen when
considered against the underlying history of each story's individual
creation.

W. C. Atkinson has pointed out that the stories fall into a nearly perfect
pattern of alternations, each idealistic story being followed by a realistic
one.[33] Temporally, this arrangement is suggested by the arrangement of
the last two. The *Coloquio* is generative of the *Casamiento*, and together
they form a unity which transcends either story and projects the author
and reader beyond both. In the same way other early stories are generative
of the later ones. In isolation, *Rinconete y Cortadillo*, *El licenciado
Vidriera*, *El celoso extremeño*, and *El coloquio de los perros* all present
opposition between self and others great enough to produce endings either
inconclusive or destructive of the central characters. In the context of their
environment within the collection, however, the internal dialectic gives
way to an external one. Surrounding each of the early stories are stories
offering a reconciliation of the self and the others, a union discoverable
beyond opposition, that suggests that the early stories are to be seen in the
context of the later stories. The *Casamiento-Coloquio* serves as a coda in a
composition which is built on opposing types of stories. The opening statement of theme, with *La gitanilla* and *El amante liberal*, is consistent with

---

[32] ". . . yo soy el primero que he novelado en lengua castellana; que las muchas
novelas que en ella andan impresas, todas son traducidas de lenguas extranjeras, y
éstas son mías propias, no imitadas ni hurtadas: mi ingenio las engendró y las
parió mi pluma, y van creciendo en los brazos de la estampa" (VP, 770).

[33] "It will be observed that, were the order of *La ilustre fregona* and *Las dos
doncellas* reversed, the sequence of the collection would show a regular alternation
of new and exemplary with old and stereotyped; and it would be easier to accept
an incidental disturbance of the order of those two in the process of printing than
an absence of designs of the author in so ordering the others" ("Cervantes, el
Pinciano, and the *Novelas ejemplares*" [1948]: 194).

the final one in *Las dos doncellas* and *La señora Cornelia*. Between these opening and closing statements of harmonious resolution beyond conflict are the stories presenting visions of life as untranscendable opposition, interspersed with stories which repeat the original theme. *Rinconete y Cortadillo* is followed by *La española inglesa; El licenciado Vidriera,* by *La fuerza de la sangre; El celoso extremeño,* by *La ilustre fregona.* The work as a whole thus participates in—and transcends—the oppositions revealed in each of its particular parts. The reiterated relationship between opposition and resolution suggests, in the generative period—in the long years before the publication of the collection in 1613—an actual development from anguished alienation to artistic fulfillment and integration, culminating in Cervantes's confident presentation of himself in the prologue as author of a collection of stories exemplary individually and as a whole. Fully the author, like the Ensign Campuzano after Peralta's reading, he offers not only the present collection, but ambitious promises of more to come. The Ensign Campuzano is the last step, within the collection, out to Cervantes himself.

IV. TRANSITION II. *LA GITANILLA* AND *LA ILUSTRE FREGONA*

*L*a gitanilla and *La ilustre fregona* while offering no assurances regarding their dates of composition, provide several hints which lead to general agreement that they were written after 1606.[1] Both stories reflect Cervantes's tendency, which appears full-blown in the *Persiles*, to adapt to Spanish prose fiction characteristics of the Greek novel. Fortune, rather than character autonomy, plays the dominant role in plot development; in both tales the denouement hinges on a recognition scene in which the major characters are restored to their true origins, and in both stories the major characters

---

[1] In *La gitanilla*, the court is mentioned as being in Madrid. Included among the romances sung by Preciosa is one commemorating Queen Margaret's mass after the birth of Philip IV in the summer of 1605. The earliest date of the work's composition, therefore, would be 1606, shortly after the return of Philip III's court to Madrid. Interior computations, based on the fact that Preciosa was stolen as a baby in 1595 and was, at the story's ending, fifteen years old, have made many commentators conclude that the work was written in 1610. (E.g., Francisco Rodríguez Marín, *El Loaysa de "El celoso extremeño"* [1901], pp. 217–18; and Julián Apraiz, *Estudio Histórico-crítico sobre las "Novelas ejemplares" de Cervantes* [1901], p. 35). Narciso Alonso Cortés (*Cervantes en Valladolid* [1918], p. 103) finds in both *La ilustre fregona* and *La gitanilla* traces of the Madrid-Valladolid controversy, leading him to the conclusion that both works were written in Madrid shortly after 1606. James Fitzmaurice-Kelly affirms the work to be post-1606 for the same reason ("Introduction," *The Exemplary Novels* [1902], p. xxi). Joaquín Casalduero (*Sentido y forma de las "Novelas ejemplares"* [1969], p. 10), on the other hand, suggests that *La gitanilla* was written expressly to be placed at the beginning of the collection of exemplary novels and was, therefore, among the last to be written. Agustín G. de Amezúa (*Cervantes, creador de la novela corta española* [1956–58], 2:23) bases his belief that *La gitanilla* was one of the last written on its perfection. William Entwistle ("Cervantes, the Exemplary Novelist" [1941]: 108) also considers *La gitanilla*, along with *La ilustre fregona*, to be among the last-written works in the collection.

La ilustre fregona offers less concrete evidence regarding its late dating. The mention of *Guzmán de Alfarache* (pub. in 1599) and the Count of Puñorrostro (1597) pushes the earliest possible date for the story's composition quite far back in time. However, the discussion regarding the Argales fountain in Valladolid and the mention of the town of Mojados, between Valladolid and Madrid, has led Amezúa and Alonso Cortés to suggest that the story was written after Cervantes left Valladolid to follow the court to Madrid. It is the similarity with *La gitanilla* in style, subject-matter, and denouement, especially, that has led many commentators to se *La ilustre fregona* as a work contemporary with *La gitanilla*.

are exemplary. Yet the continued presence of local color, the alternation between characters of high and of low social standing, and Cervantes's willingness to give prominence to antisocial orders and points of view suggests not his last works, but works written in a transitional period.

In both *La gitanilla* and *La ilustre fregona* a young man, captivated by the grace and beauty of a young lady of apparently different station, abandons everything in order to pursue her. In each case the young man is rewarded for his subsequent self-abnegation by marriage and the discovery of the loved-one's disguised noble birth. The success of the male protagonists distinguishes these stories from the earlier ones. The male characters enter the story in their home territory, are called by their parents by their given names, and are dressed in the clothes of gentlemen. Their noble birth and the prolonged period, within the story, of contact with their origins before assuming their disguises distinguish these Cervantine characters from their earlier counterparts.

The effect of these differences is to break down the sense of alienation that propelled so many of the characters in the earlier stories. There is no indication that Diego de Carriazo and Tomás de Avendaño doubt their identity or that they truly reject their background in *La ilustre fregona.* Their flight to the underworld of *pícaros* is shown to be motivated not so much by feelings of hostility toward their family or society as by their high-spirited desire for adventure and freedom. *La ilustre fregona* begins with Carriazo's return to his family in Burgos after three years with the tuna fisheries in southern Spain. The return reveals that the young man is willing to maintain ties with his family and that his family has not rejected him. The rebellion in which Avendaño and Carriazo later engage takes place within the context of their families' system of values. They do not want to break entirely with their past as they journey to their adventures with the tuna fishermen. Neither they nor Don Juan, in *La gitanilla,* suffer a crisis of identity which makes them feel that they must forge out of an assumed existence a reality which will sustain them. Much of the desperation of the earlier characters is gone, replaced by a good-natured, almost whimsical attitude of adventure.

The difference in the attitude of the male characters is paralleled by the different stance the narrator takes with respect to the characters whose lives he is presenting. In *La ilustre fregona,* Cervantes allows the narrator's voice to dominate the scene. He replaces the tentative presentation of the story's main character, typical of the early stories, with an exposition of the characters' home town, the names of their fathers, and a brief account of Carriazo's picaresque exploits. The narrator takes time to add his own feelings regarding the main characters' actions and shows a strong propensity to introduce his own voice into the story, establishing a firm relationship between himself and the reader. The reader is regularly reminded that the story is only a story and is prevented from having direct contact with the two main characters until the point when Avendaño reaches the inn where he has heard that a beautiful young girl called Costanza works. At that point, Avendaño's voice penetrates for the first time the web of narration the author has thrown over him. Only then do the two characters begin truly to chart their own course.

A few quotations from the beginning of *La ilustre fregona* will illustrate the marked change of tone in this work from the ones analyzed to this point: "In Burgos, that illustrious and renowned city, there lived, not too many years ago, two wealthy gentlemen of rank. One of them was called Don Diego de Carriazo, the other, Don Juan de Avendaño. Don Diego had a son he named after himself, and Don Juan had one he baptized Tomás. These two young gentlemen, who are to be the heroes of this story, we shall call for the sake of brevity simply by their family names, Carriazo and Avendaño."[2] Further delaying the appearance of the main character, the narrator enters into a digression on the picaresque life: "Oh, all you kitchen scullions, dirty, fat, and shiny, all you false beggars, sham cripples, pickpockets of Zocodover Square and of Madrid, eagle-eyed blind reciters of prayers. . . . Lower your mainsails, reef in your top: you have no right to call yourselves rogues if you have not taken two courses at the tuna fishing academy!"[3] The paragraph continues in such a tone. In the next paragraph, the narrator makes explicit reference to himself (". . . all this sweetness *I* have described" [*italics mine*]).[4]

The emphasis on the story-telling aspects of the tale and the use of narrational asides to the reader continue through the next several pages, but these quotations establish the point that there is an interconnection between the character's noble birth, his more relaxed and delayed effort to

---

[2] "En Burgos, ciudad ilustre y famosa, no ha muchos años que en ella vivían dos caballeros principales y ricos: el uno se llamaba don Diego de Carriazo, y el otro, don Juan de Avendaño. El don Diego tuvo un hijo, a quien llamó de su mismo nombre, y el don Juan otro, a quien puso don Tomás de Avendaño" (Cervantes Saavedra, *Novelas ejemplares*, 2 vols. [1915–17], 1:221; edited by Francisco Rodríguez Marín. Hereafter referred to in footnotes as RM, with pertinent volume number and page).

This and all subsequent translations of *La ilustre fregona* come from "The Illustrious Kitchen Maid" in *Six Exemplary Novels*, translated by Harriet de Onís (1961), pp. 240–97. Other pages on which translations occur from this source are pp. 89, 91, 102, 104, 107, and 108.

[3] "¡Oh pícaros de cocina, sucios, gordos y lucios, pobres fingidos, tullidos falsos, cicateruelos de Zocodover y la plaza de Madrid, vistosos oracioneros, esportilleros de Sevilla, mandilejos de la hampa, con toda la caterva inumerable que se encierra debajo deste nombre *pícaro*! Bajad el toldo, amainad el brío, no os llaméis pícaros si no habéis cursado dos cursos en la academia de la pesca de los atunes" (RM 1:225).

[4] "Pero toda esta dulzura que *he* pintado" (RM 1:227).

define himself, and the fuller assertion of control by the narrator. The characters become objects to be manipulated by the narrator to the extent that they allow themselves to be defined by their background. When their background is a generally comfortable and generous one, the characters show less need for independence. The narrator carefully points out that Carriazo does not leave his family out of a sense of desperation: "Carriazo was about thirteen or a little over, when, seized by a roguish impulse—*and without any harsh treatment on the part of his parents having a share in it, but just following his pleasure and whim*—he cut loose, as the young say, from his parents' home" [*italics mine*].[5] At the same time, he makes it clear that the picaresque life Carriazo has chosen does not negate his previous one as a nobleman's son: "In spite of the fact that the poverty and hardships that went with this way of life were foreign to Carriazo, he bore himself like a prince in it. A mile off, in a thousand different ways, he gave evidence of his gentle birth, for he was generous and liberal with his comrades."[6]

Don Juan, in *La gitanilla*, is also introduced as of noble birth. He first appears to Preciosa dressed as a gentleman. The next time Preciosa and the reader meet him is in his family's house. The narrator describes Preciosa's first glimpse of Don Juan's father: ". . . she saw a gentleman of some fifty years, venerable of aspect and bearing, displaying the insignia of the Order of Santiago on his breast."[7] In his father's house, Don Juan is "Don Juanico." Like Carriazo, Don Juan is careful to hide from his father the true reason for his plan to leave the house, saying that he is going to Flanders to fight and leaving open the possibility of his return and reacceptance by his family. Also, like Carriazo, his noble blood distinguishes him even in a context which would appear most antithetical to the values of the nobility.

In *La gitanilla* the narrator begins with a statement regarding gypsy

---

[5] "Trece años, o poco más, tendría Carriazo, cuando, llevado de una inclinación picaresca, sin forzarle a ello algún mal tratamiento que sus padres le hiciesen, sólo por su gusto y antojo, se desgarró, como dicen los muchachos, de casa de sus padres" (RM 1:221–22).

[6] ". . . pero con serle anejo a este género de vida la miseria y estrecheza, mostraba Carriazo ser un príncipe en sus cosas: a tiro de escopeta, en mil señales, descubría ser bien nacido, porque era generoso y bien partido con sus camaradas" (RM 1:223–24).

[7] ". . . vió en ella a un caballero de hasta edad de cincuenta años, con un hábito de cruz colorada en los pechos, de venerable gravedad y presencia" (RM 1:51).

This and all subsequent translations of *La gitanilla* come from "The Gipsy Maid" in *Six Exemplary Novels*, translated by Harriet de Onís (1961), pp. 91–162. Other pages on which translations from this source occur are pp. 90, 91, 92, 94, 95, 96, 97, 98, 100, 101, and 108.

life and habits and continues by introducing Preciosa and her putative grandmother. The presence of the narrator is revealed in his predisposition for commentary of a general nature. He begins: "It would seem that gypsies, men and women alike, came into the world for the sole purpose of thieving. They are born of thieving parents, are reared among thieves, study to be thieves, and end up as polished and perfect thieves, in whom the impulse to steal and stealing are one and the same thing, extinguished only by death."[8] The second paragraph ends: "There were even poets who gave them [ballads and songs] to her; for there are poets who make deals with gypsies and sell them their works, just as there are those whose customers are blind street singers for whom they invent miracles and receive a share of their earnings. Everything is to be found in the world, and this business of hunger drives wits to turn out extraordinary things."[9] The general tone of narrational control and confidence distinguishes *La ilustre fregona* and *La gitanilla* from the earlier works analyzed here.

Another factor which suggests the later composition of *La gitanilla* and *La ilustre fregona* and is concomitant with the character's relative satisfaction with his family and social situation is the reduced tone of criticism of society in these works. In the earlier stories, the characters' alienation from their origins results in their taking up antisocial roles from which society can be more clearly seen and criticized. In *La gitanilla* only a brief mention of the weakness of the society from which Don Juan has escaped would imply the superiority of the adopted one. Never, however, is it suggested that gypsy society is preferable to that of the Spanish nobility. The gypsy world is only the vantage point from which certain obvious defects in the courtly life are revealed. Little is made of the frailties of social justice and of corruption among civil servants or ecclesiastics.[10]

---

[8] "Parece que los gitanos y gitanas solamente nacieron en el mundo para ser ladrones: nacen de padres ladrones, críanse con ladrones, estudian para ladrones, y, finalmente, salen con ser ladrones corrientes y molientes a todo ruedo, y la gana del hurtar y el hurtar son en ellos como accidentes inseparables, que no se quitan sino con la muerte" (RM 1:3). This commentary, of course, is not entirely gratuitous, since it prefigures the end in which Preciosa is discovered to have been herself a victim of the gypsy's stated propensity for stealing. The statement also serves to establish the basis for the contrast between Preciosa and Andrés and the gypsies among whom they live.

[9] ". . . y no faltó poeta que se los diese; que también hay poetas que se acomodan con gitanos, y les venden sus obras, como los hay para ciegos, que les fingen milagros y van a la parte de la ganancia. De todo hay en el mundo, y esto de la hambre tal vez hace arrojar los ingenios a cosas que no están en el mapa" (RM 1:5).

[10] In *La ilustre fregona* the two muleteers whom Carriazo and Avendaño overhear speaking discuss the injustices of the Count of Puñorrostro. In comparison, praise is offered to the gentlemen of the high court: "Long life to those gentlemen. They are the fathers of the wretched and the refuge of the afflicted. How many poor

The similarity in the endings of *La gitanilla* and *La ilustre fregona* provides a sharp contrast with earlier stories. The earlier works were either left unfinished, with promises of continuation (*Rinconete, Don Quixote I*), or were finished in the complete collapse of the hopes of the main protagonist (*El licenciado, El curioso, El celoso*). In the early tales, when the character reaches a standstill, the narrator does so too, for the narrator always gives up control of the story's forward movement to the character as soon as his outlines have been established. Notable in *La gitanilla* and *La ilustre fregona*, however, is the fact that the protagonists' successful quest is coupled with the narrator's greater control and self-confidence. In the later stories as much as in the earlier ones, the narrator's attitude toward his work reflects that of his characters toward their lives. The relative self-assurance of Andrés or Carriazo or Avendaño is matched by the more expressive and more self-confident manner of the narrator, who now appears able to round off a story and bring it to a happy and successful denouement.

Also typical of the later stories is the dominance of the narrator over a plot whose peripeties are more complicated than they were in earlier

---

devils are eating dirt only because of the ire of some all-powerful judge, or some magistrate who is either badly informed or prejudiced! Many eyes see more than two, and the venom of injustice does not poison many hearts as quickly as one." ["—¡Vivan ellos mil años—, dijo el que iba a Sevilla—; que son padres de los miserables y amparo de los desdichados! ¡Cuántos pobretes están mascando barro no más de por la cólera de un juez absoluto, de un corregidor, o mal informado, o bien apasionado! Más veen muchos ojos que dos: no se apodera tan presto el veneno de la injusticia de muchos corazones como se apodera de uno solo" (RM 1:237–38).] Though this is spoken by rustic characters who may be prejudiced in favor of more lenient jurisdictional practices, the passion of the commentary, its gratuity within the context of the story in which it is included, and Cervantes's own unhappy experiences in jail make it likely that the author's own feelings are betrayed in the muleteer's statement. For more discussion of the statement, see Amezúa (*Cervantes, creador*, 2:312–16). The fear the Corregidor inspires in the innkeeper also suggests criticism of the system of justice in *La ilustre fregona*: ". . . just as when a comet appears it arouses forebodings of misfortune and calamities, so the law, when suddenly and in mass it enters a house, frightens and dismays the most innocent conscience." [". . . así como los cometas cuando se muestran siempre causan temores de desgracias e infortunios, ni más ni menos la justicia, cuando de repente y de tropel se entra en una casa, sobresalta y atemoriza hasta las consciencias no culpadas" (RM 1:296).]

In *La gitanilla* the officers of the law are represented as brutal and choleric: "The mayor would have been in favor of hanging him [Andrés] immediately if it had been in his power. . . . They did not move him until the next day, and during the one he spent there [in jail] Andrés underwent great abuse and sufferings at the hands of the mayor, his subordinates, and all the villagers." ["Bien quisiera el Alcalde ahorcarle luego, si estuviera en su mano; pero hubo de remitirle a Murcia, por ser

works. The emphasis on the thieving of the gypsies and the many hints that Preciosa does not truly belong with the gypsies who brought her up prepare the reader for the final revelation of her noble birth. In *La ilustre fregona* also, the reader is prepared, from the first description of Costanza, to expect that her origins are not so humble as they appear. Both stories depend on a surprise ending built upon a complicated chronology. The stories begin *in medias res*, when the girls, Preciosa and Costanza, are already nearing womanhood. The ending sheds light on the time, years before, when each girl was taken from her true parents. This flashback technique is not employed in any of the early stories analyzed, but does occur in the *Persiles, Las dos doncellas, La señora Cornelia,* and, to some extent, in *Don Quixote* II.[11]

---

de su jurisdición. No le llevaron hasta otro día, y en el que allí estuvo pasó Andrés muchos martirios y vituperios, que el indignado Alcalde, y sus ministros, y todos los del lugar le hicieron" (RM 1:110).]

Preciosa makes several comments, while in the house of the Lieutenant Governor, that reveal criticisms of high society and of the officials who govern. Though the well-born women fawn over Preciosa and beg her favors, they find themselves penniless when it comes to recompensing her. In the poem stating the Governor's wife's fortune, Preciosa says: "If perchance you had been a nun/ You would rule your convent today/ Because you are the stuff/ Abbesses are made of." ["Si a dicha tú fueras monja,/ Hoy tu convento mandaras,/ Porque tienes de abadesa/ Más de cuatrocientas rayas" (RM 1:30).] Her words suggest a possible relation between Doña Clara's penury and that of the abbesses of the convents. When the Lieutenant Governor arrives, he is just as incapable as the others of finding money for Preciosa: "Putting his hand in his purse, the Lieutenant Governor made as if to give her something, but after searching it, shaking it, and turning it upside down repeatedly, he finally brought out his hand empty." [". . . y poniendo la mano en la faldriquera, hizo señal de querer darle algo; y habiéndola espulgado, y sacudido y rascado muchas veces, al cabo sacó la mano vacía" (RM 1:32).] His wife said, "To make sure she will come back again, I am not going to give Preciosa anything now." ["Pues porque otra vez venga, no quiero dar ñada ahora a Preciosa" (RM 1:32).] Preciosa tells the Lieutenant Governor: "Accept bribes, my lord, accept bribes, and you will have money; don't institute new customs or you will die of hunger!" ["Coheche vuesa merced, señor Tiniente; coheche, y tendrá dineros, y no haga usos nuevos: que morirá de hambre" (RM 1:32–33).] Finally, Preciosa comments, upon the Lieutenant Governor's suggestion, that with her wisdom she should be at court, "They may want me for a jester, and I am not suited to that. . . . If they should want me for my wise counsel, they could use me; but in many palaces the jesters fare better than the wise." ["—Querránme para truhana—, respondió Preciosa, —y yo no lo sabré ser, y todo irá perdido. Si me quisiesen para discreta, aun llevarme hían; pero en algunos palacios más medran los truhanes que los discretos" (RM 1:34).]

[11] E.g., when Cide Hamete reveals Maese Pedro's true identity after the wiley puppeteer has left the inn; and when he carries on the simultaneous recounting of Sancho's and Don Quixote's activities during the period when they are separated. This style of narration contrasts with the almost purely chronological development in Part I.

When Avendaño overhears two young muleteers discussing the great beauty of the serving girl at the Inn of the Sevillian, his curiosity and imagination are captured and he begins, for the first time, to assert his control over the action by inducing Carriazo to go with him to the inn and to remain in Toledo a few days rather than hasten to Zahara and the tuna fisheries. The remainder of the story results from this initial deviation, by Avendaño, from the journey on which the two boys had embarked. Just as Avendaño and Carriazo had escaped from the plan of life that their fathers had established for them because of Carriazo's fascination with the picaresque life, so they escape from their own plan because of Avendaño's attraction to Costanza, the serving girl. Though to a lesser extent, these characters still show, like the earlier ones, a need to control their own lives and not simply to follow the destinies preestablished for them. So Carriazo, the leader of the expedition to the tuna fisheries, will become follower in Avendaño's sojourn to the inn in Toledo.

Both of these boys, having chosen a new way of life, have accepted the demands it has placed on them. They move not out of established society to a situation entirely of their own making, but from one preexisting pattern of life to another. This is why the narrator takes times to praise Carriazo for his perseverance in the most difficult school for rogues. When Avendaño falls in love with Costanza's beauty, he accepts a new role as servant to the innkeeper. Avendaño's attitude toward his goal is different from that of his pre-1606 brothers: the desperation which leads to scheming and the undertaking of steps toward complete control of others is replaced with patience. Avendaño, according to Costanza, has made no advances and has not in any way violated her decorum. Before declaring himself to her he transforms himself into her image, becoming, like her, hard-working, patient, and passive. With no reason to hope that Costanza will be interested in him, or that her station is in fact more elevated than he had supposed, he awaits his fate, leaving it finally in someone else's hands.

Avendaño, then, is author of his life in a new way. He does not try to control his own future by transforming the identity of everyone around him. The distinction between the attraction one feels toward something and the right he has to claim it for himself is emphasized in *La gitanilla*. Don Juan (who changes his name to "Andrés" when he joins the gypsies) must not only transform himself into the image of Preciosa without promise that she will reward his self-abnegation, but he must learn, by overcoming jealousy, to have faith in her. The will to possess is here clearly linked with its failure. To the extent that Andrés shows jealousy, Preciosa threatens to give him up. Andrés and Avendaño, in exact opposition to their defeated counterparts in earlier Cervantine fiction, engage in successful dialectic with something outside themselves—with the loved one, with poetry, with reality—by modeling themselves after the loved object, rather than by trying to remake all the objects in conformity with an abstract vision of what they believe they should be.

This leads to a consideration of the object of the quest itself. Unlike earlier Cervantine characters, whose goals were either undefined, or too abstract to be found in reality, Andrés and Avendaño seek nothing more than marriage. Fame and praise surround both Costanza and Preciosa. Everyone, from the rudest serving boys to the most refined gentlemen, agrees on the charms of both girls in their respective stories. Since both remain indifferent to the initial advances of the young men, much of each story will involve the difficulty of the enterprise on which the male characters have embarked. But the drama, despite the emphasis in this analysis up to this point, depends not exclusively on the manner in which the young gentlemen approach the girls of lower station, but on the manner in which both parties engage in a process of self-transcendence.

The process can be most easily demonstrated in the case of Andrés and Preciosa. Although neither the reader nor Preciosa is supposed to have any knowledge of the gypsy girl's true origin, the numerous hints the author gives the reader are reinforced both by popular acclaim ("Some cried: 'God bless the girl!' Others: 'What a pity the lass is a gipsy. In truth she might be the worthy daughter of some great gentleman.' "[12]); and by Preciosa's unexplained conviction that she is something special ("I, kind sir, though a gypsy and low and humbly born, have a certain whimsical spirit here within me which urges me on to great things."[13]) The speech with which Preciosa follows these introductory words suggests that she does not conceive of her uniqueness as something which would transcend the gypsy life, which is the only one she remembers. Yet her answer to Andrés's marriage proposal is ambiguous, for at the same time that she wants Andrés to become a gypsy for two years before she will consent to marry him, she insists on making sure that he is as wealthy and noble as he has said. Like Andrés, who does not tell his father that he is going to join the gypsies and who kills his mule for fear that it might be identified and his escape discovered, Preciosa is conscious of inhabiting a special world which neither completely includes nor completely excludes the two with which she is brought into contact.

Preciosa's attitude toward Andrés is initially noncommital and aloof. She insists on keeping her freedom and remaining unencumbered by Andrés's jealousy. Her promise to marry him suggests no particular attrac-

[12] "Unos decían: '¡Dios te bendiga, la muchacha!' Otros: ¡Lástima es que esta mozuela sea gitana! En verdad que merecía ser hija de gran señor' " (RM 1:9).

[13] "Yo, señor caballero, aunque soy gitana, pobre y humildemente nacida, tengo un cierto espiritillo fantástico acá dentro, que a grandes cosas me lleva" (RM 1:38).

tion: "If you wish to be my spouse, I shall be yours."[14] The author describes her attitude toward Andrés after he returns to Madrid: She was "somewhat touched (but with kindly inclination rather than love)."[15] At the house of Andrés's father, Preciosa both encourages Andrés to carry out his promise and teases him about not carrying it out. When the gentlemen read a love sonnet addressed to Preciosa by the page-poet, Preciosa tries to ease Andrés's fears at the same time that she chides him for his jealousy. The most emphatic statement of her continued noncommitment comes after the ceremonies introducing Andrés into the gypsy society: "Situations alter cases; you know the terms I have laid down; if you are willing to abide by them, it may be that I will be yours, and you mine; contrariwise, the mule has not yet been killed, your attire is sound, and not a penny of your money is gone. . . . These gentlemen have the power to surrender my body to you, but not my soul, which is free and was born free and will remain free as long as I wish. If you decide to stay, I shall think highly of you; if you leave, I shall not misprize you."[16]

Preciosa discourages Andrés's attraction to her beauty and rejects the gypsy rule that allows men to leave their women when the women grow old. She explains to Andrés that she is insisting on a two year wait before agreeing to marry him because she wants his love to be based on more than a fascination with her beauty: ". . . for I do not govern myself by the barbarous and insolent license employed by these my kinsmen, who leave their wives or punish them whenever they see fit."[17] Preciosa's willfulness is based on her refusal to be treated as an object. This willfulness makes her stand out as unique, for it does not reflect the background in which she has been brought up.

Preciosa's refusal to allow Andrés to react to her solely on the basis of her external attributes is the same as her refusal to be treated as an object. But there is, on the other hand, no proof that she is anything apart from what she appears to be. It may be that her faith in her uniqueness is a delusion created by the excessively enthusiastic response her more superficial talents have accorded her. The first step, the refusal to rush into

[14] "Si quisiéredes ser mi esposo, yo lo seré vuestra" (RM 1:39).

[15] ". . . algo aficionada, más con benevolencia que con amor" (RM 1:48).

[16] "Condiciones rompen leyes; las que te he puesto sabes: si las quisieres guardar, podrá ser que sea tuya y tú seas mío, y donde no, aun no es muerta la mula, tus vestidos están enteros, y de tu dinero no te falta un ardite. . . ." "Estos señores bien pueden entregarte mi cuerpo; pero no mi alma, ques es libre, y nació libre, y ha de ser libre en tanto que yo quisiere. Si te quedas, te estimaré en mucho; si te vuelves, no te tendré en menos" (RM 1:71–72).

[17] ". . . que yo no me rijo por la bárbara e insolente licencia que estos mis parientes se han tomado dejar las mujeres, o castigarlas, cuando se les antoja" (RM 1:72).

marriage with a nobleman, is made in a void. Preciosa exposes herself to the ridicule of the other gypsies and to the insult of Andrés by insisting that he wait until attraction to her beauty has worn off and the gypsy life's fascination no longer holds him, in the possibly deluded belief that she is greater than her beauty or her particular circumstances. This explains her ambiguous attitude toward Andrés. On the one hand, he is a threat to her will to become something more than what she appears to be and, on the other hand, he is her only means of confirming her subjective existence. She must at the same time not discourage his interest in her beauty and not encourage him to see only that.

As the time of waiting passes, there does begin to develop between Andrés and Preciosa a more profound mutual appreciation. During the two-year trial period Preciosa begins to show a commitment to Andrés. He, in the process of discovering her less obvious virtues, is also capturing her interest in him. From Preciosa's earlier comments she apparently considered her own reaction to Andrés unimportant—she was simply allowing him time to see her own more complex virtues. What in fact happens is that just as the full expression of her uniqueness cannot be achieved without outside confirmation from Andrés, so the full expression of Andrés's interest cannot be achieved without commitment from Preciosa.

Creation, whether it be in fiction or in life, cannot take place in a void. The miracle of the initial attraction will become delusion, ending in self-destruction, without a concomitant response from the attracting object. That is, the creator and the thing he would create must in fact be seen as equally independent entities who recreate each other and themselves through their interaction. Cervantes's earlier works provide ample precedent for an unresponsive Preciosa. Gelasia in *La Galatea* and Marcela in *Don Quixote* I are examples of pure feminine flight. Marcela and Gelasia are never particularized—never captured either within the novel or within their lives—and thus remain pure appearance. Their lovers, trapped within their delusions, become mad. In *La gitanilla,* Cervantes presents an expression of the means by which two absurd dreams—that a nobleman should marry a gypsy, and that a gypsy should be more noble than the thieving band with which she is brought up—when believed in enough to be acted upon, literally create their actuality. Preciosa becomes more than she is, simply by acting and talking as if she believed it. And Andrés, believing it, makes it possible for her to be something more than she appeared even to him to be.

Within *La gitanilla* several signs mark the progress of Preciosa's interest in Andrés and her simultaneous self-creation. The narrator says: ". . . little by little she began to fall in love with the wit and goodly behavior of her lover; and likewise his love, if it were possible for it to increase, grew."[18] Alonso Hurtado, the page-poet whose love sonnet to Preciosa had earlier threatened to upset Andrés's determination to follow her into the gypsy band, appears again at the moment when the narrator has declared a new level of mutual attraction between the two. Alonso, known also as "Don Sancho," and by the gypsies as "Clemente," represents on several levels the delicacy of the task of mutual creation in which Preciosa and Andrés are engaged. As a character, the page-poet remains totally undefined: he appears at night, apparently from nowhere and without being able to state a convincing destination. In Madrid he had described himself as a poet and yet not one, as neither rich nor poor, as a page and yet more than that. Later, in telling his story to Andrés he confesses that he was serving a nobleman, but not as a servant. He has written Preciosa two love poems, one in popular and one in courtly style, yet he confesses to Andrés that he is not in love with Preciosa, for "Madrid has beauties who can and do steal away the heart and conquer the soul as well and better than the most beautiful gypsies."[19] In short, this character is undefined, either by name, family, station in life, occupation, inclination, or destination. As such he represents a threat to both Andrés and Preciosa, for he offers each the suggestion that the other is, like Clemente himself, totally uncommitted.

When Andrés suspects that Clemente has come to the gypsy encampment in search of Preciosa, he accuses her of having fooled him: "Ah, Preciosa, Preciosa, how clear it is becoming that you wish to pride yourself on having more than one devoted swain! If this is the case, finish me off first, and then kill this other, and do not sacrifice us together on the altar of your deceit, that is to say, your beauty."[20] When Clemente successfully clarifies his position, the subsequent close friendship that develops between him and Andrés gives rise to Preciosa's expression of fear. She is the only one of the gypsy band who wants Clemente to leave. For just as, in his indefinition, Clemente represents to Andrés the possibility of Preciosa's fickleness, he represents to her the possibility of Andrés's returning to the city. She says to Clemente: "I want you to [refrain from] reproaching Andrés for the lowliness of his intention, [and not to] point out to him how ill it becomes him to continue in this state; for although I

---

[18] "[Preciosa] poco a poco se iba enamorando de la discreción y buen trato de su amante, y él, del mismo modo, si pudiera crecer su amor, fuera creciendo" (RM 1:80).

[19] ". . . que hermosas tiene Madrid que pueden y saben robar los corazones y rendir las almas tan bien y mejor que las más hermosas gitanas" (RM 1:91).

[20] "¡Ah, Preciosa, Preciosa, y cómo se va descubriendo que te quieres preciar de tener más de un rendido! Y si esto es así, acábame a mí primero, y luego matarás a este otro, y no quieras sacrificarnos juntos en las aras de tu engaño, por no decir de tu belleza" (RM 1:85).

imagine that his will is the prisoner of mine, yet I should regret to see him give evidence, however slight, of any repentance."[21] She fears that Andrés had confided his true identity to Clemente in anticipation of his escape from the gypsy camp. The steps toward mutual assimilation and recreation, then, are precarious, as the emotion of jealousy reveals, and each participant in this creative process suffers occasional doubts that perhaps he is mad, a fool, and a dupe, and that his hopes are nothing but delusions.

In the culminating scenes of the story, the threat to the successful completion of Andrés's and Preciosa's union comes not from within them as individuals beset by the fears of their respective isolations, but from outside. Juana Carducha and the authorities in Murcia combine treachery with insult by attributing to Andrés the base characteristics associated with gypsies at the precise moment when he is revealing most fully his nobility. Andrés's rejection of Juana Carducha's advances and his killing of the soldier who slapped him reflect his loyalty both to Preciosa and his sense of honor. But to the townspeople his actions only confirm his gypsy appearance, and they are quick to throw him into jail on charges of robbery and murder.

Preciosa's beauty saves her from a similar fate. She is taken in by the Corregidor's wife, who remembers in Preciosa her own lost daughter, Constanza. Preciosa's old gypsy grandmother cannot resist revealing finally that the beautiful girl is in fact the Corregidor's daughter, whom the old woman had stolen fifteen years before. With this discovery the story turns full-circle from the beginning: it is now Preciosa who is of noble blood and who is obedient to her parents yet secretly in love with Andrés; and it is Andrés who appears to be nothing but a gypsy. Like Preciosa, when she entered the house of Andrés's father, it will now be Andrés's turn to appear, dressed as a gypsy, in the house of Preciosa's father.

Without Preciosa's intervention, Andrés would not have been set free. At the climax of the novel, the character who initiated the project of winning the gypsy girl to him—analogically, the author of this episode—is totally dependent on her. The apparent cruelty of the Corregidor in testing Andrés by making him think that his death would follow his marriage to Preciosa represents accurately the meaning of the creative act in which Andrés has so devotedly engaged. In his marriage to Preciosa he must transcend his disguise as Andrés—the disguise that made the marriage possible. The false identity is a necessary fiction which must die, or be transfigured, by the end of the work.

---

[21] ". . . quiero que me pagues en que no afees a Andrés la bajeza de su intento, ni le pintes cuán mal le está perseverar en este estado; que puesto que yo imagino que debajo de los candados de mi voluntad está la suya, todavía me pesaría de verle dar muestras, por mínimas que fuesen, de algún arrepentimiento" (RM 1:100).

It is because of Andrés's careful obedience to Preciosa that he has won the commitment from her that in turn makes her plead for his life. On the other hand, without Andrés's attractiveness and sense of honor, Preciosa would never have discovered her origin: Andrés's noble instincts got him into trouble with the authorities, but they also prepared the way for Preciosa's discovery of her own noble birth. So in a novelistic sense, as well as a symbolic sense, Andrés has led Preciosa to the point where confirmation of her nobility is possible. Then she, also both novelistically and symbolically, is able to restore him to life.

The discovery of Preciosa's noble birth has often been criticized as contrived, "idealistic," or even hypocritical, in that it appears to accord to nobility of spirit a racial, materialistic, or genealogical analogue. How could Cervantes at the same time believe that "every man is the son of his works," and yet propose that Preciosa could transcend her surroundings solely on the basis of her noble blood? The only explanation is that her discovery of her origin follows a logic inherent in the story. The careful development of Andrés's and Preciosa's love shows that at every step in the process of self-creation the other is necessary. The interior feeling of transcendence of one's environment must have an exterior correlative or else be ultimately qualified as mad. Preciosa's insistence that Andrés respect her feelings as well as her beauty is only the first statement of this general principle of external and internal concordance. Since only someone outside of herself can confirm this essential unity of being which she intuits, Andrés plays a critical role in creating out of a sea of gypsies, or, as Clemente would have it, a sea of beautiful faces, a being separate and integral. But just as Preciosa alone cannot confirm the unity of her appearance and her thoughts (even Don Quixote had to have someone else declare him knight), so the newly created entity Andrés-Preciosa requires external confirmation to prove its nondelusory quality. The episode with Clemente proved that mutual acceptance, which had been achieved before he came upon the camp, was not enough to cement the relationship. What is lacking is exterior confirmation—social confirmation of the sensed nobility of the two major characters. For without that final solidification the whole structure collapses. The delicacy of the process by which the two characters move from total separation and alienation to full integration of themselves as individuals, as husband and wife, and as essential members of the community, is shown at every step along the way. Each step depends on the one behind it. The story does not end with the discovery of Preciosa's and Andrés's noble birth. A final step of confirmation is required before the full integration of the two is possible. The priest who has been called in hastily to marry the two refuses to officiate without their first following the orders for marriage established by the Council of Trent. The marriage can only finally take place when it is affirmed as a sacrament. The social form, like Preciosa's beauty, is a mere relic without its spiritual completion. Preciosa's nobility is simply another link in a chain that leads from alienation to integration. Only in the discovery of her nobility is the church marriage possible through which Preciosa escapes that "barbarous and insolent license employed by [her] kinsmen, who leave their wives or punish them whenever they see fit."[22]

The lesson of the story seems to be that individual integrity is not antithetical to, but rather, intimately bound up with, social cohesion; that individual disorientation and alienation is symptomatic of social disorientation. This is why, even in the post-1606 stories, the main characters are seen in disguise and out of the context in which they were born. For social cohesion cannot precede or coerce individual integrity. Across the scope of several novelas we can see the dialectic emerge which leads to the fulfillment of *La gitanilla*. The initial search for freedom proves to be illusory in such novels as *Rinconete y Cortadillo* and *El licenciado Vidriera*. The later novels, such as *La gitanilla* and *La ilustre fregona*, retain the search for freedom and its illusory quality, but place that search in a context which requires the illusory freedom as a step toward true freedom. The true freedom integrates the individual need for separation and the social need for obedience. Alienation, in the later stories, becomes not a source of despair and self-destruction, but an essential aspect of fulfillment. This is why in both *La gitanilla* and *La ilustre fregona* a strong sense of the social context of the main male characters is introduced before they emerge as characters outside that context. The extreme deference all the characters show in the presence of their fathers suggests that they become characters in their own right only away from home.[23] This explains the light-hearted, indulgent tones with which Carriazo's picaresque experi-

---

[22] ". . . la bárbara e insolente licencia que estos mis parientes se han tomado dejar las mujeres, o castigarlas, cuando se les antoja" (RM 1:72).

[23] Luís Rosales makes this same point: "Cervantes piensa que la vida social impide al hombre seguir su propia ley. Es necesario romper con ella. Sólo a partir de este desgarramiento de nuestro mundo—recuérdese el sentido religioso de esta actitud—realiza el hombre su verdadera libertad.

"Mas tampoco nos acaba de aclarar esta consideración la actitud de Preciosa. El abandono total de cuanto constituye nuestro 'mundo' no significa más que un paso para alcanzar la verdadera libertad. . . . El hecho decisivo consiste en dominar nuestras inclinaciones naturales o, mejor dicho, en espiritualizar nuestra naturaleza." ["Cervantes thinks that society impedes man from following his own law. It is necessary to break with it [society]. Only from this breaking away from our world—remember the religious meaning of this attitude—can man experience true freedom. But this consideration doesn't succeed either in making Preciosa's attitude clear. Total abandonment of everything that constitutes our 'world' only represents one step in the search for true freedom. . . . The decisive fact consists of dominating our natural inclinations, or, rather, of spiritualizing our being."] (*Cervantes y la libertad* [1959–60], 1:307). This idea of dominion over oneself corresponds to the idea stated

ences or Carriazo and Avendaño's deception of their fathers is described. For both the escape and the return are seen as essential to the full development of character in these later novels.

We must finally look at Preciosa as a symbol of poetry, since so many commentators have seen her as the embodiment of the page-poet's definition.[24] As Casalduero has pointed out, the page-poet's definition excludes reference to form—to concrete situations—exalting instead the interior, noncommunicable delights poetry offers.[25] Poetry, according to the page-poet, is not for every day. It is special, rarefied, and removed from the common spate of experiences that mark daily living. The definition he gives is preceded by his denial that he is a poet: "I am not a poet, but only one given to poetry."[26] When Preciosa asks "Is it such a bad thing to be a poet?" the page answers: "It is not bad, but to be just a poet I do not consider very good."[27] When this same page-poet appears later at the gypsy camp, what seems to be respect from a distance for a beauty far beyond his grasp becomes, rather, indifference. If Preciosa is to be linked with the "beautiful maiden, chaste, modest, wise, understanding, retiring,"[28] of the page's definition, then the page shows both in his attitude toward poetry in the abstract and Preciosa in particular that he is incapable of full commitment to her. The page is not a poet for the same reason that he is not in love with Preciosa: he cannot concentrate enough energy on any one thing to convert its abstract essence into a meaningful concrete reality. The stage having been set for the association—through the page's definition and his occasional poems dedicated to Preciosa—of Preciosa with poetry, it is Andrés who becomes the true poet by dedicating his life exclusively to the effort to make particular and concrete the beauty and charm which enchants all who see it. It is he who will, through self-abnegation and dedication, ennoble and exalt Preciosa by extracting and socializing her essence from the wild natural surroundings in which he

---

earlier that the struggle in Cervantes's later work shifts from a social to a personal focus. It is interesting that Rosales also links Preciosa with Don Quixote and Dulcinea, Persiles and Sigismunda, Ricardo and Leonisa (*El amante liberal*), and Recaredo and Isabela (*La española inglesa*), all characters from late works, in her passion for chastity. Rafael Lapesa ("En torno a *La española inglesa* y *El Persiles*" [1950]), who is more directly interested in chronology, makes the same point as Rosales regarding the spiritualization of natural instincts in Cervantes's later works.

24 See, for example, Karl-Ludwig Selig, "Concerning the Structure of Cervantes' *La gitanilla*" (1962): 273–76; José María Chacón y Calvo, "El realismo ideal de *La gitanilla*" (1953): 246–67; and Casalduero, "*Novelas ejemplares*" (1969), p. 58.

25 Casalduero, "*Novelas ejemplares*" (1969), p. 77.

26 ". . . yo no lo soy, sino un aficionado a la poesía" (RM 1:48).

27 "—¿Tan malo es ser poeta? —replicó Preciosa. —No es malo—, dijo el paje—; pero el ser poeta a solas no lo tengo por muy bueno" (RM 1:49).

28 ". . . bellísima doncella, casta, honesta, discreta, aguda, retirada" (RM 1:49).

found it. The lover's journey, then, is also the artist's journey. Poetry, like the discreet woman, only yields her favor to those who would set aside everything for her. The reward is mutual enrichment. *La gitanilla* is not a story with an artificially happy ending. It is a story which binds together the possibility of fulfilled love with the author's celebration of literary success after years of dedication and near despair.

Despite the great differences between Preciosa in *La gitanilla* and Costanza in *La ilustre fregona*, the description of the two young women's virtues is remarkably similar. Like Preciosa, Costanza surpasses all other women in her beauty and stands out for her discretion while remaining in circumstances which would ordinarily undermine or compromise it. Costanza, like Preciosa, finds herself in the midst of life—at a crossroads where men, wealthy and poor, are constantly coming and going, none, apparently, indifferent to her charms. Both Preciosa and Costanza reveal beneath a rustic or uncivilized appearance the ideal feminine virtues of the dominant class: beauty, intelligence, chastity, and self-reliance.

Costanza, however, is the reverse image of Preciosa. Whereas Preciosa's presence dominates the story of *La gitanilla*, Costanza rarely appears in *La ilustre fregona*. Costanza's disjunction with her origin does not expose her to an opposing culture, but to one which, perhaps even more rigidly than that of her true parents, adheres to the norms of the dominant society. If Preciosa is the best dancer and singer and the most charming in a society which nurtures these talents, Costanza is the most devout, hardworking, and obedient in a society which honors these virtues.[29] Like Preciosa, Costanza's very excellence allows her to remain aloof at the same time that it enhances her attractiveness.

The innkeeper describes Costanza's relationship to him as neither servant nor relative. She is a cleaning girl who doesn't clean, an illustrious girl of unknown origin. When a party is held at the inn, she forms its absent center. The sonnets and ballads composed for her by Don Pedro, the Corregidor's son, are heard by everyone but Costanza. Tomás (Avendaño) explains to Lope (Carriazo) ". . . to the many praises the guests address to her, her only answer is to lower her eyes and not open her lips."[30] In her few appearances, Costanza is always represented in

[29] Ana María Barrenechea ("Estructura de *La ilustre fregona*" [1961]: 16, n.5) points out the traditional aspects of the obedient daughter in Spanish literature. Only in the pastoral, or in the portrayal of gypsy societies, were women given active roles. She notes that Preciosa, on discovering her noble origins, immediately gives up her characteristic willfulness and shows the submissive manner expected of girls of her station.

[30] ". . . y a muchas que los huéspedes le dicen, con ninguna otra cosa responde que con bajar los ojos y no desplegar los labios: tal es su honestidad y su recato, que no menos enamora con su recogimiento que con su hermosura" (RM 1:264).

attitudes of compliance, apparently allowing herself to be controlled by everyone around her. They all define her, they all wish to control her, yet she eludes their efforts to capture her. Costanza is in fact more similar to Preciosa than was at first apparent. Like Preciosa, Costanza allows her beauty and perfection to operate automatically in an environment from which she withholds individual commitment. She remains detached while appearing to engage in her daily round of activities. Preciosa can make her detachment explicit, since she is portrayed as an active character. She tells Andrés what she rejects in the gypsy philosophy, at what point she considers her will to supersede the gypsy rules, and why she values her interior voice over the beauty of her external appearance. Costanza's refusal to show any face but the one expected of her suggests the same sort of withholding of particular traits which would reveal a rounded character.

All of Cervantes's fully developed characters are shown not only in the appearance they select for themselves, but in the process through which they select that appearance. In periods of confidence with a friend the effort to sustain the appearance is allowed to drop. The reader thus accustoms himself to a double vision of the character: a vision of the character's public image and one of the character's private struggle to control the public image. With Costanza, however, there is no behind-the-scenes acquaintance with her true personality available to the reader. She offers no deviation from the rules of comportment imposed on her through which particularizing traits could be exposed. But it is precisely through the willful withholding of these particularizing traits that Costanza can be recognized as sharing with Preciosa a faith in her superiority which reveals a character of great strength and will.

The difficulty of the author in presenting such a character is to allow her to make toward Avendaño the necessary signs of acceptance without compromising the aloofness which characterizes her. Costanza's strength is revealed in her capacity for denial. When Tomás sends her the promised prayer which will make her tooth better, a prayer which is in fact a declaration not only of his desire to marry her but of his disguised noble birth, he asks that she not betray him until he has had a chance to prove his claims to great fortune. Her answer, while appearing to reject his proposal, actually accepts it. By tearing into little bits the paper on which his statement of love was made, she is carrying out the one thing he asked of her, that is, that she not betray his intentions to the others, since that would mean his banishment from her presence. The negation, as Avendaño himself properly perceives, allows him to continue in her presence and is therefore simultaneously an acceptance. In their next encounter, it is she who initiates the conversation, although again the words she uses appear to reject him rather than to accept him. At the same time that this gives the reader the first opportunity to see Costanza anticipate a situation rather than react to it, her statement offers her explicit promise that she will not denounce Tomás. He finds further consolation in the fact that she delivers her somewhat negative speech "without anger in her eyes or any other gesture that might indicate the least severity."[31] The nature of both Costanza's character and the role she imposes on Avendaño prevents further development of their mutual trust and acceptance. The story, however, like Preciosa's, has a dual development. The threads leading toward marriage and the discovery of noble origins are, as was shown in the discussion of *La gitanilla*, interrelated yet independent of one another.

Because of Preciosa's more active role, attention in *La gitanilla* could be focused on the development of her acceptance of Andrés, with the question of her true origin left as a side issue. In *La ilustre fregona*, however, the emphasis has been throughout the story on the events exterior to Costanza which affect her actions. The roles, therefore, of the innkeeper, his wife, and Costanza's mother and father, receive an emphasis far greater than those in *La gitanilla*, but one which is consistent with the terms of the story itself. The creative and risky piecing together of Costanza's being is shown not so much from within as from outside. In the involved process through which Costanza's origin is discovered, the conflict between base and generous motives is analyzed and the succession of ultimately generous acts, all forming a chain of dependencies, finally results in Costanza's self-discovery and, simultaneously, her marriage. As with Preciosa, the final outcome depends on the successful linking of will and external circumstance. Though Preciosa and Andrés finally proved their honest will to accept each other, only the step made by the old gypsy grandmother in revealing Preciosa's true origin, a step completely beyond the control of either Andrés or Preciosa, could convert their willed mutual acceptance into an external possibility. Tomás and Costanza, also, having both indicated their inclinations from within the scope of their respective possibilities, can only depend on circumstances external to them for the final outcome of their intentions.

Immediately after Costanza tells Tomás that she will not denounce him, the Corregidor appears at the inn to inquire about Costanza and to initiate the discovery of her origin. As the pieces of the story fall in place, like the cut parchment which awaited its other half in order to be understandable, it turns out that Costanza is the result of a competing or alternating series of evil and generous acts. Costanza's mother, as the innkeeper is forced to explain to the Corregidor, was noble and honorable, leaving the

---

[31] ". . . sin mostrar ira en los ojos ni otro desabrimiento que pudiera dar indicio de riguridad alguna" (RM 1:295).

innkeeper and his wife responsible for the only partially explained illegitimate child she gave birth to in their inn. The good breeding, the wealth,
the discretion, and the generosity of the noblewoman are anomalously
combined with her secretive pregnancy and the subsequent abandoning of
her child to strangers. As for the innkeeper and his wife, the motives of
financial gain as well as the opportunity for free labor compete and lose
out against the more noble instincts of love for the child born in such
mysterious circumstances and concern for her well-being.

Even more unusual than the mother's conduct is that of the man who
turns out to be not only Costanza's but Carriazo's father. Don Diego confesses to the Corregidor and the innkeeper that he has just learned of
Costanza's existence and has come to acknowledge both his paternity and
his guilt in having forced himself upon Costanza's unsuspecting mother.
Through his story it is explained that he had not found out until Costanza
was fifteen that she had even been born, because the steward to Costanza's
mother had kept secret the child's existence in order to profit from the
money the mother had left for the girl on her death. The mother, having
died thirteen years before the action of the story, had left to her steward
the task of notifying Don Diego of the existence of his daughter and turning over to the father money left for the girl's care. Only on his deathbed
did the steward feel compelled by conscience to reveal the secret he had
hidden so long. Again motives of conscience find ultimate, though tardy,
victory over motives of greed and selfishness. In both Costanza's everyday
circumstances and in the history of her origin a battle is carried out between instincts which would appear to enhance one's well-being through
unscrupulous actions and instincts which would, through generosity, enhance the social order. Only when the steward and then Don Diego admit
their fault and confront the one whom they have wronged can the other
half of the parchment be found and the "true sign" revealed.

Like *El curioso impertinente* and *El celoso extremeño*, *La gitanilla* and
La ilustre fregona form a pair of stories, exploring through different em-
phases the same basic situation. *La gitanilla*, like *El curioso impertinente*,
is a much more internalized story, focusing on the process through which
characters create themselves and each other; while *La ilustre fregona*, like
El celoso extremeño, deals more with the role external events play in shap-
ing the lives of the central characters. Both of the latter stories have a
more diffuse structure, much time being given to the activities of secondary characters. The character of Andrés, for example, is substituted by two
characters in *La ilustre fregona*: Carriazo represents the adventuresome
and physically skillful aspects of the major male character, while
Avendaño represents the obedience and patience of the hopeful lover.
While in *La gitanilla* the accompanying gypsy girls who sing and dance

with Preciosa are not even named, in *La ilustre fregona,* the two other serving girls, La Argüella and La Gallega, are given a rather prominent role.[32] Also the innkeeper and his wife are seen in humorous dialogue, while their counterpart in *La gitanilla,* the old gypsy woman, is never seen apart from Preciosa, and is always in a secondary position. Finally, both parents in *La ilustre fregona* are given a chance to present their separate stories, which constitute in themselves a drama of great interest, while Preciosa's real parents are never described outside the scene which reunites them with their daughter.

In *La ilustre fregona,* the external questions of origin and parentage clearly receive more attention than the internal problem of a young man and young woman discovering their particularity and uniqueness. In both stories, however, the central questions revolve around the relation between these two apparently separate and opposing drives. The simultaneous fulfillment of personal dreams and integration in the highest orders of society appearing in both works suggests that the coincidence in each story is not fortuitous, but is the result of a changed view on Cervantes's part of the comparative strengths of the conflicting motives that rule men's actions and of the role of the author in portraying those actions. In the earlier pair of stories referred to—*El curioso impertinente* and *El celoso extremeño* —the narrator oversees the process by which the major characters destroy themselves and each other because of the lack of faith in powers beyond their own which characterizes the early protagonists. The narrator's benevolent intervention is absent in the earlier stories because the characters, who are after all his mirrors, cannot believe that anything beyond their own plans for themselves will have any effect on their lives. In the later stories, however, the major characters all show a tremendous capacity for self-abnegation. Rather than take their fates into their own hands, they are able to wait for circumstances to prove their intuitions to be correct. In each of the two later stories under discussion the characters who try to force circumstances or the will of others (La Carducha in *La gitanilla;* La Argüella, La Gallega, and the Corregidor's son, in *La ilustre fregona)* are represented as evil, grotesque, or ridiculous.

In tracing the dialectic through which Andrés and Preciosa recreated themselves and each other, it became evident that the author within the story is highly entangled in the life of his character and that the character's

---

[32] Ana María Barrenechea ("Estructura") links the presence of doubles in *La ilustre fregona* with Cervantes's general proclivity for paired characters. This is certainly an interesting aspect of Cervantes's art, and one briefly considered by many commentators. For a study of how the doubles problem relates to Cervantes's basic view of life, see Avalle-Arce's "Grisóstomo y Marcela," in *Deslindes Cervantinos* (1961), pp. 114–19.

exemplarity affects not only the character himself, but the lives of those who would control him. Within both *La ilustre fregona* and *La gitanilla*, a series of controlling characters emerges in the development of the story. It is not only Avendaño and Andrés who attempt to recreate Costanza and Preciosa, respectively. In the denouements of both stories more sinister controlling forces are brought to light, forces which, in their very exposure to public view become benign and restorative, where before they were destructive. The old gypsy woman in *La gitanilla*, moved by Preciosa's predicament and the passion of the Corregidor's wife, admits the long-kept secret that she had stolen Preciosa from the Corregidor and his wife fifteen years earlier. In *La ilustre fregona*, though chance appears to play a larger role in the unraveling of Costanza's true story, it is also her beauty and modesty that inspire first the Corregidor's inquiries and then her father's recognition of her. The apparently disconnected events relating to Carriazo's troubles as water boy and muleteer in Toledo join with the fabric of the whole story when it becomes clear that surrounding Costanza are a series of evil instincts which through the mediating influence of her beauty and moral perfection are overcome and restored to goodness. Don Diego de Carriazo, father and son, are redeemed from the effects of their aimlessness, restlessness, and lust by Costanza. At the same time, their uncontrolled passions have created Costanza and have made her known (the father, directly, because of the rape of Costanza's mother; the son, indirectly, because of his leading Avendaño away from home, the step by which Avendaño discovered Costanza). In the study of virtue and passion which make up *La ilustre fregona*, passion emerges as the indispensable given which must be and yet must be transcended by self-control.

The moral dialectic duplicates the dialectic established between author and character, for the force of passion is linked in both stories with the generative impulse. In the course of creation, the generative impulse is purified and justified by the taming influence of the created character. In the ensuing struggle, which makes up the story, the creator disappears, only to reemerge at the end now linked with the character. In the denouement, the union of Andrés with Preciosa, of Preciosa with her family, and of her family with society and religion, is paralleled by the union of author with character, both of whom have been transcended through the work produced in their separation. The union of Costanza with Tomás, of Costanza and Don Diego with their father, and of Don Diego with his wife also represents the ultimate union of author and character. For both stories end not simply in marriage and reunion, but with indications that both in real life and in literature the impulse toward continued creation survives: "The story of the illustrious kitchen maid afforded the poets of the golden Tagus occasion to give full rein to their

pens in extolling and celebrating the peerless beauty of Costanza, who
still lives in the company of her good stable boy, as does Carriazo, with
three sons who do not take after their father or know that such things as
tuna fisheries exist."[33] And: "With his [Don Juan's father's] arrival the
festivities were renewed, the wedding was held, tales were exchanged, and
the poets of the city, where there are several very good ones, took it upon
themselves to commemorate the strange case, together with the peerless
beauty of the gypsy maid. The famous Master Pozo wrote in such fashion
that the fame of Preciosa will endure in his verses as long as the ages."[34]

That in both stories the denouement includes mention of the poets who
have perpetuated the story as well as the characters whose union is perpetuated suggests Cervantes's emphasis on the ultimate union of events and
the written word, a union as threatened and unstable as the union of the
characters whose stories he traced. Yet the assured tone of the narrator
that emerges in the later stories prefigures the successful resolution of the
author's struggle, just as the opening words prefigure the ultimate resolution of the characters' struggles. The important point is, however, that the
fate of the author, both within the story and outside it, is indissolubly
linked with the characters' fates in this and all the other late stories.

[33] "Dió ocasión la historia de *la fregona ilustre* a que los poetas del dorado Tajo
ejercitasen sus plumas en solenizar y en alabar la sin par hermosura de Costanza,
la cual aun vive en compañía de su buen mozo de mesón, y Carriazo ni más ni
menos, con tres hijos, que sin tomar el estilo del padre ni acordarse si hay almadrabas
en el mundo, hoy están todos estudiando en Salamanca" (RM 1:324).

[34] ". . . con cuya llegada se renovaron los gustos, se hicieron las bodas, se contaron
las vidas, y los poetas de la ciudad, que hay algunos, y muy buenos, tomaron a
cargo celebrar el extraño caso, juntamente con la sin igual belleza de la Gitanilla.
Y del tal manera escribió el famoso licenciado Pozo, que en sus versos durará la
fama de la preciosa mientras los siglos duraren" (RM 1:129).

V. ANALYSIS OF THE LATER NOVELAS

Las dos doncellas

Despite the general tendency among critics of the *Novelas ejemplares* to assume an early dating for all the idealistic tales, persistent doubts have led some critics to conclude that *Las dos doncellas* may have been a late work.[1] The major characters in *Las dos doncellas* are of noble blood. In place of the wide variety of types and accents and attitudes which competed for equal hearing in Cervantes's earlier works, there is in *Las dos doncellas* greater concentration on a single theme. The story begins *in medias res*. The action, as in *La fuerza de la sangre* and *La señora Cornelia*, begins at night. All initial signs suggest an alienated central character. He is alone and traveling. He resists the assistance of others, refuses food, and retires to his room immediately upon arrival at the inn. The emphasis on the main character's disorientation is heightened when the reader, through the mediation of Don Rafael, another guest at the inn, has access to the first character's disturbed monologue. The speaker refers to his uncertain path, the "intricate labyrinth" in which he finds himself, his lack of experience, his peregrinations, and his loss of honor. Finally the monologue reveals, in yet another representation of alienation, that the speaker is not a man but Teodosia, Don Rafael's sister.

---

[1] Adolfo Bonilla y San Martín, for example ("Una versión inglesa y algunas consideraciones sobre las *Novelas ejemplares*" [1917]: 33–70), suggests that *Las dos doncellas* was one of the first stories written by Cervantes, perhaps around 1571. In his introduction to the *Novelas ejemplares*, however, written with Rudolph Schevill, he changes the early opinion radically, concluding that matters of style suggest the work to be a product of the years 1606–16 (*Novelas ejemplares* [1925], 3:393). Joaquín Casalduero (*Sentido y forma de las "Novelas ejemplares"* [1969], 11:206–7) also suggests that similarities between *Las dos doncellas* and *Don Quixote* II (notably the incident of the Catalan bandits and the trip to Barcelona) make it likely that the novela was written late. Agustín G. de Amezúa y Mayo (*Cervantes, creador de la novela corta española* [1956–58]), while declaring that the novela is "Italianate," wavers unsteadily between an early and a late dating for *Las dos doncellas*. His very vacillation reveals all the uncertainty surrounding the chronology of the idealistic novelas and is worth quoting in part: "La contraposición de las historias de Marco Antonio y Teodosia, don Rafael y Leocadia en *Las dos doncellas*, con las de don Fernando y Dorotea, Cardenio y Lucinda en *El ingenioso hidalgo* es patente, y podrían sugerirnos la conjectura de

Teodosia, unaware that the sympathetic listener is her brother, admits that she has been deceived and dishonored by Marco Antonio. She has left home disguised as a man in his pursuit. Don Rafael resolves to help his sister find Marco Antonio. Their subsequent journey to Barcelona takes them through woods where they discover a group of travelers robbed and tied to trees by bandits. Among the victims they find Leocadia, a woman, like Teodosia, disguised as a man. Leocadia, as it turns out, is also seeking Marco Antonio since he has promised also to marry her. The story develops out of the interaction of these four characters, leading from their dishonor and disorientation toward a resolution of marriage and family reunion.

Much has been said about the appearance of doubles in Cervantes's works. Casalduero, especially, has made illuminating studies of the way such characters as Carriazo and Avendaño (*La ilustre fregona*), Rinconete and Cortadillo, Cipión and Berganza, and Don Juan and Don Antonio (*La señora Cornelia*) function in Cervantes's works. Inevitably, there has been much commentary regarding the roles of Teodosia and Leocadia in *Las dos doncellas*, most critics simply giving in to the overriding similarities of the two girls to declare them identical.[2] In the analysis below, Leocadia

---

que *Las dos doncellas* debieron de escribirse muy poco antes o poco después de su Primera Parte. En cambio, el suceso de los bandoleros y la pelea de las galeras retasarían la fecha de composición de esta novela, hasta datarla en tiempo muy cercano ya a la II Parte de la novela inmortal. Pero si por la discriminación de sus aciertos y lunares hemos de calificarla de obra endeble, pobre de psicología y escasa de observación, esta conclusión nos llevaría a la primera época novelística cervantina; aunque tampoco podamos tener seguridad en tal conjetura, ya que a esta primera época pertenecen también, y de modo indudable, novelas tan acabadas y magistrales como *Rinconete y El celoso extremeño*" (p. 329). ["The juxtaposition of the stories of Marco Antonio and Teodosia, Don Rafael and Leocadia in *Las dos doncellas*, with those of Don Fernando and Dorotea, Cardenio and Lucinda in *El ingenioso hidalgo* is obvious, and could suggest to us the conjecture that *Las dos doncellas* was written just before or just after Part I [of *Don Quixote*]. On the other hand, the episode of the bandits and the fight in the galleys would bring up the date of composition of this novela so that it could be dated very close to the second part of the immortal novel. But if through the consideration of its assets and faults we are to classify the work as weak, poor in psychology and scant in observation, this conclusion would bring us back to the first novelistic period of Cervantes; although we can't be sure of that conjecture either, since novelas so finished and magnificent as *Rinconete* and *El celoso extremeño* also belong indisputably to that period."]

[2] Schevill and Bonilla, for example ("Introducción," *Novelas ejemplares*, 3:393), as well as Casalduero ("*Novelas ejemplares*," p. 208), and Amezúa (*Cervantes, creador*, 2: 347) see the two girls as doubles. Jennifer Thompson's excellent article, "The Structure of Cervantes' *Las dos doncellas*" (1963): 144–50, seeks to reveal important distinctions between the characters of the girls, seeing the work as centered around basic *cuestiones de amor* which they dispute.

will be shown to function as an exaggeration of repressed aspects of Teodosia. Her role, like that of Don Rafael, is a secondary one, significant only as an aid to the self-discovery of Teodosia and to her subsequent marriage to Marco Antonio.

Las dos doncellas offers two nearly identical narrations by two nearly identical young women about their love for and deception by the same man. The similarities in the stories and the situations are marked. Leocadia's words describing her reaction on discovering Marco Antonio's treachery are almost identical to Teodosia's. Leocadia says: "I tore at my face, I pulled my hair, I cursed my fate."[3] Teodosia has said: "I tore my hair, as if it were to blame for my fault; I martyrized my face because it seemed to me to have given the occasion for my misadventure; I cursed my fate."[4] Like Teodosia, Leocadia has decided to leave home disguised as a man. Both steal money from their equally rich fathers and leave for Barcelona. In Leocadia's story, Teodosia finds herself represented in many ways: she hears herself named in the story she is listening to, she hears, expressed in similar words and resulting in similar responses, a story of deceived love by the same Marco Antonio who has left her without honor. Even in her initial attraction to the youth tied to the tree she intuits an identity to the one who turns out to be Leocadia.

The slight differences that distinguish the girls on every level, however, must not be discounted. Leocadia is, in general, less successful than Teodosia and at the same time more audacious. While Teodosia finds protection in the care of her brother, Leocadia meets robbers in her daring adventure alone. Leocadia's disguise is not so well accomplished as is Teodosia's, for she has left visible the holes in her ear lobes that betray her as a girl. As if to emphasize the ineffectiveness of Leocadia's disguise, Don Rafael and Teodosia catch Leocadia in a series of lies regarding her family.

In addition to the many flaws which reveal Leocadia's carelessness and weakness, differences between her and Teodosia emerge in the account Leocadia gives of her affair with Marco Antonio. Leocadia makes it clear that she was the one who initiated the love between her and Marco Antonio. She decided that Marco Antonio was the man she wanted for her husband. She says: ". . . with this thought, I began to look at him [Marco

---

[3] ". . . maltraté mi rostro, arranqué mis cabellos, maldije mi suerte" (Cervantes Saavedra, *Obras Completas*, edited by Angel Valbuena Prat, 15th ed., 1967, p. 958. Hereafter referred to in footnotes as VP, with pertinent page number). All translations in this chapter are my own.

[4] ". . . castigué mis cabellos, como si ellos tuvieran la culpa de mi yerro; martiricé mi rostro, por parecerme que él había dado toda la ocasión a mi desventura; maldije mi suerte" (VP, 953).

Antonio] more carefully, and it must have been, without doubt, with more indiscretion, since he came to realize that I was watching him."[5] When Marco Antonio has sworn to be her husband, she says: "I offered myself for him to do with me whatever he wanted."[6] It was she also who insisted on the proof: ". . . but still not satisfied with his words and promises, so that the wind would not carry them away, I made him write them on a paper which he signed for me."[7] Finally, she made the arrangements by which Marco Antonio could visit her alone at night: "Having received the paper, I arranged it so that one night he could come from his place to mine and enter my room through a garden wall, where he could, without any fear, pluck the fruit which was destined for him alone."[8]

Teodosia, on the other hand, felt no special attraction on first seeing Marco Antonio. In her narration, Teodosia stresses Marco Antonio's role in initiating their love: "Sight was the intercessor and mediator for words, words for declaring his desire, and his desire for exciting mine and believing in his."[9] In describing their meeting, she emphasizes her feelings and not the manner by which the love tryst was arranged: ". . . without knowing how, I gave myself to his power without my parents' knowledge."[10] Like Leocadia, Teodosia has received from Marco Antonio a signed statement of marriage. Leocadia had insisted that he write it and had supplied him with paper and pencil. Teodosia, on the other hand, does not even mention, until the end of her story, that Marco Antonio had given her a diamond ring in which he had inscribed "Marco Antonio is the husband of Teodosia." A final difference between the two girls' claims on Marco Antonio is that, while Teodosia is pursuing Marco Antonio in order to get him to accept her or to kill him to defend her honor, Leocadia, believing that Marco Antonio is already married to Teodosia, seeks only vengeance against her rival.

Though analysis of the differences between Teodosia's and Leocadia's situations would suggest that Teodosia has the stronger claim on Marco Antonio and is the more exemplary of the two young women, the parallels

---

[5] ". . . con este pensamiento le comencé a mirar con más cuidado, y debió de ser, sin duda, con más descuido, pues él vino a caer en que yo le miraba" (VP, 958).

[6] ". . . me ofrecí a que hiciese de mí todo lo que quisiese" (VP, 958).

[7] ". . . pero aun no bien satisfecha de sus juramentos y palabras, porque no se las llevase el viento, hice que las escribiese en una cédula que él me dio firmada" (VP, 958).

[8] "Recibida la cédula, di traza cómo una noche viniese de su lugar al mío y entrase por las paredes de un jardín a mi aposento, donde sin sobresalto alguno podía coger el fruto que para él solo estaba destinado" (VP, 958).

[9] ". . . fue la vista la intercesora y medianera de la habla, la habla de declarar su deseo, su deseo de encender el mío y de dar fe al suyo" (VP, 952).

[10] ". . . sin saber cómo me entregué en su poder a hurto de mis padres" (VP, 952).

which unite the two narrations cannot be ignored. To stress either the sameness or the difference in the two accounts would be to distort the true relation between the two female characters in the story. For hidden beneath the surface of Teodosia's narration are hints that she may be more responsible for her undoing than she would admit. When Teodosia is muttering and tossing in her bed before she tells her story to Don Rafael, she is heard debating with herself the extent of her guilt: ". . . oh me, a thousand and one times, that I so freely let myself be carried away by my desires! Oh false words, which so truly obliged me to respond with deeds! But of whom am I complaining, unfortunate one? Am I not the one who wanted to be deceived? Am I not the one who took the knife in my own hands with which I cut down and threw to the ground my reputation? Oh treacherous Marco Antonio! How is it possible that the sweet words which you spoke to me could be tainted with the bile of your arrogance and disdain?"[11] In the story she narrates to Don Rafael, however, the passive role she paints for herself and the bitter denunciation she makes of Marco Antonio reflect an effort to justify herself. Teodosia may denounce Marco Antonio, but her monologue reveals that she is repressing the more haunting fear that she herself is to blame for her present predicament.

In Leocadia's story, the motive of jealousy is pronounced. Convinced that she has been abandoned for another, Leocadia seeks not to reclaim Marco Antonio but to kill her rival. Teodosia appears to have more reasonable hopes in her pursuit of Marco Antonio, for she has no reason to believe that he is married. Yet, tucked within the opening sentences of her narration is passing mention of the fact that Marco Antonio's parents had promised him to another girl. Teodosia's knowledge of this makes her in fact guilty of the treachery of which Leocadia accuses her. The existence of a rival also makes Teodosia subject to Leocadia's fear that Marco Antonio has married someone else.

Leocadia's story reverses the importance of a combination of themes which are present in Teodosia's story. Factors that Teodosia has underplayed in her narration appear in highlighted form in Leocadia's story. In place of the desire to restore her honor—Teodosia's stated goal—is the less noble desire to wreak vengeance on her rival which Leocadia stresses. In place of the complaint of having been abandoned which Teodosia makes against

[11] "¡ay de mí una y mil veces, que tan a rienda suelta me dejé llevar de mis deseos! ¡Oh palabras fingidas, que tan de veras me obligaste a que con obras os respondiese! Pero ¿de quién me quejo, cuitada? ¿Yo no soy la que quise engañarme? ¿No soy yo la que tomó el cuchillo en sus mismas manos, con que corté y eché por tierra mi crédito? . . . ¡Oh fementido Marco Antonio! ¿Cómo es posible que en las dulces palabras que me decías viniese mezclada la hiel de tus descortesías y desdenes? (VP, 951).

Marco Antonio, Leocadia introduces the feeling of terror at having been superseded, which leaves the dishonored girl no hope. The passive girl who emerges in Teodosia's narration is countered by a more assertive lover in Leocadia's version. Leocadia's story appears to develop the worst features of Teodosia's, suggesting that it serves as an obverse, rather than as a repetition, of Teodosia's story.

Like the other Cornelia in *La señora Cornelia*, or Carriazo in *La ilustre fregona*, Leocadia is Teodosia's dark shadow, exaggerating the dangers of her situation, the baseness of her motives, and the extent of her complicity in the destruction of her honor. This is why it is Teodosia and not Don Rafael who is shown to be so curious about Leocadia from the beginning, and Teodosia who looks at her long and hard only to discover another disguised girl like herself. The other girl also comes from a wealthy family in Andalusia and is pursuing the same gentleman for the same reasons. Leocadia is the image of Teodosia's self-doubts, having no real claim to a separate identity. The only truly dishonored character is Teodosia, who has actually given herself to Marco Antonio and who, in accordance with the customs of the day, is legitimately his wife.

In the effort to rediscover peace and union with self and society that marks the struggle of all of Cervantes's later characters, the character must come to see himself in perspective, beyond the blind passions that motivated his initial actions. He must recognize his weaknesses and errors and accept absolute standards and rules outside himself to govern his choices. The individual struggle of each character to gain a true perspective on himself through which he can be relieved of his suffering and alienation is part of the collective effort of all the characters to reestablish the bonds of union that passion and selfishness have broken. In *Las dos doncellas*, the struggle of Teodosia to achieve marriage with Marco Antonio depends on the success of their individual confrontations with their respective weaknesses. Teodosia, in the course of the story, discovers her identity in that which is beyond herself—in her brother, in her rival, and finally in her future husband. It is this recognition of her being beyond the particular role in which she has been cast that allows her to achieve the union that marriage symbolizes in all Cervantes's idealistic tales. The selfishness of both main protagonists can only be transcended when each is forced to see himself as insignificant—as a character in a story controlled by a will greater than his own. Leocadia sees herself in full perspective through Leocadia's tale. Marco Antonio discovers his vulnerability when he is nearly killed in the battle in which he participates in Barcelona.

Marco Antonio is the principal deceiving author in the story and Teodosia is the principal redeeming character. Marco Antonio, in his freedom, exaggerates his power and elusiveness, while Teodosia, in her captive state, exaggerates her passivity. Only through the miraculous reversal of these roles—a miracle which represents both literary creation and religious salvation for the Cervantes of the late works—can balance be restored. Teodosia's job is to insist on Marco Antonio's responsibility to her without abandoning the essentially passive nature of her role. To do this, she assumes the disguise of a man and later accepts the intercession of Don Rafael and Leocadia. In each successive stage in her approach to Marco Antonio the figure which represents her becomes both more distant from her and more similar to her. The disguise as a man lacks the requisite distance and does not accurately represent her. Don Rafael introduces some distance as mediator between Teodosia and her author-deceiver, but is still too closely involved with Teodosia herself. Leocadia finally successfully intercedes to bring Marco Antonio within Teodosia's reach. She is at the same time the closest representation of Teodosia available and the character emotionally most distant from her. In this final dispassionate self-externalization Teodosia is able to make her claim on Marco Antonio.

When Teodosia catches up with Marco Antonio in Barcelona, it is not her words that persuade him to recognize her, but his acceptance of his character role in a larger scheme of things. The deathbed scene is essential to his conversion, for there he sees that he is as helpless as Teodosia. In the context of his mortality he is able to see himself particularized and circumscribed by experience: as character as well as author. Like so many of Cervantes's male characters, Marco Antonio wished for freedom and some years in Italy. He thought of marriage as relinquishing his freedom. The freedom he dreams of, however, when placed in the context of death, becomes an illusion.

Faced with death, Marco Antonio is made to undergo, in a brief moment, the self-confrontation which Teodosia has undergone in the course of her travels. In the process, he sees himself finally as subject to a will whose higher authority he cannot dispute. Almost all the idealistic stories end with references to God or to heaven as the origin of designs beyond the comprehension of the characters. As in *La gitanilla*, the marriage is accepted only in relation to the larger social and religious order. The author, Marco Antonio, once having considered himself absolute and free, now descends to a limited situation, while his character Teodosia, completely controlled and without legitimate existence because of Marco Antonio, is elevated, through the author's acceptance, to life and a meaningful existence. Both give way to the authority of a higher law.

This analysis has slighted somewhat the interaction between Teodosia and Marco Antonio. Both have confronted separately their individual responsibility and their dependence on forces outside themselves. Their relationship to each other, having been so little stressed, appears to be of secondary importance. In order to see the way in which the two have operated directly on one another, it must be remembered that Leocadia has no independent meaning in the story, being representative of Teodosia's repressed active self. Leocadia is consistently aggressive both in her self-representation and in her subsequent actions. She takes the lead in rescuing Marco Antonio when he has fallen into the water, maintains her place at his side during all the turmoil that follows, and then pushes forward to present her position to him on his deathbed. Without her intercession, Marco Antonio might have drowned or, if he recovered from his illness, he might never have connected the gravity of his wounds with his obligation to Teodosia.

Though Leocadia must be considered an unworthy image of Teodosia— unnatural both in her aggressiveness and in the weakness of her claims on Marco Antonio—she plays an important part in the work because of her mediating role between Marco Antonio and Teodosia. She represents to both of them the guilt which they share in having reached so perilous a position in their separate lives, and she provides the means by which they can interact. For the aggression needed by Teodosia in order to regain Marco Antonio is antithetical to the role required of proper young ladies. Teodosia must remain shy, hidden, and protected, at the same time that she must expose herself, be bold, and act aggressively. This is the impossible task of creation: to be both oneself and the other at the same time. Don Rafael and Leocadia combine to externalize the various characteristics which Teodosia must now adopt. At the same time they allow Teodosia to preserve her modesty and passivity.

Teodosia's importance, in contrast to that of Leocadia and Don Rafael, can be seen not only because the story begins with her search for Marco Antonio and ends with her marriage to him, but because Teodosia is the only character who plays opposite roles at the same time. In the parallel love stories narrated by the two girls, Teodosia is the only one to have been both narrator and listener. Don Rafael had only been listener, while Leocadia had only been narrator. As listener, Teodosia repeated the role played earlier by Don Rafael and, as narrator, she repeated the role played by Leocadia. Teodosia is also the only character who is simultaneously recognized as a man and a woman. To Don Rafael she is a woman, while Leocadia thinks she is a man. Symbolically and literally she is author and audience for her own story, active collaborator and passive receptor in Marco Antonio's advances, the deceived one who saves her deceiver, a man and a woman. For his part, Marco Antonio must become passive, having conceived himself only in the active role. He must be saved in order to save. The two characters must, in other words, merge by discovering each other within themselves, thus seeing that their originally conceived selves are actually a composite of forces, some of which are suppressed in conformity with socially imposed roles, but all of which must be understood before the other can be accepted as equal. The equalization of author and character and of husband and wife results in the recognition of a higher controlling order and the rejection of license on the part of the apparently controlling half of the dialectic. This accounts for the religious tone that permeates the last stories of Cervantes, the sudden appearance of female characters in major roles, and the regularity of happy endings.

A final point must be made about the relationship between deception and art. A fundamental deception—that by Marco Antonio of Teodosia—underlies the whole story, giving it its initial impulse. This deception unleashes a whole chain of deceptions through which the confusion caused by the initial one is resolved. Deception is the *sine qua non* of the work but not its ultimate goal. Just as Don Rafael used deception to gain access to Teodosia's room, only to discover a truth and purpose he had never suspected, so it is through Marco Antonio's deception that both he and Teodosia discover the truth of their life, their marriage, the church, and society. On the moral plane, it is through sin that salvation is made possible. This is why Cervantes reveals such tolerance, not only through his characters, but in his own words. In *Las dos doncellas*, Don Rafael rejects Teodosia's suggestion that he kill her, because it seemed to him that "fortune still had not closed once and for all the doors to her salvation."[12] At the end of the same story, Cervantes warns his readers not to hasten to "condemn similar liberties until they look within to see if they have ever been touched by what are called the arrows of Cupid, which, in effect, represent an irresistible force."[13] Sin, which is life's course and the story's course, opens the door to salvation, the end toward which narrator and character alike are oriented.

Many aspects of the skeletal story of *Las dos doncellas* are reminiscent of Dorotea's story in *Don Quixote*, Part I. In order to sustain the theory that *Las dos doncellas* is a late work, it must be contrasted with Dorotea's story in such a way that the elements that define Cervantes's later work can be seen as absent in the earlier version that appears in *Don Quixote*. In Dorotea's story, a major complicating factor is her low birth. This affects both her reaction to Don Fernando's importunings and his later abandonment and reluctance to accept her claims over him. Dorotea's much longer tale is partially explained by her effort to prove her honesty and good up-

---

[12] ". . . aún no había cerrado la fortuna de todo en todo las puertas a su remedio" (VP, 954).

[13] ". . . vituperar semejantes libertades hasta que miren en sí si alguna vez han sido tocados de estas que llaman flechas de Cupido, que, en efecto, es una fuerza . . . incontrastable" (VP, 968).

bringing to her listeners. There is also much more detail in her story concerning her difficulties once outside her father's house. The attempted rape by her serving boy, whom Dorotea must push over a cliff in self-defense, and a similar attempt by a farmer whom she has served in disguise add much in the way of concrete and lascivious detail which does not appear in the later more abstract and streamlined story. In the final scene of reconciliation, there is no evidence that Don Fernando appreciated his role in a larger scheme of things. His life is in no way in danger. He simply succumbs to the pressure of the circumstances: to Lucinda's manifest and reciprocated love for Cardenio, to Dorotea's tears and reasoning, and to the prodding of the entire surrounding company. No pilgrimage or special relating of the sanctity of marriage to religion and society, although implicit, is indicated. In *Las dos doncellas*, Cervantes makes such a point of the restitutive force of marriage, that rather than end there he has the protagonists make a pilgrimage to Santiago before going home to establish peace among their by now warring families and celebrate a magnificent wedding feast. It is the rounding out of the story, the dramatization of the return to the true meaning of religion and society, coupled with the emphasis on the salutary alternative to "freedom" that gives *Las dos doncellas* the flavor of the later works.

La señora Cornelia

Although *La señora Cornelia* is often labeled "Italianate," a surprising number of critics have concluded that the work was written after 1606. Despite absence of historical reference within the work, or of detail that might suggest the period in which it was written, stylistic traits and the changed attitude toward verisimilitude and character psychology in *La señora Cornelia* have led many to intuit similarities with the *Persiles* and *Don Quixote* II that suggest a late dating.[14]

La señora Cornelia conforms in almost every way with the characteristics isolated in this study as typical of Cervantes's work after 1606. Like

[14] E.g., James Fitzmaurice-Kelly, "Introduction," *The Exemplary Novels* (1902), pp. xxviii–xxix; Schevill and Bonilla, "Introducción," *Las Novelas ejemplares*, 3:397; Amezúa, *Cervantes, creador*, 2:362. Meregalli ("Le *Novelas ejemplares* nello svolgimento della personalità di Cervantes" [1960]: 334–51) notes the similarity to the *comedia* in many of the idealistic novels, including *La señora Cornelia*, using this to suppose a late dating for the novela. Peter Dunn, in an article to appear in *Suma Cervantina*, says of *La señora Cornelia*: "The quality of vision, and the subtlety of execution . . . seem to me to mark it as a late work of Cervantes."

the other idealistic stories, this novela offers very little in the way of local color or historical detail. All the major characters are of noble birth. The plot—centering around the questions of honor and marriage—abounds in peripeties and recognition scenes, begins *in medias res* and ends with all characters happily united. The narrator, though not often intervening directly in the work, dominates the opening paragraphs and shows none of the earlier hesitancy to give the names and backgrounds of the major protagonists. The country priest is sympathetically portrayed and lends religious support to the marriage which ends the work. In short, *La señora Cornelia* reflects the influence of the Greek novel and the contemporary Spanish *comedia* as well as Cervantes's own *Persiles* and appears to have been written during the same period that produced his other idealistic stories.

Like *La fuerza de la sangre* and *Las dos doncellas*, the action which first engages the characters takes place at night and in an atmosphere of confusion. Don Juan has left his apartment and his companion, Don Antonio, for a walk alone at night, an activity greatly at variance with his normal custom. The two young men are Spaniards studying at the University of Bologna. Don Juan, with no one to talk to, decides to return home, having walked only a few blocks. A double darkness accompanies his return. "The darkness of the night and that caused by the doorways," prevent him from discerning the origin of a hissing sound that appears to beckon him. When he hesitates, a door half opens, and a whispered voice asks if he is "Fabio." Don Juan answers "yes" without thinking, and a bundle is thrust into his arms.

This beginning plunges both character and reader into the midst of a story about which nothing is clear. The contents of the bundle, which turns out to hold a newborn baby, remain unknown to Don Juan and the reader. Don Juan continues to grope blindly with a reality too mysterious for comprehension. He returns to the place where the infant was smuggled to him after taking the baby to his housekeeper. Hearing the sounds of a struggle, he jumps to the defense of an unknown man who wails that he is besieged by too many attackers. Though his new-found companion falls, Don Juan manages, with the help of the police, to rout the attackers. In the subsequent search for his hat, he mistakenly puts on that of the other man, whose identity remains shrouded in mystery. When Don Juan returns home, it is with someone else's hat, after an evening of highly unusual adventures, the meaning of most of which remains obscure to reader as well as character. On his way home, Don Juan finds Don Antonio, who also has had some unusual adventures. Don Antonio relates his encounter with a disguised woman who asked him to protect her. She, like the man whom Don Juan defended, has not given her name.

Long before the denouement, the story presents a series of subcrises in which recognition and peripety are fully exploited. The action begins because a maid mistakes Don Juan for "Fabio." Cornelia, the young woman who put herself in Don Antonio's charge, mistakes Don Juan for the Duke of Ferrara when she sees through the window the top of the hat Don Juan has put on. She makes another mistake in identity when she fails to recognize her infant son because of the poor clothing in which he is wrapped. Later, when the infant is restored to his original rich garments and presented to Cornelia, her surprise offers a classic case of recognition. Mistakes and their corrections are the impulses which, operating together, carry the story forward. Throughout the story, in conformity with El Pinciano's precepts, details are called into prominence by characters who must prove their legitimate connection with others in the story: the hat reveals the Duke's identity and re-identifies Don Juan when he later goes to seek the Duke; the baby's garments determine the recognition and non-recognition of its mother; and Cornelia's jewels later identify the baby to its father.[15] Words and memory can also be used as a means of recognition. Don Juan recalls to the "doncella" who mistook him for Fabio the conversation they had that night, thus convincing her that it was he who had taken the baby; Don Antonio believes he can prove that Cornelia is in his room by describing her jewelry to the Duke.

La señora Cornelia is a highly improbable story. The chances that a baby would be handed over to an unknown man whose best friend would be asked by the baby's mother for protection and that both would wind up in the same house are very slight. That the brother of the young woman would ask Don Juan's help the next day without knowing of his involvement with his sister and her child is equally unlikely. On the other hand, the story is carefully built up to exclude any impossible actions. The narrator explains why Don Antonio and Don Juan went out separately that night, why the baby was given mistakenly to Don Juan, why he took the baby to his house, and why he returned to the place where the baby was given to him. Don Juan joins in the struggle for the same noble reasons that impelled him to protect the baby and promise help to its mother. His getting the wrong hat is also explained, as is the reason why the young woman mistook him for the Duke. Don Lorenzo, Cornelia's brother, seeks out Don Juan for help because as a foreigner the young Spaniard is un-

---

15 See López Pinciano, *Philosophía antigua poética* (1953), 2:25–50, for a discussion of the use of recognition and peripety in stories. The breakdown of the various ways recognition can be achieved and the emphasis on the fact that recognition can be true or false makes the discussion applicable to the novelistic procedures of *La señora Cornelia*. It was the subtlety of Heliodrorus's treatment of recognition that elicited such praise from El Pinciano (see *Philosophía antigua poética*, 2:38–39).

likely to spread news of Cornelia's disgrace. The care with which the chance occurrences are knit together and the way in which every detail is explained reveals a controlling hand fully aware of the story's direction, despite the chaos and confusion into which the characters are thrown from the beginning.

The distance between the author and the characters in *La señora Cornelia* is great. The story begins with two rather lengthy initial paragraphs in which the names and an outline of the histories of most of the major characters are given. The full names of Don Antonio and Don Juan appear as the first words of the first sentence of the story. Their families are mentioned, their friendship, their gentlemanly interest in arms and letters, and the circumstances by which they came to study in Bologna. The Bentibollis, Lorenzo and Cornelia, are also mentioned, the latter famous in Bologna for her beauty and the former for the care with which he keeps his sister hidden, since the two are orphans and Lorenzo is the sole defender of his sister's honor.

The author reveals his overview in the story's ending as well as in its beginning. Typical of the later works, he relates not only the immediate conclusion to his story, but the long-range destiny of his characters. The smooth control of the author is also evident in the deft linking of the disparate parts of the middle. But he keeps the reader suspended by introducing author–characters who appear to take over control of the story. An abrupt change takes place after the introductory paragraphs—a change which removes the reader from the distance of the author and places him within the range of perception of the young Spanish gentlemen Don Juan and Don Antonio.

Carrying out a role similar to that of Rinconete and Cortadillo, Don Juan and Don Antonio mediate between the reader and the problems presented in the story. Don Juan and Don Antonio occupy a point in the story somewhere between the detachment of the reader or author and the involvement of the characters of the central plot. Unlike Rinconete and Cortadillo, however, they are neither degenerate nor of obscure background. Don Juan and Don Antonio represent the ideal of the young Spanish gentleman. They are noble, devout, generous, courageous, and given to a thirst for both learning and adventure. Their perfection and balance contrast sharply with the overly cerebral and self-seeking major characters of Cervantes's earlier fiction. As author–characters, they do not, as earlier characters did, seek to control their environment. The chaotic reality which they piece together into a meaningful whole through the course of the story is thrust at them. They only react to circumstances in which they find themselves, never trying to extract more from reality than that which they find. They take charge of the action when that seems to be the only noble course, and they allow things to happen as they will when they don't know what to do next.

The trust and faith Don Juan and Don Antonio show contrasts sharply with the anxiety of earlier author–characters. After hearing Cornelia's story, for example, Don Juan says: "You think and fear too much, Señora Cornelia, but give a place, among so many fears, to hope and have faith in God, and in my industry and good wishes, and you will see yours fulfilled with every happiness."[16] Don Juan throws himself into life and the story because of his noble spirit. It is his faith in his honor and in justice that leads him into action which might otherwise look dangerous.

In *Rinconete y Cortadillo* the two young mediators of the life of Seville's underworld cannot in any way affect the lives they witness, nor can they be absorbed by those whose society they offer to the reader. This is because neither they nor the world with which they come in contact is exemplary. Though Rinconete and Cortadillo are sympathetic characters, their story is inconclusive and their fate remains unresolved because Cervantes rejects for them either total alienation from or total absorption into the society they discover. Don Juan and Don Antonio, on the other hand, guide the characters whom they meet to a happy ending because they are already defined as noble, honorable, and gentlemanly. In the process of affecting positively the lives of the other characters, Don Juan and Don Antonio are in turn affected, with the result that all characters are united in an ending that is at once unifying and conclusive.

Like most of Cervantes's later stories, *La señora Cornelia* begins *in medias res*. Only after the baby has been found, the Duke's battle fought, and Cornelia has tried to feed the baby she does not recognize as hers does the reader, along with Don Juan and Don Antonio, discover something about the background of the incident in which they have found themselves immersed. Cornelia's narration introduces her name and her brother's into the story. Cornelia and Lorenzo Bentibolli are seen, through the young woman's narration, to be indeed the beautiful and wealthy orphans mentioned by the narrator at the beginning of the story. But they are also seen, in the first-person narration, to be in a state of confusion and disorder. Cornelia has given in to her love for the Duke. Now, with the Duke's child, she fears that she has been abandoned and that her brother will kill her to avenge his honor. From this point on, Don Juan and Don Antonio will serve as mediators between the various protagonists with whose story they have become involved and between those characters and the reader. The young Spaniards will seek to piece together the story frag-

---

[16] "—Mucho discurrís y mucho teméis, señora Cornelia—dijo don Juan—; pero dad lugar entre tantos miedos a la esperanza y fiad en Dios, en mi industria y buen deseo, que habéis de ver con toda felicidad cumplido el vuestro" (VP, 979).

ments they hear from each of the principal protagonists and at the same time to bring the protagonists back into a socially acceptable unity. The social order which is established through their intervention is identical to the novelistic order they create as they clarify the many misunderstandings that mark the relationships among the central characters.

Shortly after Cornelia's narration, her brother Don Lorenzo presents his. Though the stories are substantially the same, they differ in emphasis. Don Lorenzo is convinced that the Duke has fooled his sister and he asks Don Juan, as a valiant Spaniard, to aid him in his revenge. Don Juan, knowing what both Don Lorenzo and Cornelia think and expect, then hears the Duke's story and, realizing that chance occurrences have interrupted the Duke's intention to marry Cornelia, effects a reconciliation between brother and brother-in-law. At each point Don Juan knows more than the characters to whose story he listens: he knows where Cornelia's baby is when she tells her story; he knows where Cornelia is when Don Lorenzo tells his story; and he knows where all three of these characters are when the Duke tells his story. He controls all of these characters by withholding from them full knowledge of their circumstances. In his distance and manipulative powers, Don Juan carries out the role of the author within the work.

Any further examination of Don Juan and Don Antonio in *La señora Cornelia* must include consideration of their roles with respect to each other, for, like Rinconete and Cortadillo, they are distinguishable in their respective characteristics. Don Juan and Don Antonio reveal different aspects of the same creative process. Don Juan is generally shown throwing himself headlong into the action and taking active part in the story's forward movement. Don Antonio, on the other hand, is cast in a more contemplative role. It is he who chooses to stay home in prayer while Don Juan ventures out alone. The reader does not witness his discovery of Cornelia, as he does Don Juan's involvement with the baby and the Duke. Rather, he learns of Cornelia through Don Antonio's own first-person account of her appearance. Don Antonio maintains a verbal, passive role throughout the story. Reinforcing this distinction in roles, Don Antonio is the one to discover the woman, while Don Juan encounters the male members of the family. When Lorenzo asks Don Juan's aid in confrontation with the Duke, Don Antonio goes along too, but stays behind and out of sight until the agreement between brother and brother-in-law has been successfully concluded. Only then does he emerge, requesting that he be the one to tell the Duke and Lorenzo where Cornelia is. Don Juan and Don Antonio remain essentially undistinguished from beginning to end except in their role as mediators in the adventure of Cornelia. They separate only during the period of their creative involvement.

The simultaneous discovery of mother and child by Don Juan and Don

Antonio can be explained by their bifurcation into two aspects of the creative process. Though improbable in a strictly novelistic sense, the action reveals an initial splitting on the part of both the "author" (Don Juan/Don Antonio) and the "character" (mother/baby) as the essence of the story's impulse. The story proceeds from that initial splitting toward a new union which reunites not only Don Juan with Don Antonio and mother with child, but sister with brother, husband with wife, and father with child. The final dinner brings the characters together not only along familial lines, but along international and social lines. Don Juan and Don Antonio are accepted warmly into Italian society, the poorer and less noble Bentibollis are accepted by the family of the Duke, and all come together in the modest house of a simple country priest. In the end the disparate characters are united in a whole which belies the artificial separations of nationality and station in life.

Don Juan and Don Antonio, though important as author-characters, must, since all characters are shown to be subsumed into a single unity in the end, lose their dominant role in the story at some point. Their stupendous successes in drawing reality out of nothingness and then putting order into the chaos discovered must give way to a more fallible representation of them. Their serene, almost olympian control over the action leaves them emotionally uninvolved and makes them too self-confident. When Don Juan and Don Antonio leave Cornelia in the housemaid's charge and go with Lorenzo in search of the Duke, the story falls into two pieces, only one of which Don Juan and Don Antonio can control. Until that point they had acted separately while piecing together jointly the stories of the various characters they had encountered. When they leave Cornelia and the baby to the charge of the housekeeper and both go in search of the Duke and Lorenzo's conciliation, they give up control over Cornelia's action.

Until this point details of Don Juan's and Don Antonio's life have been relatively unimportant. They have been removed from the fears and doubts and miseries of the central characters because of their fuller knowledge of the entire situation. The nobility with which they act is almost as much a function of their privileged knowledge and distance from the emotions affecting the central characters as of their own inherent virtues. The appearance of the housekeeper, however, simultaneously suggests less noble aspects of their characters and wrests from their control the final outcome of the story. As with Cide Hamete or the Ensign Campuzano or Maese Pedro, to cite the most obvious authors built into Cervantes's stories, the mediator of the story within the story is never permitted an absolutely privileged position. The revelation of the author's weaknesses always serves to undercut his authority. And so it is with Don Juan and Don Antonio.

The housekeeper, now given her chance, tells Cornelia that her young tenants are not so noble that their word should be fully trusted. She suggests that, rather than wait there as expected, she and Cornelia and the baby go to a priest's house in a village outside of Ferrara. Breakdown in trust of those who had, up to this point, controlled the action, coincides with a breakdown in their control.

The suggestion of moral faults in the two Spanish gentlemen is followed immediately by a scene in which Don Antonio shows how confident he has become as a result of his successes in resolving the complexities of the story. Don Juan and Don Antonio are shown to feel unreal, disconnected from the events they are controlling, at just the moment when the housekeeper has convinced Cornelia to escape their control. Don Antonio expresses this when, in asking to announce to Lorenzo and the Duke the whereabouts of Cornelia, he says: "I want to have a role in this tragicomedy, and that is to be the one who asks for congratulations on the discovery of Señora Cornelia and her son, who are in my house."[17] Like Anselmo and Carrizales, the Duke and Duchess, and even Sancho and Don Quixote, Don Juan and Don Antonio become ridiculous at just the point when they believe they are fully in control. Their illusion of control is countered by an actual situation in which they are being fooled.

A third change takes place at this juncture. The "authors" have been seen in the perspective of their activities outside the scope of the "story" they are dealing with, and they have been robbed of absolute control over that story. But also the story, until now narrated without the apparent interference of another author, opens up to reveal a control beyond that of Don Juan and Don Antonio. The narrator's voice appears briefly in *La señora Cornelia*, after Cornelia, accompanied by the housekeeper, rides off to the priest's house with the baby: "Let's let them go, since they are so daring and well-directed, and let's find out what happened to Don Juan de Gamboa and Señor Lorenzo Bentibolli."[18] The simultaneous intervention of the housekeeper and the absolute author moves the story out of the hands of the two Spanish gentlemen. Now it is Don Juan and Don Antonio's turn to become involved in the story whose action they have so successfully overseen to this point. Don Antonio, pleased with the happy ending to the story, rides ahead to tell Cornelia of the Duke and Lorenzo's imminent arrival, only to find the house empty of his charges. He experiences fear and uncertainty for the first time: ". . . they found Don Antonio

---

[17] ". . . yo quiero hacer un personaje en esta trágica comedia, y ha de ser el que pide las albricias del hallazgo de la señora Cornelia y de su hijo, que quedan en mi casa" (VP, 983).

[18] "Dejémoslas ir, que ellas van tan atrevidas como bien encaminadas, y sepamos qué les sucedió a don Juan de Gamboa y al señor Lorenzo Bentibolli" (VP, 980–81).

sitting in a chair, with his cheek in his hand and with the color of death."[19]

As author–characters, Don Juan and Don Antonio pass through three distinct phases in the work. In the first phase they are prominent as characters. They are engaged in the work, shown acting and conversing, and are very little in control. The narrator describes them and introduces the events with which they are confronted. Until Cornelia's narration, they are the central characters and are deeply confused and amazed by the strange series of events that have taken place on the night the story begins. In the second stage, Don Juan and Don Antonio give way in prominence to Cornelia, Don Lorenzo, and the Duke, all of whom, in this section of the story, narrate their versions of the events that affect them. Don Juan and Don Antonio, while still important in the story, are no longer confused about the reality with which they are dealing. They are important only as mediators between the three characters with whose lives they have come in contact. In this second period, the two Spanish gentlemen become increasingly confident of their skill in dominating the conflicting visions of reality presented to them and begin to move too far away from the character roles assigned to them. This distancing is signaled by Don Antonio, who, on seeing that Don Lorenzo and the Duke have been successfully reconciled, announces that all problems are solved, since he can lead them both to Cornelia and the baby. Don Antonio's statement indicates that too great a distance has been established between the Spanish gentlemen and the Italian family whom they are helping. In the final stage, Don Juan and Don Antonio find themselves once again fooled by the reality they thought they completely understood. They return home only to find that Cornelia, the housekeeper, and the baby have disappeared. From this point until the end, Don Juan and Don Antonio drop from sight entirely, only to reappear as characters fully engaged in the story and participating in its happy ending.

From a beginning carved out of nothingness—the groping union of a baby with a stranger on a dark street near midnight—*La señora Cornelia* moves, in the hands of its author–characters, toward a clarity in which all things are explainable and controllable.[20] But clarity itself is finally over-

[19] ". . . hallaron a don Antonio sentado en una silla, con la mano en la mejilla y con una color de muerto" (VP, 983).

[20] It is this schematic, typically Baroque underlying construction that Peter Dunn so successfully highlights in his article to appear in the *Suma Cervantina* (I have had to rely on an early draft, kindly supplied to me by Professor Dunn, for this reference, as the work has not yet been published). He shows how the work moves from darkness to light, from separation to union, from the moral condition of the Fall to spiritual restoration within a sanctified social organization. *La fuerza de la sangre* would lend itself equally well to this type of analysis. The works are remarkably similar in their use of symbolic oppositions.

whelmed by a reality that continues to elude the grasp of any particular perceiver of it. The fallibility of each character's vision of the world is demonstrated again and again in *La señora Cornelia*. Significantly, this fallibility extends even to characters who appear to have a more privileged and distant view of reality. Cervantes's emphasis on religion combines with his representation of the author as limited to reveal in his later works a sense of one's dependence on a truth, beyond the reach of all people, which dissolves social distinctions.

The use of recognition and peripety in *La señora Cornelia* reveals not simply Cervantes's exploitation of a literary technique much discussed by literary theorists and used by playwrights and imitators of Heliodorus. It also suggests a critique of the use of reason and perception as guides to true understanding. Words and appearances are used in *La señora Cornelia* as often to confuse as to disabuse the characters. Don Antonio and the Duke are told that "Cornelia" is in bed with a page, but discover, upon investigation, that the same name has two different referents. Later the Duke announces to Don Lorenzo, Don Juan, and Don Antonio that he plans to marry a serving girl because he cannot find Cornelia. In this case the same young woman is designated by two different names. Words, clearly, are playthings of the characters and only tangentially connected to the objects to which they refer. This dissolution of the bond uniting words and objects is the subject of all of Cervantes's fiction, as is the concomitant challenge to the author such a dissolution proposes. Carried to its ultimate conclusion, the disjunction of words and things undercuts not only fiction but all human intercourse. This is why the emphasis in the analysis of the later stories has fallen on the connection between the way author and character are staged in the work and the social crisis which forms its content.

Lorenzo, Cornelia, and the Duke, because of the intensity of their fears of the loss of honor and life, are incapable of restoring to their lives the desired stability of a place in a defined social order. The mediator, who has more knowledge than they of the various elements involved in a given situation, can build theories and manipulate the feelings and actions of the afflicted characters. In the interchange between "character" and "author," the author is able to present choices to the character, but cannot force his response. The character, for his part, draws the author into his reality by allowing him to participate in his feelings. In the end, as in this story, their mutual dependence produces a higher reality in which all share peace and fulfillment. Mother-father, brother-brother-in-law, mother-son, and father-son are all partial expressions of an overall unity which has no name. In that final unity the separate categories of author and character are also destroyed within the story so that Don Juan and Don Antonio, once strangers, become characters indistinguishable from the rest. From their role as outsiders, the authors have become one with the story they helped to evolve and transmit.

La fuerza de la sangre

L*a fuerza de la sangre* has been praised by some as Cervantes's most accomplished work and condemned by others as his least tasteful and least convincing.[21] The work presents perhaps the greatest difficulties of all the idealistic tales for the reader unattuned to the concepts of honor and religion in seventeenth-century Spain. For the modern reader it is almost impossible to understand how a girl could fall in love with and marry the same man who had raped her seven years earlier.[22] But neither the plot nor the characters are to be evaluated by realistic or naturalistic standards. Cervantes presents in *La fuerza de la sangre* a skeletal, abstract combination of forces whose initial oppositions finally dissolve within a greater unity. The violence of the beginning contrasts sharply with the glorious almost theatrical finale, offering

[21] One of the earliest admirers was Jean Pierre Florian (*Oeuvres de Cervantes* I [1796], pp. 13–21), who called *La fuerza de la sangre* the most interesting and best developed of all the novelas. Julián Apraiz (*Estudio histórico-crítico sobre las "Novelas ejemplares" de Cervantes* [1901], p. 70) also considers the work one of Cervantes's most perfect, as does Menéndez Pelayo (*Orígenes de la novela* [1962], 2:140). More recently, Amezúa (*Cervantes, creador*, 209, 210, 215); Luís Astrana Marín (*Vida ejemplar y heroica de Miguel de Cervantes Saavedra* [1948–57], 5:427), and Casalduero ("*Novelas ejemplares*," pp. 150–63) have admired the stylistic perfection of the work. Casalduero (ibid.) and Robert V. Piluso ("*La fuerza de la sangre*: un análisis estructural" [1964]: 485–90) discuss the structure of the work in terms of its oppositions and parallelisms, defending it against accusations that it is psychologically implausible. Franz Rauhut ("Consideraciones sociológicas sobre *La gitanilla* y otras novelas cervantinas" [1950]: 143–60) also makes a case for understanding the work not in nineteenth- or twentieth-century terms, but in the context of literary expectations of the time in which it was written.

Detractors of the novela also come from among the most distinguished critics of Cervantes's work. Paolo Savj-López (*Cervantes* [1917], p. 157); Alfredo Giannini ("Introduzione," *Scrittori Stranieri, M. Cervantes, Novelle*, [1912], p. 87); and G. Hainsworth (*Les "Novelas ejemplares" de Cervantes en France au XVII\u1d49 Siècle* [1933], p. 20) all criticize the work for lack of good taste and convincing psychological insight.

[22] Rauhut ("Consideraciones sociológicas," pp. 155–56) points out that even Hardy, in his *La force du sang* (1626) based on Cervantes's novela, fills in some of the gaps in the psychology, making Leocadia's love for Rodolfo appear to grow out of her love for her son, and making her parents less ready to agree to the marriage.

Cervantes's most extreme affirmation of faith in the harmony which beauty and virtue can produce. The structural perfection and the accomplished descriptions in *La fuerza de la sangre* have led many commentators to consider it a late work, though the absence of historical references within the work has impeded speculation from many other critics. In its recourse to character types to present the universal problems of sin and salvation, its use of religious symbolism, its absence of historical or social detail, and its careful structuring of scenes, *La fuerza de la sangre* conforms to the pattern established here for Cervantes's later works.

As in many of Cervantes's other stories, the characters who instigate the action—which is always associated with disruption and disorder—represent evil forces. Rodolfo's rape of Leocadia in *La fuerza de la sangre* is the impulse which sets a story into motion. Rodolfo is the author of Leocadia's misfortune and the one whom Leocadia, through her faith, will eventually overcome, transposing his initially evil act into one out of which a transcendent goodness can be achieved. In the later works, the major author-character initiates the fiction by carrying out an evil act and disappearing. He returns to be reintegrated into society through the combined efforts of the other characters whose lives he affected and the good will of the author. This pattern, typical of the idealistic stories, suggests the evolution of the author-character in Cervantes's work from one whose cerebral construction brought him only to despair and self-destruction, to one whose more concretely evil actions lead eventually to his restitution.

La fuerza de la sangre offers Cervantes's most extreme characterization of an irresponsible son of the wealthy nobility. The economy with which Rodolfo and his friends are described suggests an incisive insight into the character whom Cervantes had long dealt with in his fictional works. The type represented by Rodolfo emerges in Cervantes's idealistic stories as a familiar category to be used symbolically to introduce not the failures of a particular social class but an abstract force very much related to the creative process. In *La fuerza de la sangre* Rodolfo epitomizes all the tendencies outlined in other characters of this type. Yet he is depicted with such precision and intensity that his youthfulness, his freedom, his lascivity, his selfishness, and his impetuosity can be captured in the single deed of rape which ignites the story in a moment in which beauty and the desire for its possession are compressed in the smallest space of time.

The story begins with opposing forces in direct confrontation. The first paragraph introduces two groups which will meet headlong in the second. A peaceful family of five, innocent of malice, is slowly returning home from a picnic in the fields beyond Toledo. They are a unit, self-sufficient, and yet, as they soon discover, exposed to the threats of disorder. They occupy the time and space which typically represent chaos in Baroque literature:

the story begins at night and outside the city. The setting, in fact, is so familiarly inauspicious that the narrator gives nothing away by making explicit reference to the disaster which is about to befall the characters. The misfortune alluded to projects the destiny of the "buen hidalgo" forward many years, linking him with the young gentleman who appears on the scene: "But since most misfortunes which happen are unexpected, against all their expectations one happened to them which upset their happiness and gave them cause to weep for many years. Almost twenty-two [years] was the age of a gentleman from that city."[23] The warning of impending disaster forms the bridge between the two forces which will meet in the next paragraph. The young man is contrasted with the old man, the unattached individual with the father of a family. As against the "twisted inclinations" by which the young man is known, the members of the family are characterized as "well inclined people." They are peaceful while the young man is daring.

In the second paragraph the symbolic aspect of this confrontation is strengthened when it becomes clear that Rodolfo is accompanied by four others—"all young, all fun-loving, and all insolent"[24]—and that they are moving in a direction opposite to that of the other group of five. The old man and his family walk uphill toward the city. Rodolfo and his friends ride their horses downhill away from the city. The opposition has symbolic significance, since ascent connotes hard work toward meritorious goals while descent suggests the facile movement toward degradation. Likewise, the movement toward the city suggests an orderly civilizing intent, while movement away from the city suggests the opposite. Cervantes underlines the moral opposition of the two groups, who have now become "squadrons": "The two squadrons met, that of sheep with that of wolves."[25]

Such an introduction and such a series of indications of danger, both explicit and implicit, prepare the reader for an inevitable conflagration. The old man is vulnerable because he is the father of an attractive sixteen-year-old girl. Rodolfo individualizes the girl, gives her a name, and draws her into the scope of the story by separating her from her family and introducing her to the emotions of anguish and despair. After the rape, Rodolfo disappears to Italy, leaving Leocadia to suffer the consequences of his impulsiveness. Leocadia's public and private lives will now be rent asunder by her need to dissimulate. Her ingenuity, her faith, and her discretion will all be called upon to reconstruct, out of the void of her dishonor, an

---

[23] ". . . pero como las más de las desdichas que vienen no se piensan, contra todo su pensamiento les sucedió una que les turbó la holgura y les dio que llorar muchos años. Hasta veintidós tendría un caballero de quella ciudad" (VP, 890).

[24] ". . . todos mozos, todos alegres y todos insolentes" (VP, 890).

[25] "Encontráronse los dos escuadrones, el de las ovejas con el de los lobos" (VP, 890).

appearance of honor. Like all Cervantes's characters, Leocadia must engage in the maintenance of false appearances. Dissimulation, though not an end in itself, will be essential to her survival within society.

Rodolfo's rape has robbed Leocadia of her honor and has the effect of killing her socially.[26] Yet even in the earliest scenes, symbols of rebirth accompany symbols of death. Leocadia's fainting and the darkness and strangeness of her surroundings represent her social death. That Leocadia's virtue has not been killed along with her honor, however, is shown when she, fully conscious, resists Rodolfo's second rape attempt. The distinction between "honor" and true virtue will remain throughout the story until the denouement in which these terms are reunited. Leocadia begins the process of rebirth almost immediately by taking from Rodolfo's room a crucifix, which provides the only link between her and her assailant.[27] If Rodolfo, in terms of the social code of his day, robs Leocadia of her life, she robs him of the symbol of its restoration. The initial, violent interaction between Rodolfo and Leocadia promises the ultimate union of opposites and the discovery of life in death, of hope in despair. For the rape results in the birth of a son, Luisico. It will be these two symbols of renewal—the crucifix and the boy—that will, coupled with the virtuous determination displayed by the conscious Leocadia, mediate between her and Rodolfo, restoring the two to life both in society and in religion.

In no other story is the period of "courtship" so foreshortened, nor the period of anguish so extended. Only in the period of dismay and anxiety is a character creatively engaged with his own life in Cervantes's works. Leocadia becomes a named character at the point when she is removed from the peaceful nest of her family and thrown into that uncertain world in which she belongs neither to them nor to her husband, where she is respected by her neighbors yet without honor, where she is both mother and cousin to her son. This is the world which Cervantes's fictional characters inhabit. Their normal peaceful lives surround the fictional moment, but exist apart from fiction which is, for Cervantes, the place where disorder is captured. When Leocadia awakens from her faint she says: "Where am I, unfortunate one? What darkness is this? What shadows surround me? Am I in the limbo of my innocence or in the hell of my wrongdoings?"[28] It is in this state that she qualifies for existence in Cervantes's fiction.

[26] See Piluso ("*La fuerza*," pp. 486–87); Américo Castro ("Algunas observaciones acerca del concepto del honor en los siglos XVI y XVII" [1916]: 1–50, 357–80; *El pensamiento de Cervantes* [1925], p. 361; *De la edad conflictiva* [1964], pp. 66–78); and Amezúa (*Cervantes, creador*, 1:207–9; 2:212–14).

[27] John J. Allen, "*El Cristo de la Vega* and *La fuerza de la sangre*" (1968): 271–75.

[28] "¿Adónde estoy, desdichada? ¿Qué oscuridad es esta, qué tinieblas me rodean? ¿Estoy en el limbo de mi inocencia o en el infierno de mis culpas?" (VP, 891).

Beauty and deception—impulses repeatedly used in Cervantes's work—combine to inspire an act through which a new reality is created. But, since beauty belongs to the object and deception to its beholder, it can be seen that even in its most elemental stages the act of creation is one of communication. Creation and communication involve interaction between the self and another. In the subsequent dialectic the self and the other exchange roles. Rodolfo, having once created Leocadia fictionally by killing her socially, will then drop out of the story to become the extreme other, the totally absent and unknown one without whom there would be no story, no Leocadia, apart from the unnamed sixteen-year-old daughter of the good "anciano hidalgo," and no Luisico. Just as radically other had Leocadia been when Rodolfo acted out his desire for union with her. Though the distance between the two could not be more extreme, the mutual desire for union could not be more intense. The creative act (rape vs. patient dissimulation) and the motivating drive (passion vs. honor) are different to the point of being opposite for the two characters, but the essential need of each for the other at different moments in the story is what gives it its forward impulse. There is an undeniable dialectic between man and woman, author and character, which underlies the story and gives it life.

Religion, in *La fuerza de la sangre,* holds the promise for the faithful characters of transcendence of, and at the same time incorporation in, society. It offers a position of hope through which human frailties can be transformed. The religious perspective is predicated on the prospect of redemption and does not depend on a rigorous rejection of humanity and social arrangements, such as can be found in the work of Mateo Alemán. Two religious symbols occur in the first encounter of the two main protagonists which auger their eventual reconciliation: the crucifix, and the church to which Rodolfo leads Leocadia after having raped her. Religion promises the joining, rather than the separation, of Leocadia and Rodolfo, offering hope for a happy ending which is totally at variance with the apparent destinies of the two characters after the rape.

The religious dimension, however, does not obscure social weaknesses, any more than it served to inhibit Rodolfo's cruelty. Throughout the opening pages are scattered hints of social criticism. Leocadia's father distinguishes clearly between social and divine justice, having no faith whatever in the efficacy of the former. When Leocadia is first carried off, her parents find themselves without recourse, their cries for help unheard: "Her father shouted, her mother screamed, her little brother cried, the maid tore her clothes; but the voices were not heard, nor the screams listened to, nor did the crying awake compassion, nor was the tearing of any use; because the solitude of the place and the hushed silence of the night and the cruel entrails of the evil-doers covered up everything."[29] This perhaps chance absence of social help when it was needed becomes a specific and intentional statement of mistrust of social justice in the next paragraph, when, upon returning home without his daughter, the old man decides against notifying the authorities: "[they were] confused, without knowing if it would be good to give notice of their misfortune to the police, fearful that they might be the principal instrument for making their dishonor public. As poor nobility, they saw themselves in need of favor; they didn't know about whom to complain except about their bad luck."[30] The implication is that not only is justice absent when it is most needed, but that without money, to alert the officers of "justice" would be to publish their dishonor and destroy the whole family.

In Leocadia's monologue after the rape, this same fear of social disgrace underlies her request that Rodolfo now kill her. When he refuses, she begs him never to tell anyone about what has happened. So fearful is she of his discovering who she is or where she lives that she pretends to enter another house on her way home, just in case he tries to follow her. Like her father, she too alludes to the vulnerability lack of money imposes on her: "You must swear," she says to Rodolfo, "not to follow me, . . . nor to ask me the name of my parents, nor my name, nor that of my relatives, who, if they were as rich as they are noble, would not be so unfortunate in my disgrace."[31]

When Leocadia returns home, her father, in refusing to kill her to cleanse the stain of dishonor that has fallen upon him, both reiterates the fear of public censure and distinguishes between the social and the spiritual criteria for sinning. "Take note, my daughter, that an ounce of public dishonor is more painful than a pound of secret misdeeds." "True dishonor is in sin, and true honor in virtue."[32] True honor and dishonor,

---

[29] "Dio voces su padre, gritó su madre, lloró su hermanico, arañóse la criada; pero ni las voces fueron oídas, ni los gritos escuchados, ni movió a compasión el llanto, ni los araños fueron de provecho alguno; porque todo lo cubría la soledad del lugar, y el callado silencio de la noche, y las crueles entrañas de los malhechores" (VP, 890).

[30] ". . . confusos, sin saber si sería bien dar la noticia de su desgracia a la Justicia, temerosos no fuesen ellos el principal instrumento de publicar su deshonra. Veíanse necesitados de favor, como hidalgos pobres; no sabían de quién quejarse, sino de su corta ventura" (VP, 890).

[31] ". . . has de jurar de no seguirme, . . . ni preguntarme el nombre de mis padres, ni el mío, ni el de mis parientes, que a ser tan ricos como nobles, no fueran en mí tan desdichados" (VP, 892).

[32] ". . . advierte, hija, que más lastima una onza de deshonra pública que una arroba de infamia secreta . . . la verdadera deshonra está en el pecado, y la verdadera honra en la virtud" (VP, 893).

then, are different from honor and dishonor as popularly conceived.[33] Criticism of society is evident in this passage, as it is in the characterization of the sons of the wealthy nobility, yet in both cases it is underplayed. The family does not reject the daughter, in accordance with society's rules, nor do they reject society in accordance with the rules of truth as they conceive them. They continue in both worlds—the world of true religion and the world of social regulation—preferring dissimulation to outright rejection. The dissimulation, however, cannot be construed simply as timid resentment, for the father expresses the confidence that in time and with faith, the religious hope will become the mediator of social justice, rather than its opponent: "What you must do," the father counsels his daughter, "is keep it [the crucifix] and give yourself to it, for since it was the witness to your disgrace, it will provide a judge who will defend your rights."[34]

The ultimate severing of religion and society, or a view of their absolute irreconcilability, would make novelistic resolution of Leocadia's problem impossible. For Cervantes's aversion to the use of magic or miracles to solve novelistic problems would prohibit a solution issuing simply out of God's grace.[35] Thus, the resolution to Leocadia's problem comes out of the material world and her strength of character. Leocadia left Rodolfo's room not only with his crucifix but with the seed of his child. It will be Luisico, having attained the age of seven, who will initiate for his mother, the movement back to social acceptance and union with herself and with her husband. Each step, from the accidental trampling of Luisico by the horseman to the marriage of his mother and father at the end, is carefully explained. Chance events are combined with the discretion and *industria* of the protagonists to produce a satisfactory ending to the story without recourse to the supernatural. At the same time, however, the narration is filled with references to divine assistance ("They agreed to wait to see what God intended for the wounded [child]";[36] "it was God's will that he was trampled, so that, on bringing him to your house, I too would find myself in it, as I hope I will find myself";[37] and "he believed it, by the

---

[33] This question has been considered extensively by Castro (see n. 26) and by Marcel Bataillon, *Pícaros y picaresca* (1969), pp. 203–42.

[34] ". . . lo que has de hacer . . . es guardarla y encomendarte a ella, que pues ella fue testigo de tu desgracia, permitirá que haya juez que vuelva por tu justicia" (VP, 893).

[35] The most explicit statement of Cervantes's rejection of magical solutions can be found in his criticism of the *Diana* and the Sabia Felicia in the "escrutinio" scene of *Don Quixote* (I, 6). Philosophic foundations can be found for rejection of the *Deus ex machina* resolution in the *Philosophía antigua poética* (2:87–88).

[36] ". . . acordaron de esperar lo que Dios hacía del herido" (VP, 895).

[37] ". . . permisión fue del Cielo el haberlo atropellado, para que, trayéndole a vuestra casa, hallase yo en ella, como espero que he de hallar" (VP, 896).

divine will of Heaven"³⁸). Leocadia divides her time equally between Rodolfo's mother and the crucifix when she reveals the name of her abductor and Luisico's father. She addresses first the one and then the other before fainting. The naturalistic explanation for the grandfather's recognition of his grandson is combined with the supernatural explanation of God's intervention, just as the combined presence of the boy and the crucifix is used as evidence of the truth of Leocadia's story.

When the chain of mediators finally brings the two main protagonists into direct contact, for the first time since the rape scene at the beginning of the story, the efforts of the other protagonists produce a tableau calculated to elicit from the audience an esthetic response. The skill of Rodolfo's mother, Doña Estefanía, creator of the scenario, has extended not only to the preparation of the scene to be viewed, but to the audience. She keeps Rodolfo ignorant of Leocadia's presence in the house and tricks him into confessing his overwhelming passion for feminine beauty. At the table, the mother pretends to have forgotten to call her house guest to dinner in order to delay Leocadia and Luisico's entrance and to allow the entire company to focus its attention on her when she appears. The narrator underscores the artifice of the whole proceeding by noting: "All of this was her arrangement, and Leocadia was advised and warned about everything that she was to do."³⁹ Leocadia makes her appearance dressed in black velvet and adorned with pearls and diamonds and gold. She is preceded by two young girls who hold candles to illuminate and heighten her beauty. This carefully developed scene excites such admiration that the principal respondent, Rodolfo, is moved to attribute divinity to the creature he sees before him: "God save me! What is this that I see! Is it by chance some human angel that I am looking at?"⁴⁰

The tendency by the characters to assign divine origins to pleasing visions or events is shown here combined with the author's careful explanation of the human industry by which the pleasing vision is produced. This drama within the story sheds light on the relationship between the reader or the characters and the overall author: apparently fortuitous actions, resulting in pleasing consequences, are brought about by the benevolence and artistry of the author in anticipation of the reader's or character's response. When the two concur, that is, then the author's skill produces in fact what the reader or character expects, the result appears divinely inspired. Unlike God, however, the author is not absolute, as further analysis of Doña Estefanía's role reveals. For the control that she exhibits

³⁸ ". . . él lo creyó, por divina permisión del Cielo" (VP, 896).
³⁹ "Todo esto era traza suya, y de todo lo que había de hacer estaba avisada y advertida Leocadia" (VP, 897).
⁴⁰ "¡Válame Dios! ¡Qué es esto que veo! ¿Es, por ventura, algún ángel humano el que estoy mirando?" (VP, 898).

over Rodolfo and Leocadia slips quickly out of her hands when Leocadia, more than simply an object of beauty after all, faints in the fear that her hopes will not finally be fulfilled. At that point not only does Rodolfo jump to reveal prematurely the passion that Leocadia's beauty has excited in him, but the parents of Leocadia and the priest, who had remained hidden, rush to the scene "breaking the order of Estefanía." After Leocadia regains consciousness, the impetuousness of Rodolfo and the generally high tension among all the guests causes Doña Estefanía again to abandon her original plan: "Doña Estefanía wound up not carrying any further her original plan, telling the priest to marry her son and Leocadia right away."[41] Doña Estefanía's representation of the author reveals once again the dialectic established between his will and that of the protagonists. Her arrangement of the scenes and the order of the action can only partially anticipate the final outcome of the drama, for the intervention of actual emotions and desires can interrupt at any moment the previously determined pattern and take it in an entirely new direction.

What the characters in the story see as the will of God in their lives will be recognized by the reader as the combined will of the author and the characters: the first presenting the situation out of which the other seeks his destiny. Not only within the work, but in the relationship between the work and its author, therefore, a correspondence is established between supernatural and natural causes, neither one usurping or replacing the role of the other. For this reason, Rodolfo's acceptance of Leocadia as his wife is viewed with benevolence and is taken as sacramental, despite the fact that it was motivated by desires originating out of his lust and love for beauty. The result is the same, whether moral or physical reasons have inspired the action, just as the result is the same whether it was caused exclusively by the mediation of Luisico's face, or whether the crucifix did in fact have a spiritual role to play. In this work human truth and justice are allowed to run the full gamut from the most debased to the most spiritual. In the end, nothing is rejected, and the union of Leocadia and Rodolfo is a hymn to the ultimate reconcilability of all things.

The reconciliation of opposites so forcefully represented in the final union of Leocadia and Rodolfo within the laws of the church and society is developed stylistically in the presence of oppositions which become fused into a single event when repeated later in the story. What appear at first to be opposite terms emerge ultimately as the constitutive elements of a greater whole. When Leocadia faints the first time in the arms of her abductor, the reader has been led, through the carefully developed sets of

[41] ". . . acabó doña Estefanía de no llevar más adelante su determinación primera, diciendo al cura que luego desposase a su hijo con Leocadia" (VP, 898–99).

oppositions already analyzed, to see in the rape the destruction of innocence and honor by the blind forces of desire. But when, at the end, Leocadia again is shown awakening from a faint in the arms of Rodolfo, the meaning of the entire act has been transformed. The repetition at the end of the same actions carried out at the beginning causes the reader to reinterpret the initial act and to see it as a life-giving force as well as a death-giving force. The repetition of the actions of the characters at the end of the work also reveals the disparity between the appearance and its meaning, for it shows that the same actions can have opposite interpretations, depending on the surroundings in which they occur.

Rodolfo's bedroom also appears twice in Leocadia's life, the second time inverting while duplicating the meaning of the first time. It is on the bed where she was raped that Leocadia, seven years later, finds Luisico, who has been trampled by a horse and rescued by Rodolfo's father. The repetition of the room and its site as the place where Luisico is twice given life establishes a parallelism and at the same time suggests a reversal of themes. The bed is now the first link in the chain that will lead Leocadia back to her honor, having originally been the place in which it was destroyed. The double appearance of Rodolfo's bedroom reinforces the initial supposition that, even in the first scene, it was host not only to Leocadia's destruction, but to her subsequent resurrection. Again the same external setting is the scene first for the destruction and then for the resurrection of Leocadia's honor. The co-presence of destruction and resurrection, however, cannot be apparent to the characters who must live out the consequences of destruction and forge the means for restitution through time. Succession, for the living characters, replaces the perception of simultaneity available to the reader through the mediation of symbols.

Luisico's accident occurs at midpoint in the novela. In that event nearly all the thematic currents of the work converge. Luisico is, of course, the embodiment of the actual and potential union between Rodolfo and Leocadia. He is the result of the initial union and the cause of its subsequent legal and sacramental consummation. He is mediator not only of the lives of his parents and of their families, but of the beginning and the end of the story. His near-death recaptures and intensifies the fainting scenes with which the story of the union of Rodolfo and Leocadia begins and ends. His near-death, in fact, is inseparable from the discovery of his true identity. It is pivotal because it illustrates the necessity of loss of self in the process of its salvation and marks the beginning of Leocadia's recovery of her honor. In Luisico the theme of the coexistence of opposites is expressed on all levels.

In considering the appearance, within the work, of characters who represent the author, it can be said that Rodolfo and Doña Estefanía represent the impetus that initiates a work and that they are in this sense surrogate authors. But unlike earlier author–characters such as Carrizales or Anselmo, the ones in *La fuerza de la sangre* are not highly conscious of themselves. Because no particular motives are attached to their actions, except curiosity or an attraction to beauty, and because they exert so little control over the action once they have initiated it, these later characters, when considered as authors, serve as almost abstract representatives of the most elemental, primitive creative drives. Still, they are like Anselmo and Carrizales in that they drop out of the action as soon as they have inspired a new direction in the story line, to be replaced by characters who, created out of their actions, undertake the restoration of the imbalances caused by the initiating characters. Inspiration, then, appears to be greatly separated from "industry," the initial drive being succeeded by long periods of patience, careful planning, and tedious work. Anselmo and Carrizales tried to carry on both functions. Possibly this is why they both failed in their projects. The creative process becomes whole when the characters, through their work and hope, rediscover the identity of the author who created them. This only happens when all have recognized, simultaneously, their mutual dependence.

VI. THE LAST WRITTEN NOVELAS

El amante liberal

Of all the idealistic tales, *El amante liberal* is the one most often considered early, even by critics who have suggested that such stories as *Las dos doncellas* and *La señora Cornelia* were written late.[1] *El amante liberal* is regularly denounced by twentieth-century critics for its supposed weakness of character development, lack of psychological insight, unconvincing dialogues, and affected style. Although the plot seems implausible on modern standards, the work conforms, nonetheless, to seventeenth-century precepts for verisimilitude and reflects the Canon's prescription (*Don Quixote* I:47) for an intellectually satisfying adventure story. Cervantes protects the story's credibility by making even the most unlikely episodes appear at least possible and by placing his fictional characters in a well-known historical situation. The story begins with a dramatic monologue by one of the main characters, Ricardo, who links his misfortune with that of Cyprus. Cyprus, two years before, had been taken by the Turks. Ricardo, held prisoner by the Turks on Cyprus, identifies his misfortunes with those of the island. He mentions his father's heroism and close relationship to Charles V, and he recalls the fighting in Cyprus, Sicily, and Constantinople, all familiar battlefields to readers of Cervantes's day. The careful description of the process of succession to power in Turkish custom adds further to the historic interest and gives the author a chance to display his knowledge. The factual and historical grounding of the story in a time and place somewhat but not greatly distant from the reader of Cervantes's day lends it the necessary air of authenticity and removes it from the criticisms leveled at the chivalric novels for their total divorce from reality.

---

[1] E.g., Rafael Lapesa, "En torno a *La española inglesa y El Persiles*" (1950): 376, n. 16; Agustín G. de Amezúa y Mayo, *Cervantes, creador de la novela corta española* (1956–58), 2:51; William J. Entwistle, "Cervantes, the Exemplary Novelist" (1941): 105; Francisco Icaza, *Las "Novelas ejemplares" de Cervantes* . . . (1916), p. 128; and Rudolf Schevill and Adolfo Bonilla, *Comedias y entremeses de Cervantes* (1915), 4:79. Others, however, have proposed a later dating. Among them are Angel Valbuena Prat, in the prologue to *El amante liberal* found in his *Obras Completas* (1967) of Cervantes, p. 807, and Ciriaco Morón Arroyo, in his review of Dietrich Rossler's *Voluntad bei Cervantes* (1971): 325. Both propose a 1610 dating for *El amante liberal*.

The question of verisimilitude was very much colored, in the sixteenth and seventeenth centuries, by extra-literary concerns. Reflecting the earlier neo-Platonic belief that fiction was simply a lie about reality and therefore inherently inferior to history and unjustifiable on its own terms, seventeenth-century neo-Aristotelian theory dictated that fiction be factually accurate with regard to any details capable of being corroborated. This left a large realm open to the author's imagination, for if he either removed the sphere of action from everyday reality, as in the first two books of the *Persiles*, or introduced turns of events explainable within the terms of naturally occurring phenomena, he could be free of charges of inverisimilitude.[2] The preoccupation with accurately presented factual details left room for considerably more license than a modern reader would accord a work of fiction, for a string of coincidences that might be perfectly acceptable to the seventeenth-century reader appears contrived to modern tastes.

Another central neo-Aristotelian tenet—that a work of fiction should contain within an overall unity a wide variety of interesting events—is reflected in *El amante liberal*, as well as in the *Persiles* and *La española inglesa*. This tenet is discussed in the *Philosophía antigua poética* and is also stated by the Canon in *Don Quixote* I:47.[3] *El amante liberal* offers

---

[2] In the *Philosophía antigua poética*, Fadrique points out that Virgil, in the *Aeneid* Book I, presented a number of false facts, describing a port in Africa which was actually in Spain and mentioning the hunting of deer which were not present in Africa. After Ugo has answered the objection, Fadrique amplifies the explanation: ". . . y assí verdaderamente lo que yo entiendo es que en estos dos lugares, aunque lo parece, no está contradicha la verisimilitud, porque pudo ser auer puertos semejantes, auerlos el tiempo escondido, como otras muchas cosas. Y lo mismo digo de los cieruos de Africa, q[ue] pudo ser en algún navío llevado algunos y auer produzido y criado el tie[m]po q[ue] fue Eneas en aquellas riberas" [". . . and thus truly, what I understand is that in these two places, even though it seems so, verisimilitude is not violated, because it could have been that there were ports, and similar ports, that time has hidden, as it has many other things. And I say the same thing about the deer in Africa, that it could have been that they were taken there in some ship and that they produced and were raised during the time that Aeneas was on those shores."] (*Philosophía antigua poética*, 2:78–80). The speakers conclude that the only thing the poet cannot alter is geography, cosmography, and natural history: ". . . es mal hecho escriuir mala doctrina y falsa: y assí no conuiene que el poeta la altere, porque lo natural es perpetuo" [". . . it's a bad thing to write bad and untrue doctrine; and thus it is not a good idea for a poet to alter it, because the natural is perpetual."] (*Philosophía antigua poética*, 2:81). For further discussion of this point, see Alban Forcione's "Cervantes and the Freedom of the Artist" (1970): esp. 251–53.

[3] Ugo says: "Bien puede tener, no sólo argumento, pero la fábula toda, diversas acciones, mas que sea la una principal, como en el animal vemos que tiene muchos miembros y el coraçón es el principal principio y fuente de todos" ["It could easily

to the reader shipwrecks, a ceremony commemorating the changing of governors at Nicosia, a battle between Ricardo and Cornelio, the description of the beautiful Leonisa and the costly raiments in which she is put up for sale in Hazán Bajá's tent outside of Nicosia, a battle at sea among the three Turkish rulers who are seeking possession of Leonisa, and a colorful return to Sicily by the band of Christians who dress themselves in Turkish costumes to frighten the townspeople. All the action, however, is closely bound to the fate of the two main protagonists.

Even the seemingly extraneous discussion by the renegade Mahmut of the procedure for changing governors becomes important in the development of the story. Only because the old governor is paying tribute to the new governor and because the latter must hear, in the presence of the former, the complaints of his people against the old regime, are the two of them, along with the town high priest, assembled together in the tent. And because of this chance for the people to appear before the new governor, the Jew who wishes to sell Leonisa can appear. Because the three powerful men, Alí Bajá, Hazán Bajá, and the Cadí are all equally enamored of Leonisa, the scene will become an important part of the denouement, which rests in part on the mutually destructive rivalry Leonisa's beauty has introduced among the three. The episode of the Cadí and his wife Halima, who fall in love with Leonisa and Ricardo, is, while amusing, also

---

have, not just the plot, but the whole story, many actions, but let one be the principal one, just as in the animal we see that it has many parts, but the heart is the main center and source of all the others."] (*Philosophía antigua poética*, 2:41). That an overall unity does not prevent inclusion of a wide variety of incidents is made even more explicit by the Canon in *Don Quixote* 1:47. The epic allows, "a good mind to display its true worth, [offering] a broad and spacious field over which the author's pen might run without impediment, describing shipwrecks, tempests, battles, and encounters; depicting a valiant captain with all the qualities requisite to such a character, showing him as prudent, capable of anticipating the stratagems of the enemy, an eloquent orator in persuading or dissuading his soldiers." [". . . el sujeto que ofrecía para que un buen entendimiento pudiese mostrarse en ellos, porque daban largo y espacioso campo por donde, sin empacho alguno, pudiese correr la pluma, describiendo naufragios, tormentas, rencuentros y batallas, pintando un capitán valeroso con todas las partes que para ser tal se requieren, mostrándose prudente previniendo las astucias de sus enemigos, y elocuente orador persuadiendo o disuadiendo a sus soldados; maduro en el consejo, presto en lo determinado, tan valiente en el esperar como en el acometer" (Cervantes Saavedra, *Obras Completas*, edited by Angel Valbuena Prat, 15th ed., 1967, p. 1251. Hereafter referred to in footnotes as VP, with pertinent page number). The English quotation of *Don Quixote* is from *The Ingenious Gentleman Don Quixote de la Mancha*, vol. 1, translated by Samuel Putnam (1949). For a thorough and stimulating discussion of the Canon's discourse, see Alban Forcione, *Cervantes, Aristotle and the Persiles* (1970), pp. 91–104; and also his "Cervantes, Tasso, and the *Romanzi* Polemic" (1970): 433–43.

closely woven to the fate of the two captives. Earlier examples of Cervantes's prose fiction, such as *La Galatea* and *Don Quixote* I, do not show adhesion to the principles of unity in diversity in the same way as the later works do. Like *Don Quixote* II and the *Persiles*, the great variety of detail in *El amante liberal* is closely linked to the fortunes of clearly defined central characters.

Finally, there is the question of moral instruction, which appears, from the title of the collection of stories published in 1613 and from the prologue to that collection, to have been a concern of the later Cervantes. The lessened concern with direct imitation of reality is justified by an increased interest in exemplarity.[4] Read allegorically, the fantastic adventure stories, such as *El amante liberal,* can be seen as dramatic representations of the interior passions of the major characters and the trials through which those passions are purified. The shipwrecks, the fainting, the attacks, the storms, the unharnessed passions of the captors, and the miseries and uncertainties of the captive's life are the embodiment of the

---

[4] The question of exemplarity opens the door to considerably more license with the precepts of verisimilitude through allegorical interpretation, as some discussions in the *Philosophía antigua poética* reveal: ". . . digo que aquellos vocablos que declaran la naturaleza de Atlante son metaphóricos: la cabeça significa cumbre del monte; el pecho, la baxada; y assí de lo demás. De a do se colige no ser aquella descripción fabulosa, sino histórica y verdadera" ["I say that those words which declare the existence of Atlas are metaphorical: the head signifies the peak of the mountain; the chest, the slope; and so on for the rest. From which one gathers that that description is not invented, but rather, historical and true."] (*Philosophía antigua poética,* 2:64). In the continuing discussion, it becomes clear that imitation of reality includes conformity with the religious law subscribed to by the poet: "Supuesto que el poeta deue guardar versimilitud en todo, la deue guardar también en la religión. . . . Digo que Homero, Virgilio y los demás no hizieron agravio a la imitación, mas fuéronla conseruando con mucha perfección en general, porque en el tiempo que ellos escriuieron, el Sol era tenido por Dios y Cibela por diosa, y los ríos y fuentes, dioses juzgados por su perpetuydad" (2:65). ["Supposing that the poet ought to maintain verisimilitude in everything, he ought also to maintain it in religion. . . . I say that Homer, Virgil, and the others did not violate imitation, but rather they preserved it in general with great perfection, because at the time when they were writing, the sun was considered to be God and Cibela was a goddess, and rivers and springs were considered, because of their self-perpetuation, to be gods."] (See also *Philosophía antigua poética,* 2:92–93; 3:174–76.) For further discussion of the use of allegory in neo-Aristotelian poetics, see Jean-François Canavaggio, "Alonso López Pinciano y la estética literaria de Cervantes en el *Quijote*" [1958]: 34, 73; and Robert L. Montgomery, "Allegory and the Incredible Fable: The Italian View from Dante to Tasso" [1966]: 45–55. Especially interesting in the context of Cervantes is Montgomery's study of Tasso's interpretation of allegory, p. 54. The question of verisimilitude clearly becomes involved in the question of the double goal of fiction: to please and to instruct. (And in the question of unity and variety. See Robert Durling, *The Figure of the Poet in Renaissance Epic,* [1965], pp. 200–10).

nightmares of characters who must prove their worth by discovering the power of their own will, their dependency on God's will and, ultimately, out of these two discoveries, the mutual dependence among highly individualized characters which makes marriage their proper terrestrial goal.

In *La gitanilla* and *La ilustre fregona*, self-discovery and mutual acceptance among the lovers develop out of their interaction in everyday circumstances. The feelings of the main characters are highlighted to reveal the difficulties inherent in the process of forming a unity out of two distinct entities. In *El amante liberal* and *La española inglesa*, however, the near misses and the petty passions that interrupt the consummation of true marriage are all represented as outside of and beyond the control of the two main protagonists. The main characters in the latter two works are seen as they are swept up in these passions, but it is as if the passions were divorced from them entirely, being represented instead in the evil schemes of the Turks or the heartless calculations of jealous Protestants. The main characters in *El amante liberal*, Leonisa and Ricardo, appear to be innocent of the evil which enmeshes them.

Careful examination of Ricardo and Leonisa's actions while still at home in Sicily, however, reveals them as less than entirely exemplary characters. Ricardo's initially demanding and impulsive nature is directly related to his subsequent capture by the Turks. And his ultimate overcoming of his weaknesses, once he returns to Sicily, is related to the control over himself that he learned as a captive.[5] The character development of not only Ricardo, but Leonisa as well, from the beginning to the end, commands a more serious look at the fantastic adventures which make up the middle of the story. For, if considered allegorically, the adventures can be seen as externalizations of the weaknesses against which both main characters must successfully struggle in order to be granted salvation.

In Ricardo's story, told to the renegade Mahmut at the beginning of *El amante liberal*, Ricardo reveals that it was his own impetuousness and aggressiveness that caused him and Leonisa to be captured by the Turks. He explains that he had spent all his time from his early youth serving Leonisa in the hope that she would marry him. He refers to the obligations that his many gifts to her have placed on her and how unworthy his competitor Cornelio was, having only wealth and good looks, while Ricardo had love, devotion, ardor, and determination behind his claims on Leonisa. Having nonetheless received no encouragement from Leonisa and her

---

[5] In Casalduero's study (*Sentido y forma de las "Novelas ejemplares"* [1969]), Ricardo's capture is directly related to his character weaknesses. For a good analysis of the structural regularity underlying the process of capture and return in *El amante liberal*, see Jennifer Lowe's "A Note on Cervantes' *El amante liberal*" (1970–71): 400–3.

family, Ricardo tells how he flew into a jealous rage when he heard that she and Cornelio were at a picnic together. In a passion he had challenged Cornelio by verbally abusing him and finally had won the rancor of Cornelio's entire family, who rose to his defense by joining in an attack on Ricardo. This almost Quixotic display of pride and lack of consideration for outside realities in the pursuit of his own fabricated sense of proprietorship over Leonisa so engaged Ricardo that when a Turkish pirate ship landed, he did not flee as the others did, but remained, along with Leonisa, who had fainted, to be captured by the Turks. Ricardo's narration of this story, under the sympathetic prompting of Mahmut, marks the first step in the long process by which Ricardo will free himself, as well as Mahmut and Leonisa, from the inferno in which he finds himself. As so often happens in Cervantes's works, the narration of his misfortunes by a protagonist has a salutory effect on both the teller and the listener. The narration, in this case, prompts Mahmut to admit his desire to return to Sicily and Catholicism and seals Mahmut's determination to help Ricardo out of his captivity.

Another characteristic which links *El amante liberal* to the late stories is the prominence given to the main female character. Leonisa is a character in search of her salvation. She must learn to distinguish Ricardo's true love from Cornelio's more superficial interest in her. Ricardo and Leonisa must both participate in the struggle which frees them from the allegorical captivity in which they find themselves. As captive, Leonisa will find herself accosted time and again, her beauty an object of bargain and sale among the various infidels at whose mercy she lives. In this constant repetition and exaggeration of Cornelio's role as her lover, she must be brought to see the courage and genuineness of Ricardo's devotion. In her nightmarish captivity she will find a series of Cornelios who, if she successfully rejects them, will give way to her one true lover Ricardo. Ricardo, on the other hand, will be tested by constantly being exposed to the loss of Leonisa.

When the story begins, Ricardo believes that Leonisa is dead. His story to Mahmut will include his inability to effect her ransom, his seeing her taken off in Izuf's ship, and her apparent death in the wreck that killed Izuf and destroyed the ship. When Leonisa reappears, dressed in the costume and jewels provided her by the Jew, Ricardo must watch helplessly as the three men who control his destiny scheme over how to possess her. In this hellish fantasy the weaknesses and fears of each protagonist are exaggerated. But beneath this fantasy a sense of the developing relationship between Ricardo and Leonisa can still be detected. For, just as in *La gitanilla* or *La ilustre fregona*, the main characters not only purge themselves of their own weaknesses, but they begin to establish the bonds of trust and communication through which their union will eventually be made possible.

The first indication that Leonisa is capable of loving Ricardo as much as he is of loving her comes, also in Ricardo's opening speech, when he reveals that she saved him from the vengeance hanging which the Turks had ordered for him upon his capture. In his turn, though less successfully, Ricardo expends his energy trying to secure the release of Leonisa, in exchange for which he offers all his money and all his possessions. The Turks, however, torn between fascination with Leonisa's beauty and the desire for wealth, put the ransom so high that without a few days' search the money cannot be produced. In presenting their ransom demands the Turks link Leonisa and Ricardo, saying that either both be freed or neither would be. Although this was a ploy to disguise the high value placed on Leonisa, it serves, in the allegorical scheme of the story, to complete, on a purely external level, the union of Ricardo and Leonisa suggested already by their shared capture and the expressed will of each to save the other from death and the hands of the captors.

The next mutual expression of the will toward union is made, again under extreme conditions, during the forced separation of the two captives. Izuf succeeds in taking Leonisa for himself in a division of captives and booty, leaving Ricardo on another ship. When Ricardo watches Leonisa being led off to Izuf's ship, he faints, only to find out that Leonisa had also fainted: "On entering the gangway which was placed from the land to the ship, she [Leonisa] turned her eyes to look at me, and mine, which did not leave hers, looked at her with such a tender feeling of pain that . . . it took my sight away and without it or any feeling at all, I fell to the ground. They told me later that the same thing had happened to Leonisa."[6] In this second example, a mutually felt communication between the two is again expressed.

The next encounter linking the sentiments of union of both Leonisa and Ricardo takes place through the mediation of Mahmut. Mahmut, having heard Ricardo's story, advises him to remain hidden and to change his name to prevent Leonisa from knowing that he is also in Nicosia. Mahmut, while accompanying Leonisa to the house of her mistress Halima, then tests her interest and concern for Ricardo by inventing a story both of Cornelio's capture and of Ricardo's death. Leonisa shows only disdain for Cornelio, but sorrow at Ricardo's death, blaming herself

---

[6] ". . . al entrar por la escala que estaba puesta desde tierra a la galeota, volvió los ojos a mirarme, y los míos, que no se quitaban de ella, la miraron con tan tierno sentimiento y dolor, . . . que me quitó la vista, y sin ella y sin sentido alguno di conmigo en el suelo; lo mismo me dijeron después que había sucedido a Leonisa" (VP, 813). All translations in this chapter are my own.

for his misfortunes: "God forgive the one who caused his death, which was I, for I am the unfortunate one whom he mourned for dead; and God knows I would be happy if he were alive in order to repay him with the suffering he would see that I had over his misfortunes, he who showed such for mine."[7] Leonisa's affirmations of concern for Ricardo and self-blame for his death are duly reported by Mahmut to Ricardo, who is then prepared to undertake the next steps toward their mutual rescue.

Mahmut's invention to Leonisa about the fate of both Cornelio and Ricardo also included an indication of diminished interest by Ricardo. Mahmut says Ricardo had stipulated that: "as long as it did not exceed three or four hundred crowns, he would be glad to give them for her, since he, at one time, had had some affection for her."[8] When Mahmut turns to Ricardo to report the success of his ploy in getting Leonisa to confess her interest in Ricardo, Ricardo is exploding with joy and praise for Leonisa's beauty and spouting poetry remembered from his father. Ricardo tells Mahmut a story about a poem of praise for the beauty of a captured Moorish girl started by one poet and completed by another. The verses started by the first poet are so difficult that he gives up midway through the poem. A second poet intervenes to finish the celebration of the Moorish girl's beauty. Mahmut comments that both the repeating and composing of poetry require a dispassionate spirit. Richardo answers that poetry is also to be sung and wept. This seemingly incidental interlude captures the essence of Ricardo's predicament and reveals the importance of Mahmut's mediating mission. Ricardo has the necessary component of passion to initiate a poem or a love quest, but not the distance necessary to bring it to a conclusion through all the difficulties it presents. As he showed in the scene in the garden when he challenged Cornelio's rights to Leonisa's love, Ricardo's passion for Leonisa drives him to demand a response, making impossible for Leonisa the illusion of free choice which would be necessary if she were truly to engage in marriage. Mahmut's suggestion to Leonisa that Ricardo had lost interest in her was intended to correct Ricardo's unrestrained expression of love. Mahmut's invention is necessary for the establishment of movement from Leonisa toward Ricardo. But it is just this fictional representation that Ricardo is incapable of making. The discussion of love poetry directly relates the process of creating a union between two individuals to the artistic process.

[7] ". . . Dios perdona a quien fue causa de su muerte, que fui yo, que yo soy la sin ventura que él lloró por muerta; y sabe Dios si holgara de que él fuera vivo para pagarle con el sentimiento que viera que tenía de su desgracia el que él mostró de la mía (VP, 819).

[8] ". . . como no pasasen de trescientos o cuatrocientos escudos, él los daría de muy buena gana por ella, porque un tiempo la había tenido alguna afición" (VP, 819).

In this dream-like adventure story leading to love and marriage, the passivity which Ricardo must come to accept is imposed on him by fortune and the exigencies of captivity. Likewise, Leonisa must discover her powers to make decisions and control not only her actions but also Ricardo's by the force of external circumstances which seem to have very little to do with her personal psychology. Every change in Leonisa's attitude toward Ricardo is accompanied by a change in external circumstances which facilitate her liberation and marriage to Ricardo.

In the next step in their development toward each other and toward their liberation, Ricardo and Leonisa find themselves together and in mediating roles for their masters. When Leonisa, who has been assigned by Halima the task of representing her amorous desires to the slave Mario, discovers that the "Mario" she is waiting to see is none other than Ricardo, she must undergo the same sensation of incredulity that Ricardo underwent on seeing Leonisa unveiled before the Cadí and the two viceroys in Hazán Bajá's tent. Both Ricardo and Leonisa had thought the other dead, and each appears to have resurrected the other symbolically through the effort of recreating, to the mediator Mahmut, the image of the other as loved one, and taking responsibility for his death. It is as if each were saved by the willed restoration of the other, each created by the other at the same time that each sacrifices himself to the other. Having shared the fainting scene and now the disabusal of the assumed death of the other, the two are finally brought together, but are still held apart by the roles they must play in representing the interests of their respective masters. Leonisa reveals to Ricardo Halima's desires for him and tells him to pretend to accept her wishes. In the slow process of Leonisa's conversion, she admits at this point to being glad to see Ricardo but will not permit the meetings to be the occasion for him to beg for her love: ". . . speaking together will be easy, and it will be a great pleasure for me if we do so, providing that you never bring up anything to do with your declared intentions."[9] In *La ilustre fregona* and in *La gitanilla* the same shift in the relationship between the couples in the two stories could be seen when the girl, Preciosa or Costanza, admitted the suitor to her presence but did not compromise herself or encourage his open solicitation.

There are many implications for an understanding of the development of Leonisa's character contained in her role as mediator of her mistress's desires and many levels· in which the situation has meaning. The mediating role provides the opportunity for Leonisa to establish an aggressive

---

[9] ". . . el hablarnos será fácil, y a mí será de grandísimo gusto el hacerlo, con presupuesto que jamás me has de tratar cosa que a tu declarada pretensión pertenezca" (VP, 824).

posture toward "Mario," but it also allows her to be protected from compromise, because she only solicits Mario's love in a role imposed on her by someone else. Since Mario has been assigned the task of representing the lascivious desires of his master, Ricardo and Leonisa can meet regularly and stand in relation to each other in exactly equivalent roles. The process is instructive to both of them, for it teaches Leonisa to respect Ricardo for his gentleness and humility, while teaching Ricardo to temper his passion in Leonisa's presence. This time spent manipulating their masters while appearing to carry out their wishes allows both Leonisa and Ricardo to explore the realms of real and dissimulated activity, of honest and dishonest passion. Ricardo will learn that to achieve any goal he must dissimulate the expectations he harbors for the outcome of his activity. Leonisa will discover in the cheapened passion of her mistress the true feeling that she has for Mario-Ricardo.

Ricardo and Leonisa, though linked through circumstance, will not automatically achieve marriage and the desired return to freedom. They must work out the details of their escape on their own. The bloody escape from captivity leaves the high quality of the major characters unstained because the mutual destruction by the three Turks of their ships and sailors and soldiers grew out of their own lustful ambitions and not out of the perfidy of the Christians. The three leaders destroy each other because of their greed and treachery. The role of the Christians in finishing off the job can be seen, therefore, as defensible and at the same time as liberating, for the Turks are never presented sympathetically, but as the instruments of the captives' ill fortune and as the rather unrealistic representatives of man's weakness and perdition.

The story is cast in alien territory precisely because of its allegorical nature. The struggle between the forces of good and evil can only be externalized if the characters who are represented as evil can be seen as having no soul. The Turks are, in fact, nothing but caricatures used to represent in a semi-dreamlike tableau the various internal struggles which the main characters must suffer in the process of their self-creation and their salvation. If Ricardo, Halima's father, and her nephews resort to cutting off the heads of the few remaining Turks after the battle between the Cadí and Alí and Hazán's forces, it is because the Turks represent the final obstacle in the tortuous path of liberation, a liberation the essence of which consists of struggle and faith. Still, Cervantes is careful to show that even with respect to the enemy the Christians are capable of clemency. He does this by showing that Leonisa is willing to embrace the defeated Cadí in accordance with his final wishes. The Christians give the Cadí a boat in which to return home and some money to get him out of any difficulties he might encounter. Leonisa's act is particularly significant, for it is the first time she is shown making a movement of personal generosity toward someone else. This signals her own liberation from selfishness as well as her liberation from captivity. In the embrace, she shows that in a position of strength she will not be cruel, that is, that she has recovered from the terms of a dialectic that dictates that one be either aggressive or passive, controller or controlled. She shows that love is not something extracted from the victim by force, but given freely by a person no longer seeing herself as victim.

The final liberation of Ricardo will be signaled by his discovery that he too has a broader role to play. Just as Leonisa must discover herself to be more than victim, more than the passive recipient of the passions of others, with no criteria of her own for choice, Ricardo must see that he is limited in his control over the wills of the others. He does not entirely control Leonisa, no matter what he has done, just as she is not entirely controlled by him. Her actions had shown all along, though only negatively, that she belonged only to herself, as Ricardo says in his final speech, for she had continually rejected his and everyone else's interest in her. He, likewise, had always known, but, again, only negatively, that he could not control anyone else, for all his efforts to determine Leonisa's life and will had come to naught. Only through radical conversion made by arduous work in desperately difficult circumstances has this hopeless situation of eternal chase and eternal flight been converted into one of mutual acceptance in stable circumstances.

In *El amante liberal*, the main male character learns a lesson that none of Cervantes's early characters could learn. Ricardo discovers, through a nightmare of bizarre adventures, that union with the other is possible only if claims over the other are renounced. Like other late characters, Ricardo moves from an initial position of absolute alienation to a final position of integration, bringing with him into a final reconciliation not only Leonisa, whom he marries, but the renegades Mahmut, Halima, and her family. Ricardo's victory over his will to dominate others becomes part of a total victory of Christians over Turks and a restoration of the lost to their faith. The *in medias res* beginning and the circular pattern of the story link it in organization with the other late stories. Ricardo and Leonisa, through weaknesses in their own characters, are wrested from their homes and families and cast upon the seas and the mercy of the enemy. Through their diligence and faith, they work their way back to their point of origin, discovering in the process a fuller meaning of themselves, each other, their homes and families, and their religion. As in the other late stories, the end marks a return to the beginning while differing from the beginning. The travails that constitute the story's middle impose on the end a transcendent understanding of the elements presented in the beginning, giving the end a depth of meaning inaccessible to the characters before their adventures.

La española inglesa

The nearly absolute control of the author over the lives of the characters, the absence of individual traits in either major or minor characters, the tendency toward static description of suspended moments of time, and the intensely spiritual atmosphere pervading the work suggest that *La española inglesa* is one of the last written of the *Novelas ejemplares*. Estimates on its date of composition, however, vary more widely than for any of the other stories in the *Novelas ejemplares*. The difficulty in determining the date of its composition stems not so much from an absence of historical referents within the work as from the errors and internal contradictions it contains regarding historical facts and temporal succession.[10]

The result of the plethora of contradictory conjectures based on an effort to correlate historical and temporal details with the work of fiction itself has been to leave the question of dating unresolved. Suggestions for the dating of *La española inglesa* range from 1596 to 1611, with a

[10] Mack Singleton ("The Date of *La española inglesa*" [1947]: 329–35) and G. Hainsworth (*Les "Novelas ejemplares" de Cervantes en France au XVIIe Siècle* [1933], p. 19) both suggest that the story follows the attack on the port of Cadiz by the English in 1587. This supposition allows Singleton to build on his theory that *La española inglesa* is an early work of Cervantes. Rodríguez Marín (*El Loaysa de "El celoso extremeño"* [1901], p. 235) thinks that the attack referred to took place in 1585 at Cartagena. This permits the proposal of a relatively early dating for him, too.

Internal chronological contradictions have further complicated the question of dating. See, for example, José María Asensio y Toledo, "Sobre *La española inglesa*" (1902): 261–66; Juan Antonio Pellicer, "Vida de Miguel de Cervantes Saavedra" (1797): 133; Allison Peers and Francisco Sánchez-Castañer, eds., *La española inglesa* (1948); and Mack Singleton, "The Date of *La española inglesa*" (1947): 329–35.

The attitude toward Elizabeth I in the work has inspired still another line of inquiry. Icaza (*Las "Novelas ejemplares"* [1916], pp. 162–63) says that the work must have been written after 1605, when the English signed a treaty of peace with the Spanish in Valladolid. Rafael Lapesa ("En torno", 377–80) discusses the question at length and notes that despite the peace treaty, repression against Catholics in England was still strong enough to incur suspicion among Spaniards (see Góngora's sonnet, cited in Narciso Alonso Cortés's *Cervantes en Valladolid* [1918], pp. 75–76: "Parió la Reina; el Luterano vino . . .") in the early years of James I. He suggests that it was later, between 1609 and 1611, that the Spaniards truly began to feel that England might become a Catholic nation again. In 1611, he notes, suggestions of a marriage between James's son Charles and Philip's daughter Anne were being made. Allison Peers ("Cervantes in England" [1947]: 226–27) also notes the atmosphere of acceptance of the English in *La española inglesa*.

liberal sprinkling of intermediary dates from which to choose.[11] The most convincing arguments, however, come from Rafael Lapesa, who supports the belief that *La española inglesa* is a late work by his analysis of the development of Cervantes's thought and writing from *La Galatea* to the *Persiles*.[12]

La española inglesa begins with the mutual consent of a pair of lovers to get married with the blessing of the parents of the young man. With everything all but arranged and the marriage to take place shortly, the Queen of England intervenes to demand of the young man, Recaredo, that he prove himself worthy, on his own merits, of the beautiful young girl, Isabela. This intervention inaugurates a string of complications that end only after both Recaredo and Isabela have faced the possibility of the death of the other, and each has undergone the temptation of an alternative to their marriage. Recaredo has to reject a beautiful Scottish girl whom his parents have selected for him after an illness ravages Isabela's good looks, and Isabela has to accept Recaredo over the life in the convent for which she had prepared herself in the belief that he was dead.[13] By these tests of constancy Recaredo and Isabela exemplify the meaning and difficulty of marriage.

The work is full of displays of generosity of spirit through which the two main characters reveal themselves as exemplary. Their task is not so much to discover their love for one another, or to force recognition of the one by the other, as to explore the depths of the implications, both social and religious, of the marriage which both have already agreed to accept. In *La gitanilla, El amante liberal,* and *La ilustre fregona*, a dialectic was

[11] Singleton, "The Date of *La española inglesa*," suggests 1596. The late dating, however, is more regularly accepted, though for widely differing reasons. The following accept 1611 as the date for the composition of *La española inglesa*: Pellicer, "Vida . . . ," 133; Julián Apraiz, *Estudio . . . sobre las "Novelas ejemplares" de Cervantes* (1901), pp. 63–67; Schevill and Bonilla, Introduction to *Las "Novelas ejemplares"* (1925), 3:383; Lapesa, "En torno," p. 380; Juan Bautista Avalle-Arce, "Introducción," *Los trabajos de Persiles y Sigismunda* (1969), pp. 18–19; and idem., "La captura de Cervantes" (1968): 267, 277–79; and Luís Astrana Marín, *Vida ejemplar y heroica de Miguel de Cervantes Saavedra* (1948–57), 2:20; 7:778.
Intermediary dates are suggested by the following: Asensio ("Sobre *La española inglesa*" [1902]): 1606; Rodríguez Marín (*El Loaysa* [1901], p. 235): 1602–03; Amezúa (*Cervantes, creador*, pp. 128–29): 1604–06; Entwistle (*Cervantes*, p. 98): 1606.

[12] Lapesa's arguments find support and amplification in Avalle-Arce's introduction, in *Los trabajos*, pp. 18–27.

[13] Jennifer Lowe ("The Structure of Cervantes' *La española inglesa*" [1970–71]: 287–90) has revealed beautifully how the trials of the lovers fall into a perfect pattern. The revelation strengthens the point here that the process of self-transcendence through marriage is a mutual one in which both parties are equally engaged.

established between an overly arduous young man and an overly cautious young woman, both of whom learned to modify their positions to discover their identity in their union with one another. In *Las dos doncellas, La señora Cornelia,* and *La fuerza de la sangre,* the untamed passions of a young man had to be controlled by the solicitations of a dishonored woman and her assistants in order to bring the man and woman together in a sanctified union. In *La española inglesa,* however, neither is the young man overly passionate in his solicitations, nor is the young woman overly cautious in her acceptance of him. This story offers the only balance within the *Novelas ejemplares* of the woman's search for marriage and the man's desire for possession. In the other idealistic stories the problem of achieving victory over the self was complicated by the problem of simultaneously achieving victory over the other. In this work, however, the test is clearly seen to be one of each character's separately achieving a proper attitude toward the adversities and uncertainties that are basic to the human condition.

The act which brings the novela and the character of Isabela into being is the theft, by Clotaldo, of a Spanish merchant's only daughter during the sack of Cadiz by the English. Despite the pleas of the girl's father and the demand by the English commander that the child be returned, Clotaldo is so taken by the girl's beauty that he cannot resist bringing her to his wife, although in doing so he incurs danger to himself. The initial act is one of great selfishness and cruelty, if looked at from the point of view of Isabela's distraught parents. When the reader recalls that Clotaldo's theft of a Spanish child is only an example in microcosm of the affront carried out by the English nation upon the Spanish in that sack, a twenty-five day plunder of a port city without defense, he begins to realize the extent of Cervantes's changed perspective in the later works. The conflict highlighted in *La española inglesa* is not one between the English and the Spanish. Elizabeth and Leicester, popularly conceived of as villains in the Spanish imagination, are neutral, if not even slightly admirable characters in this novela. Rather than emphasizing Isabela's parents' anguish, Clotaldo's cruelty, or Elizabeth's antagonism toward Spain, Cervantes removes the work entirely from social or political considerations to emphasize the moral ambiguities of Clotaldo.

Clotaldo's theft of Isabela provides an example of the disjunction between faith and action imposed upon Catholics who had also to be loyal to the Queen of England. The relatively sympathetic light in which both Leicester and Elizabeth are cast suggests that the principal interest in the work is not that the English be condemned for their break with Catholicism, but that the conflict between thought and deed among English

Catholics be exposed and healed. Clotaldo's theft of Isabela represents his unsuccessful resolution of the conflict, since he participated in the sack of Cadiz and stole from a fellow-Catholic. But the stolen girl's beauty and moral perfection will allow her to extricate Clotaldo's son from the contradictions the father was unable to escape. The contradictions are made explicit when one day, shortly before the intended wedding of Recaredo and Isabela, the Queen summons Clotaldo to appear before her with the beautiful young Spanish girl whom she discovers he has been harboring. Clotaldo's greatest fear is that Isabela will expose him and his family as Catholics before the Queen. His weakness is shown in contrast to Isabela's equanimity. The exterior contradiction of being a Catholic in Protestant England is shown to have an interior correlative in Clotaldo's pusillanimity. Cervantes describes the interior rupture between belief and action in Clotaldo and his wife in the following way: ". . . even though they were spiritually ready for martyrdom, still the weak flesh refused its bitter course."[14]

The salvation which Isabela confidently promises them will not take the form any of them anticipates. For it is not the upbringing that Clotaldo and Catalina have given their Spanish captive but her beauty that fascinates the Queen. It is this beauty that causes the Queen to demand of Recaredo actions of valor which would make him worthy of her possession. Recaredo's courage will be drawn on not to test his valor and intelligence, as the Queen thinks, but to try his moral strength. For he must decide how he can both serve the Queen courageously and not compromise the respect he holds for other Catholics. In sailing against Spain in the name of the Queen, he is repeating the dilemma of his father who engaged in the sack of Cadiz. But while Clotaldo's resolution was cowardly, choosing to repay in kindness to a stolen girl the wrong done by his nation to hers, Recaredo's resolution must be daring. His feelings on embarking on the mission the Queen sets for him are described as follows:

. . . Recaredo set sail, torn between two thoughts which, among many others, had him beside himself: The one was considering whether he needed to perform deeds that would make him worthy of Isabela; and the other, that he could not do anything, if he were to remain true to his faith, which prevented him from drawing his sword against other Catholics. If he did not draw it, he would be branded as a Catholic or a coward, and all this would threaten his life and hinder the attainment of his goals. But, finally, he decided to subordinate his pleasure as a lover to his obligations as a Catholic, and in his heart

---

[14] ". . . puesto que estaban prontos con el espíritu a recibir martirio, todavía la carne enferma rehusaba su amarga carrera" (VP, 856).

he asked Heaven to offer him chances in which, while being brave, he could fulfill his duty as a Catholic, satisfying the Queen and winning Isabela.[15]

The dilemma having been presented, Cervantes places his character in a situation in which his resolve can be tested. The Baron of Lansac, Recaredo's immediate superior and commander of the two-ship fleet of which Recaredo is second in command, is reported to have died, just as Recaredo sights three ships, two of which appear to be Turkish galleons. Recaredo assuming command, the English deftly handle the attack which the Turkish ships initiate against them and manage to sink one and to capture the other, thus freeing the Christian galley slaves who then join in with the British in finishing off the Turks. The third ship turns out to be Spanish, loaded with spices and jewels from India. At this point Recaredo must show his real courage, confronting his crew as their new, young, and inexperienced commander, with the decision to let all the Spaniards go free. The climate of hostility in which this command is made by Recaredo is revealed in the suggestion by some that they kill all the captives, one by one, as they enter the ship, thus avoiding the possibility that the released Spaniards might alert their fleets and send another ship in pursuit. Recaredo, in deciding on clemency toward the Spaniards, is risking not only his own exposure as a Catholic, but his entire booty and perhaps the lives of him and his crew to Spanish vengeance. He nonetheless holds firm to his resolution, giving freedom and money and the use of their ship to the Spaniards and twenty extra Turks as well. Since they are within sight of the Spanish shore, the action is risky indeed. The drama of his decision is heightened when the wind appears to die and the crew begins to voice fears that they will not be able to escape a counterattack by the Spaniards: "The wind, which showed signs of being lasting and favorable, began to calm slightly, which calm awoke a great storm of fear in the English, who blamed Recaredo and his generosity."[16]

The repetition of the conflict in the father by the mission of the son to

[15] "Recaredo se hizo a la vela, combatido, entre otros muchos, de dos pensamientos que le tenían fuera de sí: era el uno el considerar que le convenía hacer hazañas que le hiciesen merecedor de Isabela, y el otro, que no podía hacer ninguna, si había de responder a su católico intento, que le impedía no desenvainar la espada contra católicos; y si no la desenvainaba, había de ser notado de cristiano o de cobarde, y todo esto redundaba en perjuicio de su vida y en obstáculo de su pretensión. Pero, en fin, determinó de posponer al gusto de enamorado el que tenía de ser católico, y en su corazón pedía al Cielo le deparase ocasiones donde, con ser valiente, cumpliese con ser cristiano, dejando a su reina satisfecha y a Isabela merecida" (VP, 858).

[16] "El viento, que daba señales de ser próspero y largo, comenzó a calmar un tanto, cuya calma levantó gran tormenta de temor a los ingleses, que culpaban a Recaredo y a su liberalidad" (VP, 861).

attack and conquer Catholic forces in the name of the English reveals a reversal of reactions when it becomes clear that whereas the father was the instrument for the separation of Isabela from her parents, Recaredo will be the means by which they are restored to her. The last Spaniards to leave their ship turn out to be Isabela's parents, who beg Recaredo to take them to England so they can look for their daughter. Again the author rewards the correct actions of his protagonist with fortuitous circumstances that will help him in the ultimate fulfillment of his wishes. Had Recaredo obeyed the instincts of fear and repression that were expressed by others and which surely constituted a temptation for him, he would have killed the very ones whom his father had dishonored eight years earlier. By replacing a sense of individual goodness with a sense of universal goodness, Recaredo has reversed the trend of the timid Catholicism of his parents and rectified the wrong they did in separating Isabela from her parents. His actions prove that generosity and Christian kindness cannot be reserved for a few and maintained in privacy. They must be openly demonstrated, without discrimination or expectation of personal gain. This is why Recaredo's act is shown to be dangerous to himself and at the same time accidentally redemptive of his father's weakness.

Recaredo will not know the full meaning of his act of clemency until the end when he finds his act reciprocated in Spain and Algiers. Nor is it clear to him that the fulfillment of his hopes for marriage to Isabela is contingent upon more than a question of his personal valor. For although he presented the Queen with a ship so loaded with riches that eight days were needed to unload it, and though he kept his faith intact and restored Isabela's parents to her, the overall trajectory of the novela requires much more of him. True restitution of the wrong done to Isabela must be made by returning her to Spain and reuniting her with her family, and by unifying the opposing demands of duty to Queen and duty to religion that weaken his father. Only when Recaredo can live his Catholicism openly will the individual weakness that gave initial impulse to the story be overcome. That is, he can only truly escape his father's sins by separating himself from his parents as they had forced Isabela's parents to be separated from her. The task of the author is to be sure that the union of Recaredo and Isabela is effected in a way that will provide proper punishment to Clotaldo and a·proper climate for the full expression of Catholicism for his son. Thus, the ending brings back to Spain on a deeper, more spiritual level all the things that were taken from it. By the time Recaredo appears in Seville he has fulfilled his faith by making a pilgrimage to Rome. His marriage to Isabela is more than a personal test of worth. It is a restitution of justice and the reintegration on the religious plane of characters normally held apart because of language and nationality.

When some of Recaredo's crew suggest to him that he kill all of the captive Spaniards, he answers with a statement that could be taken as typical of the exemplary characters of Cervantes's later works. "It is not well," he answers, "to remedy by means of the sword that which I can remedy by my hard work."[17] The tone is set from the beginning by the generosity with which the author presents Clotaldo, the Queen, the "Conde de Leste," and even the sack of Cadiz. But it is Isabela, within the novel, who most fully exemplifies this open and forgiving character. Although she was seven years old when taken from her family and remembers and yearns for her parents often, she shows no signs of rebelling against her English parents or showing any attitude toward them except one of love and respect. She is so generous in her attitude toward others that she does not question what they have done, but only follows what she takes to be her duty in whatever circumstances she finds herself. She says to Recaredo, when he asks her to marry him: "After the rigor or the kindness of Heaven, for I don't know to which of these extremes I should attribute it, chose to take me from my parents, Señor Recaredo, and give me to yours, grateful for the infinite kindnesses they have done for me, I decided my will would never contradict theirs. Thus, without their approval, I would take not as good, but rather as bad fortune the inestimable kindness you wish to do me."[18] In her response she shows her character to be superior to both Clotaldo's and Recaredo's. For Clotaldo contradicted authority by stealing Isabela, and Recaredo, fearing his parents' insistence that he marry the Scottish girl, had proposed to Isabela that they marry without his parents' knowledge. Isabela's position forces Recaredo not to be evasive with his parents, who turn out to be very easily persuaded of the correctness of their son's choice.

The initial cowardice of Clotaldo and Recaredo shows a weakness in their faith. Recaredo is afraid he cannot make his parents recognize the worth that he has found in Isabela. Rather than trying to make them see it, he is willing to act out his beliefs in hiding. His attitude toward Isabela at that point duplicates the attitude of his family toward their Catholicism. In contrast to Clotaldo's complicated imaginings Isabela shows a calm faith. When it is later reported by some of the envious girls at the Queen's court that Isabela is as strong in her Catholicism as she had earlier shown

---

[17] ". . . ni es bien que lo que puedo remediar con la industria lo remedie con la espada" (VP, 860).

[18] "Después que quiso el rigor o la clemencia del Cielo, que no sé a cuál de estos extremos lo atribuya, quitarme a mis padres, señor Recaredo, y darme a los vuestros, agradecida a las infinitas mercedes que me han hecho, determiné que jamás mi voluntad saliese de la suya; y así, sin ella tendría no por buena, sino por mala fortuna, la inestimable merced que queréis hacerme" (VP, 855).

herself to be in her respect for the wishes of her adoptive parents, the Queen is shown to hold her in even higher regard. Twice, then, once in opposition to Recaredo and once in opposition to Clotaldo, Isabela has shown that in the face of firmness of convictions openly expressed, the supposed opponent is not likely to be intransigent.

Isabela's parents show the same acceptance and absence of resentment as their daughter on discovering the man responsible for her theft and the Queen under whose direction the sack of Cadiz, which left them destitute, took place. Their thankful and forgiving spirit facilitates the offering of kindnesses that the Queen, Clotaldo, and Catalina bestow on them. In place of bitter resentment, Isabela and her family leave England with jewels and promises of money from the Queen, and the lasting friendship of Clotaldo and Catalina.

The kindness and acceptance that the Catholic characters show and the resultant unity of spirit they achieve is made more obvious by the presence of inferior Protestant characters who are prone to envy and desperation. Just as the advice of some of the crew to kill the Spaniards is counterposed by Recaredo's equanimity, so the jealousy and brutality of Arnesto and his mother serve as counterpoint to Isabela, Recaredo, and their families. Arnesto is represented as arrogant and high-handed. He immediately becomes desperate when his solicitations of Isabela in Recaredo's absence are to no avail. His tendency to absolute solutions and spontaneous reactions frightens his mother into petitioning the Queen for a delay in the wedding. When Arnesto's impetuousness impels him to rush to Recaredo and challenge him to a duel, the Queen interrupts the action through one of her guards and has Arnesto imprisoned. It is then the mother's turn to show her faithless desperation and cruelty. Arnesto's mother gives Isabela a nearly fatal poison. When the Queen imprisons the desperate woman, she tries to excuse herself by saying that she was doing God's work by removing from the world another Catholic and saving her son from anguish.

These characters, of course, are not only symbols of faithlessness to be compared with the serenity of Isabela and Recaredo; their actions also materially affect the lives of the major characters and represent to them the final obstacles they must overcome in the process of purifying their faith. The poison renders Isabela ugly and no longer of interest to the Queen. If her stay with the Queen represented the peak of her worldly fortunes, it also exposed her to the depths of worldly degradation. From that climax at the center of the story, Isabela must retrace her footsteps back to her origin, her physical descent—represented both by her loss of beauty and her removal from the court—being countered by a movement of continual ascent on the spiritual level. From the Queen's palace Isabela returns to Clotaldo's home to find that, since she is showing no signs of recovering her lost beauty, Clotaldo and Catalina, like the Queen before them, no longer want her to remain with them. They resurrect instead the idea of bringing Clisterna, the Scottish girl, back as wife to their son. Plans are made for Isabela and her parents to return to Spain. The rejection is not absolute, however, and this is a tribute to Cervantes's consistency of tone throughout the work. Having shown both Clotaldo and the Queen as morally complex figures, capable of generous actions within a limited scope, and having refused to oversimplify either the inherent goodness of Catholics or the inherent badness of Protestants, Cervantes allows these intermediary figures to show some responsibility to Isabela and her parents, even as they make clear the superficiality of their attachment to her. As a result, Isabela and her parents return to Seville restored financially to their position before the sack of Cadiz.

In the two years between Isabela and Recaredo's departure from England and their marriage in Seville the two undergo separately, and in conformity with their social roles, a process of spiritual purification. In Recaredo's case the purification takes the form of a pilgrimage, in which the fulfillment of religious aspirations culminates in his arrival in Rome. The difficulties of his pilgrimage include an attempted murder by Arnesto and his capture by the Moors while on his way to Spain. Isabela's spiritual purification is of an interior nature, as she suffers in the belief that Recaredo has been killed. She overcomes desperation by preparing herself to enter the convent, careful nonetheless to keep her word to Recaredo to wait two years before giving up hope. When finally Recaredo appears, on the very day when Isabela is preparing to enter the convent, the two are completely tested, both separately and together, in social as well as in religious spheres. In this triumph of faith and generosity the author rewards them for their temperance.

In *La española inglesa* can be found the most complete statement in the *Novelas ejemplares* of Cervantes's preoccupation with religion. This is the religion which requires both self-purification and acceptance of life. For Isabela and Recaredo not only culminate their struggle in marriage and end their separate tests of isolated spiritual purification in union, but each constantly acts in such a way as to accept the other. Isabela showed no hostility toward Clotaldo and Catalina, and Recaredo showed no desire for vengeance when faced with Arnesto. Their *askesis* does not, in other words, lead them away from society, no matter how corrupt, but toward it in a generosity that offers a rediscovery of human unity. The joining of Recaredo and Isabela is an example of Catholic generosity which transcends national boundaries. It is the resurrection of the dream of peace on earth and the recovery of faith in the unity of all things despite the presence of forces of disruption and disintegration.

In *La española inglesa* the voice of the narrator dominates the story. When Isabela first appears before the Queen, for example, great care is taken with the description of her dress and the effect her presence has on the spectators, the narrator clearly taking pride in the skill with which he paints her: "The hall was large and spacious. Those accompanying her took two steps and stopped, and Isabela went forward. When she stood alone, she resembled a star or a flash of light which moves through the region of fire on a calm and tranquil night, or the rays of the sun which at the break of day appear between the mountains. She seemed all this, and even like a comet which anticipated the setting afire of more than one of the souls who were there."[19] The recourse to the cosmos in descriptions is typical of Baroque poetry and also suggests the borderline between temporality and eternity, between finitude and the infinite which Cervantes seeks to capture in the idealistic tales. Isabela, in her assured faith, embodies the serenity and changelessness of the stars.

None of the characters has distinctive linguistic traits, and even the words they speak conform rather to the general and typical than to the particular and individual. The lack of attention to details in the characterizations presented has often been remarked. Queen Elizabeth, for example, says upon meeting Isabela that she knows Spanish well, yet she requires an interpreter when talking to Isabela's parents. Recaredo likewise speaks Spanish on one occasion only to need help with it on another. Isabela is never shown speaking English or Spanish with an accent, as characters such as the Biscayan did in *Don Quixote* I. She symbolizes perfection in a young lady: she is obedient, devout, beautiful, she can read and write, play musical instruments, and sing. Through all her adversities she remains serene, never resentful or self-serving. Recaredo also speaks in a way that reveals not his particular traits, but his perfection within the expectations of a young man of his position. He is ardent yet respectful as a lover, a valiant and temperate leader, handsome and just.

Unlike the other idealistic stories, no selfish passions threaten the love between the two major characters. Recaredo and Isabela cannot be said to develop in the same way as Andrés and Preciosa, or Tomás de Avendaño and Costanza. Jealousy only appears in the minor characters, the ladies at court being envious of Isabela's beauty and claim on Recaredo, and Arnesto being jealous of Recaredo. But there is development to the extent

---

[19] "Era la sala grande y espaciosa, y a dos pasos se quedó el acompañamiento y se adelantó Isabela; y como quedó sola, pareció lo mismo que parece la estrella o exhalación que por la región del fuego en serena y sosegada noche suele moverse, o bien así como rayo de sol que al salir del día por entre dos montañas se descubre; todo esto pareció, y aún cometa que pronosticó el incendio de más de un alma de los que allí estaban" (VP, 856).

that Recaredo and Isabela learn to accept each other in an increasingly spiritual way as a result of the difficulties they encounter. In this learning process, all the other characters are instruments. The lack of bitterness shown in the characterization of Elizabeth by Cervantes can be explained by the abstract conception of her role. When she commands Recaredo to prove himself valiant before marrying Isabela, her words sound like the voice of the author: "He will not be [married] to Isabela until he merits her on his own terms; that is to say, I do not want your [Clotaldo's] services to help him in this, nor the services of his ancestors: he himself must serve me and earn himself this jewel, for I honor her as if she were my daughter."[20] Explaining what she wants of him, the Queen tells Recaredo: "Take notice of the favor I am doing you. I am giving you the chance thereby so that, in a manner worthy of your station, serving your Queen, you may show the valor of your intellect and of your whole being."[21] The test to which the Queen puts Recaredo is the test of personal worth, imposed by Cervantes in the story and by God in life as necessary to personal salvation.

Arnesto likewise is an instrument of the author, playing no other role than arrogant villain in the story. He incarnates the passions which Recaredo must subdue in his quest for possession of Isabela. Beyond his role as interrupter of Recaredo's plans and his position as obverse to Recaredo's perfection, Arnesto does not exist in the story. His mother, who administers the poison which nearly kills Isabela, is also unimportant in herself. She remains, in fact, unnamed in the story, as do the women in court whose envious comments are allowed occasionally to slip into the narrative.[22]

[20] "Ni lo estará—dijo la reina—con Isabela hasta que por sí mismo lo merezca; quiero decir que no quiero que para esto le aprovechen vuestros servicios ni de sus pasados: él por sí mismo se ha de disponer a servirme y a merecer por sí esta prenda, que yo la estimo como si fuese mi hija" (VP, 857).

[21] ". . . y advertid a la merced que os hago, pues os doy ocasión en ella a que, correspondiendo a quien sois, sirviendo a vuestra reina, mostréis el valor de vuestro ingenio y de vuestra persona" (VP, 857).

[22] Avalle-Arce makes this same point with regard to the *Persiles*, whose last two books he identifies closely with *La española inglesa*: "La intención universalizadora del autor tiene, como consecuencia y contrapartida, la abstracción. Y por ello, los principales personajes del *Persiles* son todos unidimensionales y acartonados. No son cuerpos opacos de carne y hueso, sino transparentes símbolos de validez universal: Persiles y Sigismunda son los perfectos amantes cristianos, Rosamunda es la lascivia, Clodio la maledicencia, etc." ["The universalizing intent of the author has, as a consequence and counterpart, abstraction. And for that reason, the principal characters of the *Persiles* are all cartoon-like and one-dimensional. They are not opaque bodies of flesh and blood, but rather, transparent symbols of universal validity: Persiles and Sigismunda are the perfect Christian lovers, Rosamunda is lasciviousness, Clodio is the evil-tongued, etc."] ("Introducción," *Los trabajos*, p. 27).

The combination of the skill and descriptive powers of the author and the stereotyped dialogues of the characters, inhibits the presentation of autonomous characters such as those who dominated the earlier stories. In *La española inglesa* the major characters do not invent the situation in which they find themselves. Their exemplarity derives from the constancy and devotion to eternal principles they display when assaulted by the challenges of a reality characterized by corruption, flux, and decay. The other characters, to the extent that they take their fortunes into their own hands, are evil or inconsequential. The perception of exemplarity which dominates the idealistic tales also determines that the major characters will appear to be controlled by the author's will, and that they will be described more as ideal types than as unique characters. In this lessened importance of individualism, the thoughts of the characters are not stressed. The author, therefore, spends more time in description and the narration of the events which affect the characters' plans. Everything is at once more static and more external.

Only when Recaredo arrives in Seville to marry Isabela does he take on the role of narrator of his own story. Recaredo recounts to the assembled company the story of his pilgrimage to Rome, the attack on him by Arnesto, his captivity, and his release. This taking over of the narrator's role is especially interesting since in the narration Recaredo offers one of the fullest accounts of Cervantes's own captivity and release.[23] When Recaredo has finished, the ecclesiastics encourage Isabela to write the story, affirming thereby the combined role of both characters in the process of literary creation. The moral with which Cervantes ends the story suggests that the reader learn "how heaven can derive out of our greatest adversities, our greatest good fortune."[24] The reflection appears to have meaning for Recaredo and Isabela and Cervantes as well, since at the end the characters take up the author's role and narrate a story true to the life of Cervantes himself. This is the most abstract formulation of the idea, developed in the *Casamiento-Coloquio*, that through writing a man can transform his disgraces into good fortune. In the final stories, Cervantes adds a religious dimension to this understanding. It might also be pointed out that the site of the reunion between Recaredo and Isabela and the place where Recaredo will be allowed to live in harmony with his religious beliefs is the same Seville which appears in *Rinconete y Cortadillo*, the story immediately preceding *La española inglesa* in the *Novelas ejemplares*. The alternation of early and late stories in the collection takes on

---

[23] See Avalle-Arce, "La captura de Cervantes," pp. 267–68; 277–80.
[24] ". . . cómo sabe el Cielo sacar de las mayores adversidades nuestros mayores provechos" (VP, 874).

added significance if it is noted that the spiritualization achieved in *La española inglesa* elevates not only Recaredo and Isabela within the novela, but Seville, which had been portrayed in the preceding work as the seat of corruption and dissolution.

VII. CONCLUSION

Both the character's desire to escape "fiction" and to return to his original self, and the ultimate realization that there is a reality beyond the limited perspective of the normal role, introduce an air of apparent conformism in Cervantes's later works. The return to society and religion which forms the denouement of all of the idealistic tales in the *Novelas ejemplares*, as well as the *Persiles* and *Don Quixote* Part II, involves an expression of choice and free will on the part of the characters. The apparent loss of liberty is discussed by many of the male characters who finally accept marriage in the *novelas* (Marco Antonio in *Las dos doncellas*, and Ricardo in *La fuerza de la sangre*). What they come to see is that the liberty of flight which they have so cherished is illusory and that true liberty can come only through acceptance of a reality beyond the self.

What this means for the novel is a rejection of the perspectivism so often discussed as the hallmark of Cervantes's works. In *Don Quixote* Part I no choices are made between the various characters' visions of the world because Cervantes could conceive of no authority beyond that of the individual. The chaos of this vision of the world is suggested in the very structural disunity of Part I, as well as in Anselmo's disastrous enterprise (in *El curioso impertinente*), Fernando's near-rejection of Dorotea, Grisóstomo's suicide, Marcela's constant flight, and Zoraida's rejection of her father.

J. Hillis Miller, in a study on Conrad,[1] has shown very clearly how this particular vision imposes certain techniques on the novelist trying to represent it. Explaining Conrad's conception of reality as a menacing darkness out of which meanings are arbitrarily carved, he describes some characteristics of Conrad's novelistic technique which could as well be applied to Cervantes: "His habit of multiplying narrators and points of view, so that sometimes an event is told filtered through several consciousnesses, his reconstruction of the chronological sequence to make a pattern of progressive revelation, his use of a framing story—all these techniques increase the distance between the reader and the events as they

---

[1] "Joseph Conrad," *Poets of Reality* (1969).

were lived by the characters" (p. 17). In another place he says: "Conrad habitually calls attention to the conflict between the qualitative aspect of things and the interpretation of what is seen into recognizable objects" (p. 24). It is easy to see the "baciyelmo" episode in this comment. An even more specific statement of the relation between the breakdown in the concept of authority and the challenge of the word's ability to capture meaning is made by Ihab Hassan: "The suspicion of language reflects a more radical mistrust of reason, history, and social organization. At bottom, the revolt is directed against those inseparable twins, authority and abstraction. For authority in social life and abstraction in language are corollaries: they are commandments issued to the flesh, coercing private experience into objective order."[2]

The breakdown of authority and the emergence of the individual belong to the heritage of the twentieth-century critics who revel so in Cervantes's masterpiece and find his idealistic tales and the *Persiles* so difficult to understand or to appreciate. The evolution of the modern novel has clearly followed the development of the middle-class individualism glimpsed by Cervantes and fully presented by later novelists. But Cervantes belonged, after all, as Casalduero so rightly insists, to the seventeenth century and not to the nineteenth or twentieth. Like his near-contemporary, Descartes, Cervantes took a peek into the future, into the chaotic uncertainties of individual perceptions unguided by authority and without the reassurances that rational thought or empirical data could offer, and shut the door again. Despite their profound insights, or perhaps because of them, Cervantes and Descartes both rediscovered beyond individual uncertainties a benign transcendent reality the perfection of which could not include the deliberate maintenance of man in an ambiguous condition.

The rediscovery of certainty for Cervantes means that the characters can no longer appear autonomous, that the author need no longer disguise himself through a series of surrogates, need no longer, in fact, place himself as a character within the fiction he is creating. When once he accepts the reality of a truth beyond his own, he is able to assert his control over his fictional world without apology. Like God to man, Cervantes as author becomes the ultimately benevolent creator who must test his characters' faith. He puts the character through a variety of difficulties, allowing the character's hopes finally to prevail if he has maintained proper faith that his goals are in fact attainable. There is a dialectic between author and character in the later works, but it is established not within the work, but in the interaction between a character inside and an author outside. The character inside must persistently maintain his vision fixed beyond the

---

[2] Ihab Hassan, "The Dismemberment of Orpheus: Notes on Form and Antiform in Contemporary Literature" (1964).

complications which entangle him, and the author, in accordance with his character's will and faith, corresponds by gradually unraveling the web in which he has placed him.

To summarize the distinctions being made here between pre-1606 works of Cervantes and the ones written after 1606: the later works show a more tightly knit and self-contained fictional structure than the earlier ones, the characters have much more clearly defined goals, come from good families, and display no fundamental disaccord with their social or religious backgrounds.[3] The author is much more confident, in the later works, of his narrative abilities and is much more willing to manipulate his characters' circumstances. In a word, the author appears to be more self-assuredly omniscient in the later period and more removed from his characters.

The techniques used in *Don Quixote* Part I are, on the other hand, much more "modern." For Cervantes, at the time when he was writing the first part, was living in a much more modern sense of uncertainty. Américo Castro, so sensitive to the lived reality of the author on whose work he comments so extensively, points out that Cervantes, while trying always to be first in whatever he did, found himself by 1599 at the nadir of his fortunes—penniless, jailed, unrecognized, isolated.[4] As Castro has said, whether *Don Quixote* was actually started in jail, it was at least engendered in a moment of most complete personal alienation on the part of its author.[5] The underlying sense of personal disorientation which is a part of our modern Western heritage appears to carry with it certain authorial stances which have become part of the tradition of the modern novel. We can only associate Cervantes's use of Cide Hamete and the story-within-a-story structure, the perspectivism, and the verbal uncertainty, with Cervantes's own self-doubts as a man and as an author. He lets the characters create their own worlds in *Don Quixote* Part I and other earlier stories. They are—like the author—seeking definition in a reality which has left them undefined and self-alienated. The character-autonomy and the presence of a multiple-author structure attest to the insecurity and hesitancy of Cervantes with respect to his literary creations. When this is coupled with the character's own floundering sense of distance from his surroundings, the conclusion that the technique reflects the content of the work is inescapable.

Ironically, the full exploitation of his talent, which Cervantes appears

---

[3] The exception made of *Don Quixote* II has been explained by the preestablished role set for Don Quixote in the 1605 work (see chapter I, pp. 11–12).

[4] "La ejemplaridad de las *Novelas ejemplares*" (1967), p. 462.

[5] "Los prólogos al *Quijote*" (1967), p. 264: "Se ha escrito mucho sobre la cárcel en que pudo empezar a forjarse el *Quijote*; lo evidente para mí es que tuvo que ser concebido en la más apartada reclusión del ánimo cervantino, allí justamente donde toda incomodidad tiene su asiento."

to effect between 1606 and 1616, has produced little which is appreciated by the modern reader. The shift is not unlike Thomas Mann's, both in its paradoxical nature and in its direction. John Henry Raleigh[6] describes the remarkable difference between *Doctor Faustus* and *The Holy Sinner,* defending the latter, against critical incomprehension, as belonging to a universe conceived of as orderly: Catholic and classic. Leverkühn, in *Doctor Faustus,* carries the image of individualism to its extreme of despair: "Syphilitic, migrain-wracked, ridden by demons, he makes a pact with the Devil, in order to produce great but despairing music." This hero-creator—not so far from Ensign Campuzano or from Cañizares, in the *Coloquio de los perros*—gives way in another work which appears to represent a return from the haunts of a chaotic world without authority. It is literature in this atmosphere which we find difficult to comprehend. Raleigh says: "For almost a century now in the literature of our civilization it has been assumed that the sane, the simple, the unqualifiedly good cannot be taken seriously. . . . Yet it must be remembered that an art which is not a substitute for religion, that is unpretentiously benign and humanistic, would have been perfectly meaningful to many past epochs and it may well happen that it will be perfectly meaningful to some in the future." As Conrad wrote to Edward Garnett: "When once the truth is grasped that one's own personality is only a ridiculous and aimless masquerade of something hopelessly unknown, the attainment of serenity is not very far off."[7]

We can speculate on the reasons for this change in Cervantes's perspective in his later years, but the fact that such a change took place seems conclusive. Judged in the light of both the overt religious framework of the *Persiles* and the clear exemplarity of its major characters, as well as the concomitant stylistic changes that can be seen not only in the *Persiles* but in *Don Quixote* II, we can only take at face value the claim to exemplarity Cervantes makes in his prologue to the *Novelas ejemplares* and in the title he gives his collection.

---

[6] "Mann's *Doctor Faustus and the Holy Sinner,*" in *Time, Place and Idea: Essays on the Novel* (1968).

[7] Quoted from Miller, "Joseph Conrad," p. 35. I am indebted to Peter Dunn for yet another quote regarding a shift toward order and serenity in a great author's work. Quoting Northrop Frye on Shakespeare's mature romances he says, ". . . they do not avoid tragedies but contain them. The action seems to be not only a movement from a 'winter's tale' to spring, but from a lower world of confusion to an upper world of order. The closing scene of *The Winter's Tale* makes us think, not simply of a cyclical movement from tragedy and absence to happiness and return, but of bodily metamorphosis and a transformation from one kind of life to another . . . we see the action, in short, from the point of view of a higher and better ordered world."

It is well known that at least two of the early novelas, *Rinconete y Cortadillo* and the *Celoso extremeño*, were rather seriously altered before being published in the collection. Judging from this fact alone, it is hard to believe that Cervantes's arrangement of the works within the collection was fortuitous.[8] Comments in the prologue heighten this sense of the work's over-all unity, as Casalduero has pointed out. For every early work of despair and uncertainty, Cervantes countered in his collection with one of idealism and goodness. The entire work, seen in this light, culminates in the *Casamiento-Coloquio*. These final stories reveal precisely the movement by Cervantes out of despair as a man and uncertainty as an author toward a full understanding of his role in both areas. The prominent position given the *Casamiento* and the *Coloquio* underscores the idea that they most fully capture the meaning of the collection taken as a whole, for they recall the period of uncertainty and despair, while pointing a way out for an author thoroughly disabused and purged of his infirmities. By ending the collection with these two stories, Cervantes shows exactly the relation, established through the alternate pattern of stories in the collection, that he sees between "corrupt" reality and fiction. Fiction is seen to be not only the mirror of reality, but the means by which the author and the character and the reader discover and recreate themselves. The author, no less than the characters, is shown in the *Casamiento-Coloquio* to be a part of the process of deceiving and being deceived which marks our normal existence. When the fictional reader of the *Coloquio* praises the manuscript not for its credibility, but rather for its artifice and invention, we see Cervantes tracing the steps which led him out of realism, out of a sense of desperation with his unsuccessful past, and into a vision of himself, as artist, liberated from that past, and liberating, at the same time, his fantasy for fuller explorations of the now boundless realm of imaginative literature. The *Casamiento-Coloquio* marks the turning point, chronologically, between the pre-1606 novelas and those that were written later— between the realistic and the idealistic tales collected in the *Novelas ejemplares*.

In the idealistic novelas the retreat from a temporal vision of man and fiction, the retreat from individualism and perspectivism becomes increas-

---

[8] W. C. Atkinson, "Cervantes, El Pinciano, and the *Novelas ejemplares*" (1948): 194, notes the alternating pattern of what he considers early and late works: pre-Pinciano works of little value, and post-Pinciano works of considerable sophistication. Joaquín Casalduero (*Sentido y forma de las "Novelas ejemplares"* [1969]) develops a much more complex scheme for explaining the ordering of the works in the collection, which he takes to be an organic whole and not merely a composite of separate works. My own explanation for the ordering of the *Novelas ejemplares* is taken up in detail in chapter III, pp. 82–85.

ingly marked. Minor characters give up their positions as characters to become representative of various aspects of man's folly, while major characters show less and less development, standing instead as bulwarks of stability and perfection in a menacing world. In this realm of the "No-Longer,"[9] Cervantes's idealistic novelas point the way not toward the modern novel, but toward the romance, where abstraction and authority are enshrined.

The *Novelas ejemplares* capture, in a way similar to the two parts of *Don Quixote*, the trajectory of Cervantes's development as a man and as an artist. The strong differences that separate the stories into groups represent not authorial schizophrenia or senility or hypocrisy or a response to monetary pressure, but, through their intermixture in the collection, an organic whole built up through struggle and confusion toward release in a full acceptance of transcendent truths. The stories are not opposites, as their very different styles would suggest, but complementary parts of a totality perceived by Cervantes when, near the end of his life, he gathered them together in one "exemplary" collection, the value of which was to be derived "from each one in itself and from all together."

[9] I take this expression from Georg Lukacs's *Solzhenitsyn* (1970), p. 7.

APPENDIX: THE CHRONOLOGY PROBLEM

The problem of chronology in Cervantes's work is complicated by the presence of two very different types of fiction the outlines of which are noted by almost every critic of his work. The two types, conveniently labeled "idealistic" and "realistic," have led to various explanations which can be broken down into two basic approaches: (1) a chronological approach which posits a development either from idealism to realism or vice versa; and (2) an atemporal approach which suggests that Cervantes was an artist in whom the poles of realism and idealism coexisted untranscended. A variation of this later approach subordinates the idealistic tales by transforming them into an aberration originating in senility or hypocrisy.

In either case, whether the critic takes a chronological or an atemporal approach to the problem of the "two Cervantes," our modern predilection for the realistic tales tends to reveal itself in the conclusions drawn. The idealistic tales have regularly presented to nineteenth- or twentieth-century critics a problem which must be explained away. William C. Atkinson's commentary on the *Novelas ejemplares* is typical: "Seven of the tales in the collection, as every critic has noted, are divided by an aesthetic abyss from the other five. These latter—those omitted by Rodríguez Marín in his *Clásicos castellanos* edition—have no claim to be either new or exemplary. Conceived in the Italianate tradition of amorous intrigue, incredible coincidence, and total innocence of philosophic intention, they constitute an artistic anachronism in the company of the other seven."[1]

Two preconceptions tend to cause critics who adopt a chronological approach to conclude that the realistic tales represent a late development in Cervantes's work. The first is that idealism is not characteristic of Spanish literature, whose great works belong to the realist tradition. It is this attitude that contributes to the impression that Cervantes's idealistic tales are "Italianate" and are therefore a product of his early years in Italy.[2]

---

[1] "Cervantes, El Pinciano, and the *Novelas ejemplares*" (1948): 194.

[2] Franco Meregalli ("La literatura italiana en la obra de Cervantes" [1971]: 1–15) shows decisively that Cervantes's "realism" owes as much, if not more, to the Italian tradition as does his idealism, citing especially Cervantes's debt to Boccaccio and Ariosto.

The other is a product of nineteenth- and twentieth-century materialistic thought. Seeing progress in general as an inevitable movement from the abstract to the concrete, from the ideal to the real, an almost unconscious assumption has developed over the past century that Cervantes's idealism was replaced by a later realism of the sort that culminated in *Don Quixote*.[3]

The problem with any analysis which proposes that the idealistic tales are works of Cervantes's youth is that the *Persiles*, of a clearly idealistic stamp, was published in 1616. This has led many commentators to make excuses for the work: it was written early, but published late to make money;[4] or it was the product of senility.[5] On the other hand, *Don Quixote* I was finished in 1605, and *Rinconete y Cortadillo*, always esteemed by those who celebrate Cervantes's realistic tendencies, was written before that. If there is to be a development *toward* realism, the analysis forces the doubtful conclusion that after 1605 Cervantes's art did not develop at all. Yet it is precisely between 1606 and 1616 that he pub-

---

[3] E.g., Francisco Icaza (*Las "Novelas ejemplares" de Cervantes* . . . [1916]) who considers the "Italianate" tales (e.g., *Las dos doncellas*), along with the "autobiographical" tales (e.g., *El amante liberal*) to be the earliest written. Icaza's ideas are echoed by Blanca de los Ríos ("Prólogo," *Novelas ejemplares* [1916]) and by E. B. Place (*Manual elemental de novelística española* [1926]). More recently, August Rüegg (*Miguel de Cervantes und sein "Don Quijote"* [1949]) continues the assumption that the "Italianate" stories were written first. G. Hainsworth (*Les "Novelas ejemplares" de Cervantes en France au XVIIe Siècle* [1933], p. 15) follows this pattern to some extent by assuming that the "realistic" stories represent a late development in Cervantes's work, which suggests that the idealistic tales were also written late.

[4] Mack Singleton, "The *Persiles* Mystery" (1947). Though with considerably more subtlety and ingenuity, Stanislav Zimic ("El *Persiles* como crítica de la novela bizantina" [1970]) arrives at the conclusion that if not written early, the *Persiles* was written mainly for economic reasons: "Es posible que escribiendo el *Persiles* Cervantes quisiera de veras entregarse a su último sueño romántico . . ., pero es también muy posible que lo escribiera sencillamente porque por aquel entonces las novelas bizantinas estaban de moda" (p. 63). ["It is possible that in writing the *Persiles* Cervantes really wanted to yield himself to his final romantic dream . . ., but it is also very possible that he wrote it simply because at that time byzantine novels were in vogue."]

[5] Although Mack Singleton (ibid.) attributes this sentiment, without citing the source, to Menéndez Pelayo, it seems fairer to conclude that Mack Singleton himself, rather than Menéndez Pelayo, finds this plausible. Menéndez Pelayo refers, in "Cultura literaria de Miguel de Cervantes y elaboración del *Quijote*" (1956), to the *Persiles* as a work of Cervantes's old age, as Singleton correctly states. But nowhere does he imply, despite Singleton's assertion to the contrary, that the work was the product of senility. Singleton, though, makes considerable use of the term to strengthen his basic argument that the *Persiles* is a work unworthy of the full flowering of Cervantes's artistry.

lished most prolifically, when he was free to live by his writing alone, and when he was universally recognized as a writer of stature.

Commentators such as Rudolf Schevill and James Fitzmaurice-Kelly suggest, without adducing any reasons other than biographical ones, that most of Cervantes's writing was done between 1606 and 1616.[6] Although Américo Castro also considers the idealistic tales to have been written between 1606 and 1612, his position does not differ essentially from that of other critics who assume that Cervantes's artistic development traced a movement toward realism. Castro's explanation for the idealistic tales— "aquellas novelitas ingenuas"[7]—recalls his famous conclusion that "Cervantes es un hábil hipócrita."[8] Castro does not conclude that the idealistic tales were written before 1600, but only that they do not represent the

[6] Schevill, *Cervantes* (1919). "The date of composition of each tale cannot be readily determined, but it is likely that most of them were written after the publication of the first part of *Don Quixote*. Three or four of them may have been sketched during the years which preceded the issue of Cervantes's master work, but we may assume that all of them received their final form shortly before they were presented to the official censor in 1612" (pp. 296–97). See also James Fitzmaurice-Kelly's *Miguel de Cervantes Saavedra: Reseña documentada de su vida* (1944). In his introduction to Norman MacColl's 1902 translation of the *Novelas ejemplares*, pp. xx–xxix, Fitzmaurice-Kelley discusses in detail the conjectures for the dating of each of the novelas. His study is both amusing and eminently sane. The conclusions do not, for the most part, contradict mine.

[7] "La ejemplaridad de las *Novelas ejemplares*": "La mutación de perspectiva dio origen a algunas de esas novelitas, ingenuas, abstractamenta calificadas de italianizantes (*Las dos doncellas, El amante liberal, La señora Cornelia, La española inglesa, La fuerza de la sangre*), e incluso a *Persiles y Sigismunda*, obras de las cuales se hablaría mucho menos si su autor no hubiera compuesto el *Quijote, El celoso extremeño, Rinconete y el Coloquio de los perros*" (pp. 466–67). ["The change in perspective gave origin to some of those little novelas, ingenuous, abstractly called italianate (*Las dos doncellas, El amante liberal, La señora Cornelia, La española inglesa, La fuerza de la sangre*), and even to *Persiles y Sigismunda*, works about which a lot less would be said if their author had not composed the *Quijote, El celoso extremeño, Rinconete*, and the *Coloquio de los perros*."] This, of course, leaves unexplained the publication of the *Quijote* II in the midst of this change of perspective. He mentions elsewhere in the same article, "Seguro es, en todo caso, que después del éxito del *Quijote* (1605) la conducta social de Cervantes varió bastante y también el estilo de algunas obras" (p. 463). ["It is certain, in any case, that after the success of the *Quijote* (1605) Cervantes's social conduct changed considerably, and also the style of some works."]

[8] The charge is first made in *El pensamiento de Cervantes*, p. 244. Castro was not the only one to comment in this way on Cervantes's marked change of perspective in his later works. See also Ortega y Gasset, *Meditaciones del Quijote* (1958), Med. 1, #2; and Salvador de Madariaga, *Guía del lector del Quijote* (1926). But many have taken issue with this position. See, for example, Marcel Bataillon, *Erasmo y España* (1950), pp. 784–85. See also Helmut Hatzfeld, *"Don Quijote" als Wortkunstwerk* (1927), p. 119. Hatzfeld's polemic against the hypocrisy charge was

true Cervantes—that they are extraneous to his artistic and intellectual development.

The other major approach to the problem of dating is to say that the two opposing tendencies—one idealistic and one realistic—coexisted, unassimilated, in Cervantes. This is the conclusion reached by G. Hainsworth and Carlos Romero, though both admit perplexity with the idea that, for example, *Rinconete y Cortadillo* and *El amante liberal* were written at the same time.[9] Neither can find a suitable explanation for the disjunctions apparent in Cervantes's work.[10]

Finally, there are some critics who have detected a movement in Cervantes's work from realism to idealism. The most fully realized exposition of this position is made by Rafael Lapesa.[11] The assertion that Cervantes developed spiritually in the last decade of his life toward a sense of religious transcendence is echoed in the most recent work of Avalle-Arce as

---

answered by Castro in "Erasmo en tiempo de Cervantes" (1931): 329–89, especially on pages 356–62 and notes. In succeeding articles the position was slightly modified: "La palabra escrita y el *Quijote*" (1947); "La estructura del *Quijote*" (1947); and "La ejemplaridad de las novelas cervantinas" (1948).

[9] Hainsworth, Les *"Novelas ejemplares,"* p. 15; and Romero, *Introduzione al "Persiles" di Miguel de Cervantes* (1968), p. cxvii. Hatzfeld ("Das Stilproblem bei Cervantes" [1926]) and William Entwistle ("Cervantes, the Exemplary Novelist" [1941]) also tend toward the idea that no development can be established on the basis of the varying styles in the novelas: that both idealistic and realistic tales were being written in roughly the same period.

[10] Hainsworth, Les *"Novelas ejemplares,"* says: "Que l'auteur de *Rinconete y Cortadillo* ait pû concevoir, en même temps, des nouvelles que nous paraissent maintenant si invraisemblables, la fait est certes déconcertant" (p. 15). ["That the author of *Rinconete y Cortadillo* could have conceived, at the same time, novelas which now seems to us so lacking in verisimilitude, the fact is certainly disconcerting."] See, for a similar comment, Romero, *Introduzione* (1968), p. cxvii.

[11] "En torno a *La española inglesa* y el *Persiles,*" "En la segunda parte del *Quijote* es esencial la transformación espiritualista, insignificante en la parte primera; es en el *Quijote* de 1615 donde se acrisola el amor ideal del heroe y donde tiene lugar la dignificación moral de Sancho. El proceso ocurre aquí en el terreno de lo meramente humano; pero en otras creaciones de los últimos años cervantinos la regeneración tiene marcado carácter religioso, especialmente en *La española inglesa* y el *Persiles.* Habrá que relacionar esto con el hecho de que en 1609 entrara Cervantes en la Congregación de Esclavos del Santísimo Sacramento y en 1616 ingresase en la Orden Tercera" (p. 376). ["In the second part of *Don Quixote* the spiritual transformation, insignificant in the first part, is essential; it is in *Don Quixote* of 1615 where the ideal love of the hero is purified and where the moral dignification of Sancho takes place. The process occurs here, in the terrain of the merely human; but in other creations of Cervantes's last years, the regeneration has a marked religious character, especially in *La española inglesa* and the *Persiles.* This should be related with the fact that in 1609 Cervantes entered the Congregation of Slaves of the Most Holy Sacrament, and that in 1616 he entered the Third Order."]

well.[12] Other commentators, for slightly varied reasons, also suggest a projection toward the idealistic tales in Cervantes's work.[13]

Having outlined the basic approaches to the underlying problem of the "two Cervantes," a problem highlighted in the *Novelas ejemplares,* I would like to consider briefly the major studies on the *Novelas ejemplares.* Though many commentators specifically eschew the problem of chronology, their work often suggests attitudes which are useful in approaching that problem.

Casalduero's work on the *Novelas ejemplares* and the *Persiles* has gone a long way toward exposing the artistic validity of Cervantes's less appreciated works.[14] Casalduero has pointed out the approval accorded the *Persiles* and the idealistic tales by contemporary audiences, an approval which extended through the eighteenth century. In his quarrel with nineteenth- and twentieth-century positivistic thinking, he devotes to both the *Novelas ejemplares* and the *Persiles* a careful study of the literary tastes and expectations of the Baroque as opposed to the Romantic age. He admits that some of Cervantes's works have transcended the period in which they were written, while others, including Part II of *Don Quixote,* are works of art belonging very much to the seventeenth century and are therefore difficult for the twentieth-century reader to understand. While Casalduero establishes a case for the Baroque as the literary context in which Cervantes's works are to be studied, he resists becoming involved in questions of dating of specific works.[15] For the purposes of my study,

[12] Avalle-Arce, "Introducción," *Los trabajos de Persiles y Sigismunda* (1969).

[13] E.g., Franco Meregalli, "Le *Novelas ejemplares* nello svolgimento della personalità di Cervantes" (1960): 334–51; and Alessandro Martinengo, "Cervantes contro il Rinascimento" (1956): 177–222. It is worth adding that Juan Antonio Pellicer, the first critic to take up this matter (1797), offered a similar chronology for the novelas. In "Vida de Miguel de Cervantes Saavedra," *El ingenioso hidalgo don Quijote de la Mancha,* I, he identifies *Rinconete* and the *Celoso* as works written in Seville, *La gitanilla,* as written in Madrid, and *La española inglesa* as composed in 1611, which makes his speculations very similar to mine, though for different reasons.

[14] *Sentido y forma de las "Novelas ejemplares"* (1969); and *Sentido y forma del "Persiles"* (1947).

[15] *Las "Novelas ejemplares"* (1969) "Los esfuerzos de los eruditos que han tratado de establecer la cronología de las novelas han sido, por desgracia, hasta ahora inútiles" (p. 10). ["The efforts of the scholars who have tried to establish a chronology for the novelas have been, unfortunately, useless so far."] "Resolver el problema de la época en que fueron escritas las novelas sería sumamente útil para poder darse cuenta del desarrollo del arte de Cervantes. Para el estudio de las *Novelas ejemplares,* sin embargo, no creo que tenga especial importancia" (p. 11). ["Resolving the problem of the period in which the novelas were written would be extremely useful in order to become aware of the development of Cervantes's art. For a study of the *Novelas ejemplares,* however, I don't think it has particular importance."] Casalduero does attempt, in a very general way, to describe a trajectory for Cervantes's spiritual development through his works in "El desarrollo de la obra de Cervantes" (1966).

Casalduero's analyses are most helpful in that they insist upon the value of the works of Cervantes which hold little attraction for the modern reader. His analysis makes it more difficult to put these works back into the sixteenth century among Cervantes's *juvenilia*.

In addition to studies of Cervantes's work from the standpoint of literary periods and historical and social perspectives, another major trend in recent work on Cervantes has been to correlate his fiction with the literary precepts current during the late sixteenth and early seventeenth centuries. Toffanin, in *La fine dell'umanesimo* (1920), and Américo Castro, in *El pensamiento de Cervantes* (1925), are the precursors of this approach. W. C. Atkinson incorporated the question of dating into his study of the literary *preceptistas* who may have influenced Cervantes. While pronouncing El Pinciano, as opposed to earlier Italian theorists, as Cervantes's major source of theoretical understanding of fiction, Atkinson dismisses as inferior and obviously early the idealistic tales in the *Novelas ejemplares*.[16] Mack Singleton made similar assertions in two articles, arguing the early creation of not only *La española inglesa*, but the *Persiles* as well.[17] The much more thorough study of the relationship between El Pinciano and Cervantes by Canavaggio affirms Atkinson's conclusion that the *Philosophía antigua poética* was essential in Cervantes's literary development, but avoids specific mention of the *Novelas ejemplares*.[18]

E. C. Riley and Alban Forcione have made the most recent contributions to Cervantes criticism in the area of historical literary theory. E. C. Riley defends the *Persiles*'s position as Cervantes's last work by showing how fully the problems of verisimilitude, fiction and reality, and rhetorical accuracy are explored. Like Canavaggio, Riley sees in Cervantes's last work an increased preoccupation with the literary precepts presented in *Don Quixote*, but he also avoids specific consideration of their presence in the *Novelas ejemplares*. His interest in Cervantes's esthetic ideas ties him to the same conclusion as Canavaggio, that "from the first part of *Don Quixote* (1605) until *Persiles y Segismunda*, published posthumously in 1617, his theory of the novel shows in general remarkably little change."[19]

---

[16] "Cervantes, El Pinciano, *Novelas ejemplares*" (1948): 189–208.

[17] "The Date of *La española inglesa*" (1947): 329–35; "The *Persiles* Mystery" (1947).

[18] Jean François Canavaggio, "Alonso López Pinciano y la estética literaria de Cervantes en el *Quijote*" (1958): 13–107. Canavaggio avoids mention of the *Novelas ejemplares* in his excellent study, except in a final footnote which, while suggesting that in general the novelas have more in common with *Don Quixote* and the *Persiles* than with the *Galatea*, refers the reader to Atkinson's work.

[19] *Cervantes's Theory of the Novel* (1962), pp. 10–11.

Alban Forcione also restricts his study for the most part to *Don Quixote* and the *Persiles*, and does not appear to distinguish between the early *Don Quixote* and the late one or to concern himself with shifts of literary perspective to be found between 1605 and 1616 in Cervantes's work.[20]

Most other commentators do not attempt to deal with the totality of Cervantes's work, especially when engaging in philosophical questions. The great volume of Cervantes criticism generally restricts itself to *Don Quixote* as a basis for studies in the development of the modern novel, in the beginnings in fiction of the consideration of the distance between the self and the other, and in the relationship between the word and the thing. A notable exception to the tendency to study *Don Quixote* alone when exploring philosophical problems in Cervantes's work is Avalle-Arce, whose essays in *Deslindes Cervantinos* are most illuminating.[21] Ortega y Gasset, Manuel Durán, Leo Spitzer, Mia Gerhardt, Marthe Robert, René Girard, Michel Foucault, and many others have greatly enriched our appreciation for Cervantes's landmark work by their subtle analyses of the various ramifications and implications to be dealt with in

---

[20] *Cervantes, Aristotle and the "Persiles"* (1970). Forcione's discussion of the role of Clemente in *La gitanilla* develops the idea of the protean figure of the artist in Cervantes's work, but does not suggest a necessarily temporal development. There is, nonetheless, an implied chronology in his association of the artist's role in *La gitanilla* with that in *Pedro de Urdemalas*, and with Ginés de Pasamonte: "If the *Gitanilla* describes the departure of the poet from the city and the beginning of his voyage of initiation through the asocial world of the *pícaro*, *Pedro de Urdemalas* presents the completion of his journey" (p. 320). Although the main thrust of Forcione's argument is to reveal and define the anti-classical tendency found not only within the two *Don Quixotes* but in the *Persiles* as well, he resists at the same time falling into the familiar trap of the "two Cervantes" (see p. 339). In order to do this he suggests, without developing, a continuous movement toward Aristotelian precepts in Cervantes: "There is, I think, in Cervantes's *movement toward Aristotle* something far more profound than his admiration for such figures as Tasso, Virgil, and Heliodorus and his disappointment over the success of Lope's non-classical drama. At the same time the *increasingly* intense engagement with neo-Aristotelian thought awakens criticisms which transcend the limited boundaries it imposes on art" (*italics mine*). What remains unclear, however, is the reason for Cervantes's increased interest in Aristotelian poetics or the developmental sense of Cervantes's resistance to their claims to have captured the rules of art. For the examples Forcione cites to substantiate his thesis of Cervantes's continued rebellion against literalism, factualism, or the dominion of abstract systems of any sort come from the *Quijote* of 1605, 1615, and the *Persiles*. The trajectory, while asserted, is left unexplained.

[21] See especially chapter I, "Conocimiento y vida en Cervantes" (1961). Avalle-Arce has referred to the publication of a second and enlarged edition of the *Deslindes Cervantinos*, which has not become available at this writing.

discussing *Don Quixote*.[22] But their very revelations of the depths of *Don Quixote* have only widened the gap in our appreciation of Cervantes's other works, returning us to the speculation that *Don Quixote* was an unconscious creation by an author whose understanding of literary questions was limited,[23] or that Cervantes became senile after having completed *Don Quixote* II in 1615, or that all the works lacking the sophistication we find in *Don Quixote* and a few of the *Novelas ejemplares* belong to Cervantes's early fiction.

Although efforts to revive the *Persiles* have given rise to several good studies in recent years (Casalduero, Avalle-Arce, Alban Forcione, Carlos Romero and Tilbert Stegmann), the *Novelas ejemplares* have not been so fortunate. Amezúa's work tends to bog down in efforts to discover historical correlatives to the characters and situations found in the novelas.[24] Although Amezúa discusses at length the problem of dating for each story, he does not appear to be seeking a pattern through which Cervantes's artistic development can be understood. Other treatments of the *Novelas* (Hainsworth, Apraiz, Icaza, Hatzfeld, Entwistle, Fitzmaurice-Kelly) are

---

[22] Ortega y Gasset, *Meditaciones* (1958); Leo Spitzer, "Linguistic Perspectivism in the *Don Quijote*" (1948); Manuel Durán, *La ambigüedad en el "Quijote"* (1961); Mia Gerhardt, *"Don Quijote": La vie et les livres* (1955); Marthe Robert, *L'Ancien et le nouveau (De Don Quichotte à Franz Kafka)* (1963); René Girard, *Mensonge romantique et vérité romanesque* (1961); Michel Foucault, *Les mots et les choses* (1966); and David Grossvogel, *The Limits of the Novel* (1967). This list does not pretend to be exhaustive, of course, but only to indicate some of the most intriguing efforts, in twentieth-century criticism, to relate the philosophical and epistemological problems of Cervantes's work to twentieth-century preoccupations and interests in the novel.

[23] This tradition in Cervantes criticism is well known, starting with Menéndez Pelayo's famous statement that Cervantes, as a critical thinker, had ideas of limited transcendence (in "Cultura literaria de Cervantes y elaboración del *Quijote*," *Estudios y disursos de crítica histórica y literaria* [1956], p. 338). The idea continued in Cesare De Lollis's *Cervantes reazionario* (Rome, 1924), and in Rodríguez Marín's statement (in his edition of *Don Quijote*, IV: 303) that Cervantes's creation of *Don Quixote* is so profound that he could not possibly have understood its full depth of meaning. The idea of the "ingenio lego" is also continued by Ernest Merimée, *Compendio de historia de la literatura española* (1949), p. 288; and Paolo Savj-López, *Cervantes* (1917), p. 38. Unamuno's *Vida de Don Quijote y Sancho* (1938) develops this opinion to its fullest. The works of Castro, in the *Pensamiento* (1925) and of Canavaggio, Riley, and Forcione have come a long way in combating this position, but have, in the process, as Castro shows in *Hacia Cervantes* (1967) (in his own rejection of the attitudes informing his *Pensamiento*), ignored the vital circumstances affecting Cervantes's creation and understanding.

[24] Casalduero, *Sentido y forma del "Persiles"* (1947); Avalle-Arce, "Introducción," *Los trabajos* (1969); Forcione, *Cervantes, Aristotle, "Persiles"* (1970); *Cervantes' Christian Romance* (1971); and Stegmann, *Cervantes' Musterroman "Persiles"* (1971).

also useful to students of Cervantes but do not project a convincing explanation for the vast differences in style so often remarked upon in studies on Cervantes.

I have devoted a special appendix to the question of chronology in anticipation of objections that my analysis of the *Novelas ejemplares* is based on a temporal ordering of the stories which cannot be defended. I hope to have shown, in this brief summary of previous work on the novelas, that no other explanation for the problem of the "two Cervantes" is entirely satisfactory; and that other critics, by different methods, have also reached the conclusion that the idealistic tales were written late. I stress the defensibility of the chronology in the hope that objections on this level will not intervene to upset appreciation of other aspects of this study.

BIBLIOGRAPHY

Adams, Hazard. *The Interests of Criticism: An Introduction to Literary Theory*. New York, Chicago, San Francisco, and Atlanta: Harcourt, Brace & World, 1969.

Allen, John J. "*El Cristo de la Vega* and *La fuerza de la sangre*." *MLN* 83 (1968): 271–75.

———. *Don Quixote: Hero or Fool?: A Study in Narrative Technique*. Gainesville: University of Florida Press, 1969.

Alonso Cortés, Narciso. *Cervantes en Valladolid*. Valladolid: Casa de Cervantes, 1918.

Amezúa y Mayo, Agustín G. de. *Cervantes, creador de la novela corta española*. 2 vols. Valencia: Consejo Superior de Investigaciones Científicas, 1956–58.

Apraiz y Saenz del Burgo, Julián. *Estudio histórico-crítico sobre las "Novelas ejemplares" de Cervantes*. Vitoria: Domingo Sar, 1901.

Asenio, Eugenio. "En torno a Américo Castro. Polémica con Albert A. Sicroff." *Hispanic Review* 40 (1972): 365–85.

Asensio y Toledo, José María. "Sobre *La española inglesa*." In *Cervantes y sus obras*. Barcelona: F. Seix, 1902.

Astrana Marín, Luís. *Vida ejemplar y heroica de Miguel de Cervantes Saavedra*. 7 vols. Madrid: Edit. Reus, 1948–57.

Atkinson, William C. "Cervantes, el Pinciano, and the *Novelas ejemplares*." *Hispanic Review* 16 (1948): 189–208.

Avalle-Arce, Juan Bautista. "Conocimiento y vida en Cervantes." In *Deslindes cervantinos*. Madrid: Edhigar, 1961.

———. "El curioso y el capitán." In *Deslindes cervantinos*. Madrid: Edhigar, 1961.

———. "Grisóstomo y Marcela." In *Deslindes cervantinos*. Madrid: Edhigar, 1961.

———. "Introduction." *Cervantes: Three Exemplary Novels*. New York: Dell, 1964.

———. "La captura de Cervantes." *Boletín de la Real Academia Española* 48 (1968): 237–80.

———. "Introducción." *Los Trabajos de Persiles y Sigismunda*, by Miguel de Cervantes Saavedra. Madrid: Clásicos Castalia, 1969.

Ayala, Francisco. "El arte nuevo de hacer novelas." *La Torre* 21 (1958): 81–90.

Barrenechea, Ana María. "*La ilustre fregona* como ejemplo de la estructura novelesca cervantina." *Filología* 7 (1961): 13–32.

Bataillon, Marcel. "Cervantès et le 'Mariage cretien.'" *Bulletin Hispanique* 49 (1947): 129–44.

———. *Erasmo y España*. Translated by A. Alatorre. 2 vols. Mexico: Fondo de Cultura Económica, 1950.

———. *Pícaros y picaresca*. Translated by Francisco R. Vadillo. Madrid: Taurus, 1969.

Beringer, Arthur A. "*Persiles* and the Time Labyrinth." *Hispanófila* 41 (1971): 1–11.

Blanco Aguinaga, Carlos. "Cervantes y la picaresca. Notas sobre dos tipos de realismo." *Nueva Revista de Filología Hispánica* 11 (1957): 313–42.

Bonilla y San Martín, Adolfo. *Cervantes y su obra*. Madrid: Beltrán, 1916.

———. "Una versión inglesa y algunas consideraciones sobre las *Novelas ejemplares*." In *De crítica cervantina*. Madrid: Ruiz, 1917.

Brehm, E. J. "El mitologema de la sombra en Pedro Schlemihl, Cortadillo y Berganza." *Anales Cervantinos* 9 (1961–62): 29–44.

Buchanan, Milton A. "The Works of Cervantes and Their Dates of Composition." *Transactions of the Royal Society of Canada* 32 (1938): 23–39.

Canavaggio, Jean-François. "Alonso López Pinciano y la estética literaria de Cervantes en el *Quijote*." *Anales Cervantinos* 7 (1958): 13–107.

Casa, Frank P. "The Structural Unity of *El licenciado Vidriera*." *Bulletin of Hispanic Studies* 41 (1964): 242–46.

Casalduero, Joaquín. *Sentido y forma de "Los trabajos de Persiles y Sigismunda"*. Buenos Aires: Editorial Sudamericana, 1947.

———. *Sentido y forma del "Quijote"*. Madrid: Insula, 1966.

———. "El desarrollo de la obra de Cervantes." *Torre* 14 (1966): 65–74.

———. *Sentido y forma de las "Novelas ejemplares"*. 2nd ed., rev. Madrid: Gredos, 1969.

Castro, Américo. "Algunas observaciones acerca del concepto del honor en los siglos XVI y XVII." *Revista de Filología Española* 3 (1916): 1–50; 357–86.

———. *El pensamiento de Cervantes*. Madrid: Hernando, 1925.

———. "Erasmo en tiempo de Cervantes." *Revista de Filología Española* 18 (1931): 329–89, 441.

———. *Cervantès*. Paris: Rieder, 1931.

———. *De la edad conflictiva*. Madrid: Taurus, 1964.

———. *Cervantes y los casticismos españoles*. Madrid: Alfaguera, 1966.

———. "*El celoso extremeño* de Cervantes." In *Hacia Cervantes*. 3rd ed., rev. Madrid: Taurus, 1967.

———. "La ejemplaridad de las *Novelas ejemplares*." In *Hacia Cervantes*. Madrid: Taurus, 1967.

———. *Hacia Cervantes*. 3rd ed., rev. Madrid: Taurus, 1967.

———. "La palabra escrita y el *Quijote*." In *Hacia Cervantes*. Madrid: Taurus, 1967.

———. "Los prólogos al *Quijote*." In *Hacia Cervantes*. 3rd ed., rev. Madrid: Taurus, 1967.

———. *El pensamiento de Cervantes*. 2nd ed., rev. Barcelona: Noguer, 1972.

Cervantes Saavedra, Miguel de. *Don Quijote de la Mancha.* 8 vols. Edited by Francisco Rodríguez Marín. Madrid: Espasa-Calpe, 1911–13.

———. *Novelas ejemplares.* 2 vols. Edited by Francisco Rodríguez Marín. Madrid: Espasa-Calpe, 1915–17.

———. *The Ingenious Gentleman Don Quixote de la Mancha.* 2 vols. Translated by Samuel Putnam. New York: The Viking Press, 1949.

———. *Three Exemplary Novels.* Introduction and translation by Samuel Putnam. New York: The Viking Press, 1950.

———. *Six Exemplary Novels.* Introduction and translation by Harriet de Onís. Great Neck, New York: Barron's Educational Series, 1961.

———. *Obras Completas.* 15th ed. Edited by Angel Valbuena Prat. Madrid: Aguilar, 1967.

———. *Novelas ejemplares.* 13th ed. Buenos Aires: Espasa-Calpe, 1967.

———. *La Galatea.* 2 vols. Edited by Juan Bautista Avalle-Arce. 2nd ed. Madrid: Espasa-Calpe, 1968.

Chacón y Calvo, José María. "El realismo ideal de *La gitanilla.*" *Boletín de la Academia Cubana de la Lengua* 2 (1953): 246–67.

Chandler, Frank Wadleigh. *Romances of Roguery: An Episode in the History of the Novel.* London: The Macmillan Company, 1899.

Criado del Val, Manuel. "De estilística cervantina." *Anales cervantinos* 2 (1953): 233–48.

De Lollis, Cesare. *Cervantes reazionario.* Rome: Fratelli Treves, 1924.

Déguy, Michel. *Actes.* Paris: Gallimard, 1966.

Drake, Dana B. *Cervantes—A Critical Bibliography. I, The "Novelas Ejemplares."* Blacksburg, Virginia: Virginia Polytechnic Institute, 1968.

Dunn, Peter. Early draft of chapter to appear in *Suma Cervantina.* Edited by J. B. Avalle-Arce and E. C. Riley. London: Tamesis, 1973.

Durán, Manuel. *La ambigüedad en el "Quijote."* Xalapa, Mexico: Universidad Veracruzana, 1961.

Durling, Robert M. *The Figure of the Poet in Renaissance Epic.* Cambridge, Mass.: Harvard University Press, 1965.

El Saffar, Ruth S. *Distance and Control in "Don Quixote."* To be published in the Studies in the Romance Languages and Literature Series. Chapel Hill: University of North Carolina Press.

Entwistle, William J. *Cervantes.* Oxford: Clarendon Press, 1940.

———. "Cervantes, the Exemplary Novelist." *Hispanic Review* 9 (1941): 103–9.

Farinelli, Arturo "El último sueño romántico de Cervantes." In *Divagaciones Hispánicas: Discursos y estudios críticos.* Barcelona: Bosch, 1936.

Fitzmaurice-Kelly, James. Introduction to *The Exemplary Novels of Miguel de Cervantes.* Glasgow: Gowans & Gray, 1902.

———. *Miguel de Cervantes Saavedra: Reseña documentada de su vida.* Translated and revised by James Fitzmaurice-Kelly. Buenos Aires: Libro de Edición Argentina, 1944.

Flores, Angel, and Benardete, M. J., eds. *Cervantes Across the Centuries.* New York: The Dryden Press, 1947.

Forcione, Alban K. "Cervantes and the Freedom of the Artist." *Romanic Review* 61 (1970): 243–55.

———. *Cervantes, Aristotle, and the "Persiles."* Princeton: Princeton University Press, 1970.

———. "Cervantes, Tasso, and the *Romanzi* Polemic." *Revue de Littérature Comparée* 44 (1970): 434–43.

———. *Cervantes' Christian Romance. A Study of Persiles y Sigismunda.* Princeton: Princeton University Press, 1971.

Foucault, Michel. *Les mots et les choses.* Paris: Gallimard, 1966.

Frye, Northrop. *Anatomy of Criticism. Four Essays.* Princeton, N. J.: Princeton University Press, 1971.

Gerhardt, Mia I. *"Don Quijote": La vie et les livres.* Amsterdam: N.V. Noord-Hollandsche Uitgevers Maatschappij, 1955.

Giannini, Alfredo. "Introduzione." *Scrittori Stranieri: M. Cervantes, Novelle.* Bari: Laterza, 1912.

Gilman, Stephen. *Cervantes y Avellaneda.* Mexico: Fondo de Cultura Económica, 1951.

———. "Los inquisidores literarios de Cervantes." *Actas del Tercer Congreso Internacional de Hispanistas.* Mexico: El Colegio de Mexico, 1970, pp. 1–26.

Girard, René. *Mensonge romantique et vérité romanesque.* Paris: Grasset, 1961.

Green, Otis. "*El licenciado Vidriera*: Its Relation to the *Viaje del parnaso* and the *Examen de ingenios* of Huarte." In *Linguistic and Literary Studies in Honor of Helmut A. Hatzfeld.* Washington: Catholic University of America Press, 1964.

Grossvogel, David. *The Limits of the Novel.* Ithaca: Cornell University Press, 1967.

Guillén, Jorge. "Vida y muerte de Alonso Quijano." *Romanische Forschungen* 64 (1952): 102–13.

Hainsworth, G. *Les "Novelas ejemplares" de Cervantes en France au XVIIe siècle.* Paris: Champion, 1933.

Haley, George. "The Narrator in *Don Quijote*: Maese Pedro's Puppet Show." *MLN* 81 (1966): 145–65.

Hassan, Ihab. "The Dismemberment of Orpheus: Notes on Form and Antiform in Contemporary Literature." In *Learners and Discerners.* Edited by Robert Scholes. Charlottesville: University Press of Virginia, 1964.

Hatzfeld, Helmut. "Das Stilproblem bei Cervantes." *Spanische Philologie und Spanischer Unterricht* 6 (1926): 1–8.

———. *"Don Quijote" als Wortkunstwerk.* Leipzig: B. G. Teubner, 1927.

Icaza, Francisco A. de. "Algo más sobre *El licenciado Vidriera.*" *Revista de Archivos, Bibliotecas y Museos* 34 (1916): 38–44.

———. *Las "Novelas ejemplares" de Cervantes: Sus críticos. Sus modelos literarios. Sus modelos vivos.* Madrid: Ateneo de Madrid, 1916.

Lapesa, Rafael. "En torno a *La española inglesa* y *El Persiles.*" In *Homenaje a Cervantes.* Vol. 2. Edited by Francisco Sánchez-Castañer. Valencia: Mediterráneo, 1950.

López Pinciano, Alonso (El Pinciano). *Philosophía antigua poética*. Edited by A. Carballo Picazo. 3 vols. Madrid: Biblioteca de Antiguos Libros Hispánicos, 1953.

Lowe, Jennifer. "The Structure of Cervantes' *La española inglesa*." *Romance Notes* 9 (1968): 287–90.

———. "A Note on Cervantes' *El amante liberal*." *Romance Notes* 12 (1970–71): 400–3.

Lukacs, Georg. *Solzhenitsyn*. Translated by William David Graf. Cambridge, Mass.: The MIT Press, 1970.

Madariaga, Salvador de. *Guía del lector del "Quijote."* Madrid: Espasa-Calpe, 1926.

Martín Gabriel, Albinio. "Heliodoro y la novela española: Apuntes para una tesis." *Cuadernos de Literatura* 8 (1950): 215–34.

Martinengo, Alessandro. "Cervantes contro il Rinascimento." *Studi Mediolatini e Volgari* 4 (1956): 177–222.

Mele, Eugenio. "La novella *El celoso extremeño* del Cervantes." *Nuova Antologia* (1906): 475–90.

Menéndez Pelayo, Marcelino. "Cultura literaria de Cervantes y elaboración del *Quijote*." *Estudios y discursos de crítica histórica y literaria*. Edited by J. M. Cossío. Madrid: Espasa-Calpe, 1956.

———. *Orígenes de la novela*. 4 vols. Edited by D. Enrique Sánchez Reyes. 2nd ed. Madrid: Consejo Superior de Investigaciones Científicas, 1962.

Meregalli, Franco. "Le *Novelas ejemplares* nello svolgimento della personalità di Cervantes." *Letterature Moderne* 10 (1960): 334–51.

———. "La literatura italiana en la obra de Cervantes." *Arcadia* 6 (1971): 1–15.

Merimée, Ernest. *Compendio de historia de la literatura española*. Translated by Francisco Gamoneda. 2nd ed. Mexico: Botas, 1949.

Miller, J. Hillis. *The Form of Victorian Fiction*. Notre Dame and London: University of Notre Dame Press, 1968.

———. *Poets of Reality*. New York: Atheneum, 1969.

Molho, Maurice. "Remarques sur le *Mariage trompeur et Colloque des chiens*." In *Le Mariage Trompeur et Colloque des chiens*, translated by Maurice Molho. Paris: Aubier-Flammarion, 1970.

Montgomery, Robert L., Jr. "Allegory and the Incredible Fable: The Italian View from Dante to Tasso." *PMLA* 81 (1966): 45–55.

Moreno Baez, Enrique. *Reflexiones sobre el "Quijote."* Madrid: Prensa española, 1968.

Morón Arroyo, Ciriaco. Review of Dietrich Rossler's *Voluntad bei Cervantes*. *Hispanic Review* 39 (1971): 324–27.

Murillo, L. A. "Cervantes' *Coloquio de los perros*, a Novel-Dialogue." *Modern Philology* 58 (1961): 174–85.

Ortega y Gasset, José. *Meditaciones del Quijote*. Madrid: Revista de Occidente, 1958.

Osuna, Rafael. "El olvido del *Persiles*." *Boletín de la Real Academia Española* 48 (1968): 55–75.

Osuna, Rafael. "Las fechas del *Persiles.*" *Thesaurus* 25 (1970): 383–433.

Parker, A. A. *Literature and the Delinquent: The Picaresque Novel in Spain and Europe* 1599–1753. Edinburgh: At the University Press, 1967.

Payás, Armando. "La crítica social en las *Novelas ejemplares* de Cervantes." Dissertation, Florida State University, 1970.

Peers, E. Allison. "Cervantes in England." *Bulletin of Spanish Studies* 24 (1947): 226–38.

Peers, E. Allison, and Sánchez-Castañer, Francisco, eds. *La española inglesa.* Valencia: Ediciones Metis, 1948.

Pellicer, Juan Antonio. "Vida de Miguel de Cervantes Saavedra." In *El ingenioso hidalgo don Quijote de la Mancha.* Vol. 1. Madrid: Gabriel de Sancha, 1797.

Piluso, Robert V. "*La fuerza de la sangre:* un análisis estructural." *Hispania* 47 (1964): 485–90.

Place, E. B. *Manual elemental de novelística española.* Madrid: V. Suárez, 1926.

Predmore, Richard L. *El mundo del "Quijote."* Madrid: Insula, 1958.

———. "*Rinconete y Cortadillo.* Realismo, carácter picaresco, alegría." *Insula* 23 (Jan. 1969): 17–18.

Raleigh, John Henry. *Time, Place, and Idea: Essays on the Novel.* Carbondale and Edwardsville: Southern Illinois University Press, 1968.

Rauhut, Franz. "Consideraciones sociológicas sobre *La gitanilla* y otras novelas cervantinas." *Anales Cervantinos* 3 (1950): 143–60.

Riley, Edward C. *Cervantes's Theory of the Novel.* Oxford: Clarendon Press, 1962.

———. "Three Versions of Don Quixote." *Modern Language Review* 69 (1973): 807–19.

Ríos de Lámperez, Blanca de los. "Prólogo," *Novelas ejemplares,* by Miguel de Cervantes Saavedra. Cádiz: Real Academia Hispanoamericana de Cádiz, 1916.

Rivers, Elias L. "Cervantes' Journey to Parnassus." *MLN* 85 (1970): 244–48.

Robert, Marthe. *L'Ancien et le nouveau (De "Don Quichotte" à Franz Kafka).* Paris: Grasset, 1963.

Rodríguez Marín, Francisco. *El Loaysa de "El celoso extremeño."* Seville: P. Díaz, 1901.

———, ed. *Novelas ejemplares,* 2 vols. Madrid: Espasa-Calpe, 1915–17.

———. "*Rinconete y Cortadillo,*" *novela de Miguel de Cervantes Saavedra.* 2nd ed., rev. Madrid: Real Academia Española, 1920.

Romero, Carlos. *Introduziones al "Persiles" di Miguel de Cervantes.* Venice: Libreria Universitaria, 1968.

Rosales, Luís. "La evasión del prójimo o el hombre de cristal." *Cuadernos Hispanoamericanos* 9 (1956): 253–81.

———. *Cervantes y la libertad.* 2 vols. Madrid: Graf. Valera, 1959–60.

Rüegg, August. *Miguel de Cervantes und sein "Don Quijote."* Bern: A. Francke, 1949.

Savj-López, Paolo. *Cervantes.* Madrid: Casa Editorial Calleja, 1917.

Schevill, Rudolph. *Cervantes*. New York: Duffield, 1919.

Schevill, Rudolph, and Bonilla, Adolfo. *Comedias y entremeses de Cervantes*. Madrid: Impr. de D. Rodríguez, 1915.

———. "Introducción." *Novelas ejemplares*. Vol. 3. Madrid: Schevill and Bonilla, 1925.

Selig, Karl-Ludwig. "Concerning the Structure of Cervantes' *La Gitanilla*." *Romanistisches Jahrbuch* 13 (1962): 273–76.

———. "The Metamorphosis of the *Ilustre fregona*." *Filología y crítica hispánica: Homenje al Profesor Federico Sánchez Escribano*. Madrid: Ediciones Alcalá, 1969.

Sicroff, Albert A. *Les controverses des statuts de "pureté de sang" en Espagne du XVᵉ au XVIIᵉ siècle*. Paris: Didier, 1960.

Singer, Armand E. "The Sources, Meaning, and Use of the Madness Theme in Cervantes' *Licenciado Vidriera*." *West Virginia University Philological Papers* 6 (1949): 31–53.

———. "Cervantes' *Licenciado Vidriera*: Its Form and Substance." *West Virginia University Philological Papers* 8 (1951): 13–21.

Singleton, Mack. "The Date of *La española inglesa*." *Hispania* 30 (1947): 329–35.

———. "The *Persiles* Mystery." In *Cervantes Across the Centuries*. New York: The Dryden Press, 1947.

Soons, Alan. "An Interpretation of the Form of *El casamiento engañoso y Coloquio de los perros*." *Anales Cervantinos* 9 (1961–62): 203–12.

Spitzer, Leo. "Das Gefuge einer cervantischen Novelle." *Zeitschrift für Romanische Philologie* 51 (1931): 194–225.

———. "Die Frage der Heuchelei des Cervantes." *Zeitschrift für Romanische Philologie* 56 (1936): 138–78.

———. "Linguistic Perspectivism in the *Don Quijote*." In *Linguistics and Literary History: Essays in Stylistics*. Princeton: Princeton University Press, 1948.

———. " 'Y así juro por la intemerata eficacia'." *Quaderni Ibero-Americani* 16 (1954): 483–84.

Stagg, Geoffrey L. "Sobre el plan primitivo del *Quijote*." *Actas del Primer Congreso Internacional de Hispanistas*. Oxford: The Dolphin Book Co., 1964.

Stegmann, Tilbert. *Cervantes' Musterroman "Persiles"*. Hamburg: Lüdke, 1971.

Thompson, Jennifer. "The Structure of Cervantes' *Las dos doncellas*." *Bulletin of Hispanic Studies* 40 (1963): 144–50.

Todorov, Tzvetan. *Poétique de la prose*. Paris: Seuil, 1971.

Toffanin, Giuseppe. *La fine dell'umanesimo*. Turin: Fratelli Bocca, 1920.

Tomashevsky, Boris. "Thematics." *Russian Formalist Criticism: Four Essays*. Translated by Lee T. Lemon and Marion J. Reis. Lincoln: University of Nebraska Press, 1965.

Unamuno, Miguel de. *Vida de Don Quijote y Sancho*. 3rd ed. Madrid: Espasa-Calpe, 1938.

Valbuena Prat, Angel. *Historia de la literatura española*. 4 vols. Barcelona: Gustavo Gili, 1953.

————, ed. *La novela picaresca española.* Madrid: Aguilar, 1946.

————, ed. *Obras completas, Cervantes.* Madrid: Aguilar, 1967.

Valera, José Luís. "Sobre el realismo cervantino en *Rinconete.*" *Atlántida* 6 (1968): 434–49.

Vilanova, Antonio. "El peregrino andante en el *Persiles* de Cervantes." *Boletín de la Real Academia de Buenas Letras de Barcelona* 22 (1949): 97–159.

Wardropper, Bruce W. "The Pertinence of *El curioso impertinente.*" *PMLA* 72 (1957): 587–600.

————. "*Don Quijote*: Story or History?" *Modern Philology* 43 (1965): 1–11.

Willis, Raymond S. *The Phantom Chapters of the "Quijote."* New York: Hispanic Institute, 1953.

Zimic, Stanislav. "El *Persiles* como crítica de la novela bizantina." *Acta Neophilologica* 3 (1970): 49–64.

INDEX

THE JOHNS HOPKINS UNIVERSITY PRESS

This book was composed in Fairfield text with Fairfield and Caxton display by Maryland Linotype Composition Company from a design by Laurie Jewell. It was printed on Warren's 60-lb. Sebago, regular finish, and bound in Columbia Fictionette, natural finish, by The Maple Press Company.

Library of Congress Cataloging in Publication Data
El Saffar, Ruth S   1941-
    Novel to romance.

    Bibliography: p.
    1. Cervantes Saavedra, Miguel de, 1547-1616.
Novelas ejemplares.   I.   Title.
PQ6324.Z5E5   863'.3   73-19332
ISBN 0-8018-1545-2